Jamaica Kincaid:

Where the Land Meets the Body

Jamaica Kincaid:

Where the Land Meets the Body

MOIRA FERGUSON

University Press of Virginia *Charlottesville and London*

The University Press of Virginia

Copyright © 1994 by the Rector and Visitors of the University of Virginia

First published 1994

Library of Congress Cataloging-in-Publication Data

Ferguson, Moira.
    Jamaica Kincaid : where the land meets the body / Moira Ferguson.
      p.   cm.
    Includes bibliographical references and index.
    ISBN 0-8139-1519-8 (cloth). — ISBN 0-8139-1520-1 (paper)
    1. Kincaid, Jamaica — Criticism and interpretation.   2. Feminism
and literature — Antigua — History — 20th century.   3. Mothers and
daughters in literature.   4. Imperialism in literature.   5. Colonies
in literature.   6. Antigua — In literature.   I. Title.
PR9275.A583K5644   1994
813 — dc20   94–1309
                                              CIP

Printed in the United States of America

FOR LUCIANA

Contents

Acknowledgments

⚙ I have incurred many debts in the course of writing this study and I am happy to have an opportunity to acknowledge them. For their help in bringing this study to fruition, I owe a large debt of thanks to staff members at the *Outlet* newspaper in Antigua. I especially thank Editor Tim Hector for an illuminating conversation in January 1990. I am also very grateful to Phyllis Meyers, Chief Librarian of St. Johns Public Library in Antigua, for her kindness and resourcefulness and for opening up her collections to me. I thank Annie Drew for her warm hospitality and Jamaica Kincaid for helpful discussions.

For assistance in tracking down Jamaica Kincaid's periodical pieces, I thank *The Paris Review, Ms.,* Susan Moller at the *Christian Science Monitor,* Nikki de Gioia at *Rolling Stone,* Owen Ketherry at the *New Yorker,* and Transcript Services, National Public Radio. For illuminating conversations, responses to questions, and general assistance, I am grateful to Robert Antoni, Victor Holliday, Ketu Katrak, Richard Nenneman, and Donna Perry.

At my home institution, I am indebted to the circulation department and the Interlibrary Loan office for books and documentation. I also thank the Department of English for a Faculty Development Fellowship and the Research Council for a Maude Hammond Fling Fellowship that enabled me to pursue research in Antigua. Irma Nippert commented usefully on several chapters. Roma Rector typed the manuscript in her customarily expert fashion, while Kate Flaherty, Nicolle French and especially Lisa Toay offered fine assistance. For several incisive readings of the manuscript, a warm thanks to Daryl Cumber Dance. I thank Rebecca

Busker for typing the index. The chapter on *Lucy* originally appeared in *Modern Fiction Studies*. Many thanks to Patrick O'Donnell.

Last, I thank my students in Modern Fiction and Twentieth-Century Women's Literature at the University of Nebraska—Lincoln for many lively discussions.

Chronology

1 9 4 9

Born May 25, Elaine Potter Richardson, Holberton Hospital, St. John's, Antigua

Mother's family, surname Richardson, land peasants in Dominica

Maternal grandmother, Carib Indian

Grandfather's occupation, a policeman (both grandparents from Dominica)

Mother, Annie Richardson Drew, born in Dominica, homemaker and political activist

Father, Roderick Potter, a former taxi driver, now an employee of the Mill Reef Club in Antigua

Stepfather, David Drew, a cabinetmaker and carpenter

1 9 5 2

Enrolls in Moravian School

Mother teaches her to read

1 9 5 6

Attends the Antiguan Girls School

Mother gives her *Concise Oxford Dictionary* for her birthday

Apprenticed to Miss Doreen, a seamstress

Attends Princess Margaret School

1 9 5 8

First brother, Joseph Drew, born

1 9 5 9
Second brother, Dalma Drew, born

1 9 6 1
Third brother, Devon Drew, born

J U N E 1 9 6 6 – 7 3
Shortly after seventeenth birthday, Elaine Potter Richardson leaves Anti-
    gua for United States
Works as an au pair in Scarsdale, N.Y., then as a receptionist, and as a
    magazine writer for *Art Direction*
Takes classes at Westchester Community College, White Plains
Works as au pair on the Upper East Side
File clerk and secretary at Magnum Photos
Obtains high school diploma
Studies photography at New York School for Social Research
Attends Franconia College in New Hampshire

1 9 7 3
First Publication: "When I Was Seventeen"
Freelance writer, *Ms., Ingenue, Village Voice*
Changes name to Jamaica Kincaid

1 9 7 6 – p r e s e n t
New Yorker staff writer

1 9 7 9
Marries Allen Shawn

1 9 8 4
Receives the Morton Dauwen Zabel Award for fiction

1 9 8 5
Moves to Vermont
Daughter Annie is born
Finalist for Ritz Paris Hemingway Award

Returns for a visit to Antigua; informally banned from the island
Visits England

1 9 8 9
Recipient of a Guggenheim fellowship
Son Harold born

1 9 9 1
Honorary degrees, Williams College; Long Island College

1 9 9 2
Informal ban on visiting Antigua apparently lifted

Women artists are giving us new views not only of women but of men as well.

—Jamaica Kincaid

Jamaica Kincaid:

Where the Land Meets the Body

Introduction

This doubleness has become the form in which that politics is now emerging. It is the source of its particular creative power. Inside and outside, in and against every discourse. Has to be in, because there's no place to speak from except from somewhere. But at the same time as somebody has to speak from somewhere, they will not be confined to that person who is speaking and that place.—**Stuart Hall**

✸ INTERVIEWS WITH JAMAICA KINCAID probe the problematic relationship she has long had with her mother. While Jamaica Kincaid agrees that she and her mother did not always see eye to eye, she also volunteers that personal experience shapes the protagonists of her texts; she further avows that the negative influence of colonialism on Antiguan culture was incalculable. This study takes these assertions a step further.

I argue that the relationships between Kincaid's female protagonists and their biological mothers are crucially formative yet always mediated by intimations of life as colonized subjects. Jamaica Kincaid continually fuses diverse formulations of motherhood, maternality, and colonialism. Reflecting on these crossover conjunctures, she demystifies the ideology of a colonial motherland. That doubled articulation of motherhood as both colonial and biological explains why the mother-daughter relations in her fiction often seem so harshly rendered, a fact that has constantly unsettled reviewers. In the course of unraveling overdetermined responses by themselves and others, Kincaid's protagonists come to new understandings of their positions and their capacity for agency. Cultural location becomes paramount.

To implement this doubled negotiation, Kincaid foregrounds a complicated matrix of mother images that encompasses not only "her island home and its unique culture [but also] . . . the body of tropes, talismans and female bonding that is a woman's heritage through her own and other mothers. The land and one's mothers, then, are co-joined."[1] But this relationship is always fraught with fear, alienation, and ambivalence, is always about separation. To underscore this complex duality, Kincaid also experiments with "decolonizing" styles, discursive formations that refuse a Western linear modality.[2] She chooses an innovative format "as a space of radical openness."[3] Beyond that is her own double-voiced authorial vantage point, given her stated textual-biological intervention from the United States after Antigua gained independence.

More specifically, Kincaid's first text, *At the Bottom of the River,* presents a series of vignettes in which a protagonist discusses her relationship with an ambiguously represented mother — a motherland or a biological mother — who is both absent and present. Through these intricate renderings, the mystery and shifting focus of the (anti)narrative constitutes a counterhegemonic opposition to the logic of colonialism.[4]

The many discussions about motherhood and colonialism that ground each section of *At the Bottom* overlap and spill into one another. At times the physical mother mimics colonial protectors. Caught up in fear, suspicion, and a vulnerable need for safety, the protagonist craves to break loose. She can scarcely fathom where she is, let alone where she is going because the constitutive elements of her immediate family keep changing shape; her center is not holding. At a certain point this unnamed protagonist withdraws into a world of "blackness" where nothing can touch her. In the end, a transcendent vision attached to writing and hence agency empowers her to persevere.

In the precolonial world of *Annie, Gwen, Lilly, Pam and Tulip,* originally a section of *At the Bottom of the River,* a sense of impending doom inflects the conversations of the title characters. But they stand somewhat apart from the mystery and the omens, defiantly identifying themselves.

These oblique manipulations to build and ascertain identity are more keenly highlighted in *Annie John,* so much so that it reads like the second part of a bildungsroman in which the protagonist is slowly emerging from a fraught environment. Annie John's confrontation with precolonial forerunners and contemporary educators parallels an off-center mother-daughter relationship. More to the point, Annie John's antagonism toward her colonial mother helps to gloss daughterly anger and frustration and reminds us of that persistent imperial presence in everyday life.

Both *At the Bottom* and *Annie John* feature protagonists with a distinct cultural location; each is a young black Antiguan subject experiencing the rigors of British colonial rule in an environment where her mother protects and indoctrinates. As an adolescent in *Annie John,* she confronts personal and political parents simultaneously, reaching a cultural impasse that leaves little room for maneuver.[5] Both sequences involve the narrator and her parents, who are deeply but silently divided. Although diverse provisional resolutions are fashioned, the narrator eventually transcends her experiences, wins control, and repositions herself. Additionally, the critical self-claiming at the end of both texts resonates mutually. Once the speakers name themselves, they people the void, communicate, and reappropriate their space.[6]

The third text, *A Small Place,* constitutes Jamaica Kincaid's searing response to her return home after Antigua won independence from Britain. Kincaid works through what happened to the island — "a small place" — for fourteen years under black Antiguan rule. Having anticipated that the island would fare better without the British presence, she is shocked at the governmental neglect.

Thus in *A Small Place* Jamaica Kincaid represents herself as a historical subject in her own right. Constituting herself as the other of hegemonic violence, she claims to be speaking as an unmediated narrator-author who has witnessed and now wants to compare colonial and postcolonial contamination. However, rather than sarcastically referring to England as the motherland — as West Indian authors have historically done — she exposes imperial manipulation of that concept.[7]

In addition, the speaker insists on disrupting old complacencies. Cultural resistance is key — she insists — as she argues a quiet version of Fanonian opposition, the necessity for political (perhaps militant) solutions: "Without that struggle, without that knowledge of the practice of action, there's nothing but a fancy-dress parade and the blare of the trumpets. There's nothing save a minimum of readaptation, a few reforms at the top, a flag waving: and down there at the bottom an undivided mass, still living in the middle ages, endlessly marking time."[8]

In *A Small Place* Kincaid writes an unvarnished account of discordances only intimated in *At the Bottom of the River, Annie, Gwen, Lilly, Pam and Tulip,* and *Annie John.* What is redeeming about these colonizers and their legatees — if anything is redeeming, she seems to say — is the motivation they offer a formerly colonized subject to redress the balance of colonial mystification. Furthermore, through her opposition the narrator claims a visible and yet another diverse vantage point. The complex symbol of the biological mother imbricated with the "motherland" is downplayed until close to the end, when the narrator (Kincaid) and her mother together oppose exploitation by an indigenous black bourgeois ruling order.

The pitch of *A Small Place* contrasts sharply with that of *Lucy,* Jamaica Kincaid's most recent novel, published in 1990. Having vented postcolonial outrage in *A Small Place,* Kincaid transports her protagonist into a new, rather bracing space. A young Caribbean leaving a preindependent Antigua in the 1960s, Lucy travels to the United States for the first time to work as an au pair and negotiate her way into and through a white North American upper-middle-class world. Now resident in a self-avowed but bogus motherland, Lucy is an outsider in a "first world" country, looking in on colonizers and their bankrupt shenanigans. In the meaning of the phrase "the third scenario," Lucy stands in a "nonbinarist space of reflection" with its concomitant "struggle in the politics of location." A lone, courageous "emigrée," Lucy may live in seemingly voluntary exile, but that exile is psychologically and politically forced. This creative, created space tends to "provoke new relationships."[9] To occupy such a complicated position is a form of "mutual becoming."[10]

Having temporarily allied herself with a new blonde "mother" in her employer, Mariah — as if to compensate for leaving her mother and her motherland behind — Lucy is subjected to tireless efforts at assimilation by her employers and their friends. They treat her as a "find," their only silent stipulation being that she "behave herself." She must act as they dictate.

Coping on the one hand with postcolonial agents trying to co-opt her and on the other with her mother reaching out to the absent daughter, Lucy must navigate rough waters. Only reluctantly does she concede her mother's positive influence. That influence becomes increasingly more obvious as Lucy slowly constructs a more self-conscious identity. Like the narrator in *At the Bottom of the River* and like Annie John herself, Lucy proudly assumes the role of "native transgressor"; she flouts postcolonial authority. By the end, she has bought gaudy curtains reminiscent of her childhood — a form of self- and cultural claiming despised by white United States society — to fortify (and perhaps cocoon) herself in preparation for whatever happens next.

Refusing to buy the contention that dominant representations of authority are natural, Lucy ruptures their apparent seamlessness. On her own at the end, like her sister protagonists, she is ready to sound yet another postcolonial oppositional voice into the void.

This new mediation takes place in a short story entitled "Ovando," which exposes the original conquistadorian invasion in the Caribbean as anything but seamless. "Ovando" is a pièce de résistance of anticolonial excavation in which the protagonist takes an unusual cultural stance. Historically it comes on the heels of *Annie, Gwen, Lilly, Pam and Tulip.* Kincaid's new fictional venue is Hispaniola, site of the third Spanish conquest. Previous protagonists who chronologically follow Ovando share the legacy of these invasions. Taking the wide view, "Ovando" illumines a transhistorical context against which *At the Bottom of the River, Annie John, A Small Place,* and *Lucy* are played out.

Through fictionalizing the arrival of Nicolás de Ovando, the most violent conquistador, Kincaid refuses the imperial gaze on the "New World"; at the moment of colonization, the narrator gazes on conquistadorian genocide. She dissolves the perspective that privileges conquerors and their legatees.

As in *A Small Place,* "Ovando" exposes the fact that the motherland is no motherland at all but a point of embarcation for marauders bent on implementing a colonial law of the father.[11] The only mother is the narrator who welcomes Ovando into her home. Like the nameless protagonist of *At the Bottom* and *Annie John,* the unnamed protagonist of "Ovando" tries to outwit colonial agents and ends up in a state of blankness, almost eaten away by worms that are one of the story's basic elements.

This breakdown, however, coincides with the narrator's stated intent never to assist Ovando again, as she perhaps foolishly, certainly naively did at the beginning. Her refusal constitutes a transhistorical ultimatum. Resembling and in part synthesizing the respective endings of *At the*

Bottom, Annie, Gwen, Lilly, Pam and Tulip, Annie John, and *A Small Place,* the narrator in "Ovando" finally rejects her role as mimic and placator, becomes someone who discerns dual oppression, and claims an identity. By clarifying origins and historical process, she symbolically recaptures the terrain. Most tellingly, she has assumed agency, consciously at odds with imperial authority. Across centuries, the narrator of "Ovando" has become Lucy seeing through blonde Mariah. Even more to the point, she is the audacious narrator of *A Small Place* and a collective narrator of *Annie, Gwen, Lilly, Pam and Tulip* now more fully attuned to realpolitik.

Kincaid's colonial and postcolonial texts, then, are indelibly marked by opposition to the hegemonic project. In that sense, Kincaid is a voice-giver, inviting us to read against the grain, exposing the suppression of heterogeneous utterances.[12] Kincaid's resistance to illicit or corrupt authority is a form of nonviolent decolonization that complements a postcolonial agency.[13]

The collective quests of these protagonists for individual identities merge, separate, and overlap at times (it seems) with Kincaid's personal quest. Occupying a fluid position in the margins connects these people. Kincaid's representation of a plurality of identities promotes different hiding places as well as different sites from which to pounce. It fosters daring.[14] In this staging of new vantage points, Jamaica Kincaid dissolves the economy of domination.

At the Bottom of the River: *Mystical (De)coding*

Chapter 1

> I can see the great danger in what I am — a defenseless and pitiful child. Here is a list of what I must do.
>   . . . . .
> I looked at this world as it revealed itself to me — how new, how new — and I longed to go there. — *At the Bottom of the River*

✪ BY HER OWN ADMISSION, Jamaica Kincaid views her first publication, *At the Bottom of the River* (1983), as the text of a repressed, indoctrinated subaltern subject: "I can see that *At the Bottom of the River* was, for instance, a very unangry, decent, civilized book and it represents sort of this successful attempt by English people to make their version of a human being or their version of a person out of me. It amazes me now that I did that then. I would never write like that again, I don't think. I might go back to it, but I'm not very interested in that sort of expression any more."[1]

I want to argue that Jamaica Kincaid through diverse discussions of mothers sets up a subtle paradigm of colonialism that enables these repressions to be heard; the text, that is, masks and marks the role that colonialism plays in educating colonized people against their interests. For Kincaid herself, the project was a failure for the colonizers.

At the Bottom takes place on the island of Antigua, where Jamaica Kincaid was born, a geographical and psychic reality that constantly serves as backdrop. Kincaid represents the experiences of a child growing up in Antigua during the 1950s. Sometimes she mentions the fact of colonial life through intertextual references but rarely head-on, while the child's biological mother seems to double occasionally as an anticolonial target. The section entitled "Wingless" is saturated with colonial tropes, typically nineteenth-century British. Winglessness denies legitimate ontological status, deprives the narrator emotionally, and enforces limits.

The section opens on a classroom where small children "are reading from a book filled with simple words and sentences. 'Once upon a time there was a little chimney-sweep, whose name was Tom'" (p. 20). Thus does the narrator explicitly draw from *The Water-Babies,* Charles Kingsley's political allegory about nineteenth-century British industrial poverty and child abuse that foreshadows everyday situations in twentieth-century Antigua.[2] This narrator longs for the same drastic transformation experienced by the protagonist, Tom, a psychologically and physically abused chimney sweep who becomes a water baby. But she also fears that she might become an oppressor: "Perhaps I stand on the brink of a great discovery, and perhaps after I have made my great discovery I will be sent home in chains" (p. 21). The narrator and Tom could become the exiled Christopher Columbus, victim of sorts of Francisco de Bobadilla, second leader of the conquistadors, for no one is immune to corruption. Resembling the narrator in his feelings of alienation and idyllic longings, Tom miraculously has his (unconscious) wishes granted and, as a water baby, he is "adopted" by a loving mother figure named Mrs. Do As You Would Be Done By.

Consumed like Tom with a transcendent desire for change, the narrator craves her elementary teacher's attention, "that large-bottomed woman . . . I gave up my sixpences [for] instead of spending for sweets" (p. 21). Underscoring a daily life steeped in vestiges of colonialism, Kincaid refers to old British coinage (sixpences), British idiomatic usage ("sweets" for "candies"), and the ambivalence of the colonized (desiring the teacher's attention). Mimicry and insurrection uneasily interact. Descendants of freed slaves, the children are instructed in scarcely disguised postcolonial values as Antigua nominally moves toward independence.

Flashes of self-scrutiny — "Am I horrid?" — conjoin with an intimation of other subjectivities. She feels like the abused and lonely Tom though she recognizes that Tom's circumstances caused his self-deprecating and socially demeaning identity: "a defenceless and pitiful child." Announcing that she also (like Tom) swims "in a shaft of light, upside down and I can see myself clearly through and through, from every angle," she hovers on the threshold of discovery. More importantly, she is someone who does not see the authentic relationship of herself as a historical subject:

> I am not yet a dog with a cruel and unloving master. I am not yet a tree growing on barren and bitter land. I am not yet the shape of darkness in a dungeon.
> Where? What? Why? How then? Oh, that!
> I am primitive and wingless. (p. 24)

This water is clear and it moves: "Clear waters . . . produce fleeting and facile images." It takes on almost anthropomorphic qualities, echoing one critic's assertion that "the stream, the river, the cascade then have a speech that men understand rationally."[3] The narrator's longing to be free explodes through her sadness, but winglessness prevents her from taking off. Rather pointedly, this section about the need to soar heralds a singularly nuanced anticolonial interrogation between a teacher-mother (country) and a (colonized) student:

> "Don't eat the strings on bananas — they will wrap around your heart and kill you."
> "Oh. Is that true?"
> "No."
> "Is that something to tell children?"
> "No. But it's so funny. You should see how you look trying to remove all the strings from the bananas with your monkey fingernails. Frightened?"
> "Frightened. Very frightened." (p. 24)

Thus the narrator links her own colonial situation to Tom's imaginative transformation that enables him to escape a brutal apprenticeship with the vile Mr. Grimes. Wrestling for sexual power interlaces with the complex monkey trope that populates all Kincaid's texts. The monkey functions both as a trickster who can retaliate against exploitation and as a traditional symbol of the Eurocentric gaze. Mr. Grimes's name signifies the same filth that characterizes the dead ashes she rubs her toes in.[4] Everyone, the narrator states, is so on edge that black and white teachers are collectively startled (or feign being startled) when a black child succeeds. Discussing one of her former teachers, Jamaica Kincaid talked of this situation in a recent interview. If she wrote a good essay, the teacher would proclaim: "At last one of you did it right." In *A Small Place,* she also mentions the fact that the headmistress of the girls' school where she was a pupil told "these girls over and over again to stop behaving as if they were monkeys just out of trees. No one ever dreamed that the word for any of this was racism.[5]

This section in "Wingless" connects to another critical moment when the narrator remarks that no one compliments her father and goes on to describe him as a vain man who orders a brown felt hat from England every year. She represents this purchase as an act of colonial mimicry that in turn is metonymically and inversely linked to the headmistress's dread of the other. A fantasy of personal-colonial patricide follows in which "the woman I love" (the mother) reacts to a frightening man who is dressed in sticks and tree bark. Not coincidentally, the imperialists who arrived in the Caribbean were associated with bark, the fabric of their ships and a sign of their mobility: "Instead of removing her cutlass from the folds of her big and beautiful skirt and cutting the man in two at the waist, she only smiled — a red, red smile — and like a fly he dropped dead" (p. 25).

This self-critical and doubled use of language — who is mimicking whom? — this hybrid form and the self-knowledge implied in growing up fragmented yield a decolonizing of the narrator's outlook. She claims the right to what Edward Said calls "the audacious metaphoric charting of spiritual territory usurped by colonial masters." She internalizes the postcolonial impulse.[6] Issues of class, sexual difference, and race intersect with attentiveness to the mother-daughter relationship. More generally, these issues are connected to the condition of growing up in Antigua before black Antiguans win independence from the British and precipitate an uneasy alliance between a black Antiguan government, the people, and a disenfranchised ex-colonial Anglo-Saxon class.

Two other critical, imperial signs appear in subsequent references to an Anglican hymn and to night-soil men. First, the speaker in the section "Letters from Home" alludes to "All Things Bright and Beautiful." This hymn is an emblem of a nominally Anglican colonizing culture that is rhetorically featured in the book she is reading, its title *An Illustrated Encyclopedia of Butterflies and Moths:* "I leaf through the book," she says, "looking only at the pictures, which are bright and beautiful" ("Holidays," p. 29). The hymn renders corruption and human degradation invisible, or at least hints at it very gently:

The cold wind in the winter,
The pleasant summer sun.
The ripe fruits in the garden,
He made them every one.
He gave us eyes to see them,
And lips that we might tell
How great is God Almighty,
Who has made all things well.

Since her experiences growing up militate against that view, the speaker mocks the idea that the beauty of the world is evidence of God.[7] From the point of view of politically dominated people, the world cannot be beautiful as long as an unequal dynamic of power obtains. This allusion not only glosses her recognition of and resistance to cultural indoctrination but it further records her fascination with the word *thorax* because of its symbolic significance: "From my looking through the book, the word 'thorax' sticks in my mind. 'Thorax,' I say, 'thorax, thorax,' I don't know how many times" (pp. 29–30). An insect's body or middle section between the neck and abdomen, enclosed by the ribs is the place where the narrator "exists" for the expropriating colonizer-parasite. The narrator is an alienated being, an unwilling host. More ironically, however, recent entomological research prefers to talk of the insect as divided into fourteen segments and not to talk in terms of the head-thorax subdivision.[8] So to talk of thorax is to talk of artificial separation such as the daughter experiences from the mother. Kincaid later elaborates on another form of artificial separation in "Ovando." This deadness at the nerve ends is partly explained by references elsewhere, notably in "Wingless," where the narrator highlights the suppressed conditions of a take-over culture. Through the chaos of images around insects, what the narrator-representative does and does not have is subtly suggested.

Second, her discussion of the night-soil men describes their imaginative and physical impact on her life. Hard workers, they represent colonial neglect of an adequate sewage system. Underscoring their mythical as well as concrete physical presence, she discursively links them to a woman who removes her skin in a reenactment of a voodoo priestess's spiritual ritual.[9] The people's culture is still vital, despite a colonial presence. She follows this with dreams about her father, then a separate mother-love fantasy. This admixture implies that the biological and colonial layers of the narrator's life are inextricably interrelated. The narrator closes with a claim that she will marry a "red-skin" woman and live in a mud hut by the sea, invoking prehistoric allusions to caves and reptilian life.[10] The narrator is neither afraid of unconventional behavior nor too callow to perceive it as such. During this episode while the men remove feces, the narrator wet-dreams of a baby and a lamb being born and bleating, emblems of degradation and exclusion. Mud, moreover, in Gaston Bachelard's formulation, is the dust of water. It lacks clarity and forges mystery. The mud around water is an imagination, as it were, struggling to free itself. Michelet argues along comparable lines that maternal feelings emanate from mud and slime because that form of water is elemental.[11] Viscosity of water links to maternality. This introduction of water marks a critical intervention in Kincaid's texts: water suggests a preoedipal state.

One of the things the happy but fantastically married female child-pair will do in "In the Night" is "put on John Bull masks and frighten defenseless little children on their way home from school." John Bull masks signify carnival gaiety. Conventionally, the person wearing this mask has horns and a rope tied round him or her and is pulled by another disguised person. Uncle Sam's blood cousin, John Bull also stands for Britain and patriotism, as well as British values, ethnocentrically conceived. Unsure who they are — for in that age how could two women marry? — they appear to mock the insensitive British colonists who rule Antigua.[12] The speaker's complacent and rebellious side imaginatively fuse here; with the mask she creatively expropriates the colonists' power.[13] By invoking a feminocentric paradigm, she contests male colonial power. Echoing the mother's fervor, the narrator proudly proclaims: "This woman I would like to marry knows many things, but to me she will only tell about things that would never dream of making me cry; and every night, over and over, she will tell me something that begins, 'Before you were born.' I will marry a woman like this, and every night, every night, I will be completely happy" (p. 12).

The narrator veils but dialogizes her beliefs: her mask reveals her concealment.[14] In the next section the narrator recognizes the connection of her own angst to a pervasive colonial malaise. This section, "Holidays," takes the form of a letter in which another letter is embedded.

She sits facing the mountains on a visit to her grandmother's house in

Dominica. These mountains together with Kincaid's autobiographical writings about Dominica suggest that this is the island in question. The narrator checks herself physically, seeking a basic security that still eludes her: "I sit on the porch facing the mountains. The porch is airy and spacious. I am the only person sitting on the porch. I look at myself. I can see myself. That is, I can see my chest, my abdomen, my legs, and my arms. I cannot see my hair, my ears, my face, or my collarbone. I can feel them, though" (p. 31).[15]

She tries but she cannot write her name in dead ashes with her big toe; perhaps she does not accept the renaming that accompanied colonialism. When her body is being metaphorically mutilated and she has to write with a toe in the embers of her environment, she cannot identify herself. Ash, in addition, links metonymically to fire and to the sun that denies water. Perhaps even more to the point, in Bachelard's view mud and dust are connected.[14] She cannot find who she is or how she functions in this history or any other history. She tries to rectify the situation by attaching her sense of being soiled to a colonial symbol. In this way she can displace the "dirt" it engenders: "I try to clean by rubbing it vigorously on a clean royal-blue rug. The royal-blue rug now has a dark spot, and my big toe has a strong burning sensation" (p. 30). No matter where she turns, colonialism remains; the dark spot—the despoiling of the land and its people—stains the royal-blue colonial map. An anti-phoenix, she wants to script her name in the embers of a dead colonial ruling class. She will help define imperial disintegration. Not by coincidence, she then tries to suppress an involuntary matricidal desire that presses in on her, born of a different kind of history and knowledge. Her reaction also suggests her resistance to fighting back: "I remove my hands from resting on my head, because my arms are tired. But also I have just remembered a superstition: if you sit with your hands on your head, you will kill your mother. I have many superstitions. I believe all of them" (p. 31).

But her senses and her memory of indigenous culture retaliate. She remembers (and reinvokes?) obeah practices against the enemy—the so-called mother country that can eventually be destroyed. Affirming her belief in cultural practices coded by westerners as superstitions, she signals decisive opposition to the invaders through her commitment to the land and the people. Nonetheless, the mother's identity remains ambiguous. On the one hand, the narrator could be talking about a physical mother. On the other, Kincaid clearly opens the door to plural readings. This explicit letter — "Holidays" — differs considerably from the inserted letter in "Holidays" that she imagines writing. It comprises an attempt to boost her self-image even as it comments on the division between life and art she has already explored. Is the condition of her life worth memorializing? The answer seems to be yes, because it is not only a personal life but a representative history. Thus it is important to record that life and transform it into art and history. The colonizer's version of events and history must be challenged. This interior letter embryonically foreshadows her revelation at the end.

In reaction to alienation, the speaker cherishes feeling, yet is shaky enough to doubt her right to language: "Oh, sensation. I am filled with sensation. I feel — oh, how I feel, I feel, I feel, I feel. I have no words right now for how I feel. . . . It is midday. Did I say that? Must I say that? Oh me, oh my" (p. 30). Her doubled letters, exterior and interior, her jumpiness and unsureness are efforts to identify herself—however tentatively—through language. Her claim to speech intersects with a traditional femininity, replete with disclaimers and apologies, that remains an unresolved conflict.

As well as assaulting colonialism obliquely as a corrupt motherland, Jamaica Kincaid also focuses on a central mother-daughter unit that functions at the very least as a politically ambiguous relationship. She does so specifically in a section entitled "Girl," which opens the volume. In a continuous, one-sentence near-monologue of six hundred and fifty words or so, a mother intones instructions to a daughter about how to act as she grows up in Antigua. Sometimes the directives are domestically oriented, at other times they address sexual behavior: "Wash the white clothes on Monday and put them on the stone heap; wash the color clothes on Tuesday and put them on the clothesline to dry; don't walk barehead in the hot sun . . . on Sundays try to walk like a lady and not like the slut you are so bent on becoming" (p. 3).

By opening *At the Bottom of the River,* her first text, with a section on a seemingly unproblematized biological mother, Kincaid temporarily suppresses the doubled meaning of mother. Besides, according to her own testimony, she was scarcely aware of the layered political implications.

During this litany, the mother insistently assumes that the daughter will act loosely in the future—certainly not to the mother's satisfaction—suggesting some apprehension about her present behavior. Sexual difference, as the mother perceives it, features critically in how to conduct oneself: "This is how to behave in the presence of men who don't know you very well, and this way they won't recognize immediately the slut I have warned you against becoming; be sure to wash every day, even if it is with your own spit; don't squat down to play marbles—you are not a boy, you know; don't pick people's flowers—you might catch something" (pp. 4–5).

Through the word *slut* the mother presents her daughter's sociosexual and metaphysical reality as she wishes it to be. She spells out what to note, what not to become, and therefore, as later events bear out, what to desire. In psychological terms, the phallus is introduced as a primary signifier of desire, to be rejected at all costs.

This self-reiterating discourse evokes fear or self-disgust or both. The "Girl" of the title is being warned to conform in such a way as to refract what the mother-speaker did or did not do growing up in Dominica. Thus the mother is trying to prevent the daughter from doing things that might well have disrupted her own life. Hence the mother through her daughter both tries to and wants to rewrite her own script. If only through discursive repetition, the daughter is obliquely reminded that "slut" as a cultural taboo marks colonialism. Its overuse—in a quiet reference to the historical sexual abuse of black women—underscores the status of the narrator as a young black woman. The mother's admonitions illumine the critical role that history has played and is playing in everyone's lives.

The narrator responds mildly and rather unprovocatively—perhaps deliberately so. Retrospectively, Kincaid seems to have decoded these responses by the daughter as repressed. The speaker disrupts her mother's commands only twice with the briefest of comments. After her mother tells her, "Don't sing benna [calypsos] in Sunday School; you mustn't speak to wharf-rat [reform school] boys, not even to give directions; don't eat fruits or the street-flies will follow you," the daughter stoutly replies: "But I don't sing benna on Sundays at all and never in Sunday School." The mother does not want, it seems, to fracture colonial decorum in Sunday School with manifestations of Antiguan culture. First, the daughter announces her obedience and correct conduct in a clear

effort to please her mother. At a conscious level, she agrees to conform —
or so it seems. This answer also intimates a sideways refutation of any
potential charge of anticolonial opposition or of immorality intimated in
"slut" and reaccentuated in the reference to "wharf-rat boys." A further
suggestion is that the daughter knows full well what the mother is talking about. Her intentionally soft answer could be stressing how pre-
posterous she finds these charges or how meticulously she will deny
them. The reply is ambiguous.

The daughter's second reply comes after the mother tells her how "to
make ends meet; always squeeze bread to make sure it's fresh." She says:
"What if the baker won't let me feel the bread?" to which the mother
responds: "You mean to say that after all you are really going to be the
kind of woman who the baker won't let near the bread?" (p. 5). The
daughter dreads that she cannot live up to the mother's expectations but,
as her defensiveness indicates, she still admires her mother's refusal not
to be pushed around. The mother derides the very idea that the daughter
will be a pushover, obviously expecting the daughter to be strong yet
obedient at the same time. She appears oblivious to the complex bind in
which she may be positioning the daughter. At another level, too, the
mother challenges the daughter to make people expose their wares; otherwise, she commands the daughter, "call them on it."

Through her bossy directives in "Girl," the mother attempts to pre-
empt certain prejudices against black Antiguan females as sexually loose.
She wants to protect her daughter from obvious pitfalls. (We assume
rules are bent or circumstances refashioned in the case of ruling-class
white students who kick over sexual traces.) On the other hand, the
mother's anxiety may project a desire to prevent her daughter from
repeating behavior that the mother had to live down or deny in her past.

Besides, from the mother's standpoint, bringing a daughter up well
necessitates such vigilance; her attentiveness indicates lavish maternal
caring. She wants to teach her daughter "highly adaptive mechanisms
designed to promote physical and mental survival. Without such teaching the mental and physical survival of Black women would be impossible."[17] The daughter herself would feel cherished — rather than dominated — and consequently shies from separation, unconsciously craving
a closer, almost symbiotic, preoedipal maternal union. Anna Freud explains the painful fluctuations of adolescent conflict this way:

> I take it that it is normal for an adolescent to behave for a considerable length of time in an inconsistent and unpredictable manner; to fight his impulses and to accept them; to ward them off successfully and to be overrun by them; to love his parents and to hate them; to revolt against them and to be dependent on them; . . . to be more idealistic, artistic, generous and unselfish than he will ever be again, but also the opposite: self-centered, egotistic, calculating. Such fluctuations between extreme opposites would be deemed highly abnormal at any other time of life. At this time they may signify no more than that an adult structure of personality takes a long time to emerge, that the ego of the individual in question does not cease to experiment and is in no hurry to close down on possibilities.[18]

The ambiguous end of "Girl" stresses the mother's love of decision making and her persistence in trying to determine the daughter's future behavior. The end also applauds self-assertion even though the relentless litany of repetitions delivered from on high tends to crush response: "All geared to enforce the sanctioned behavior of the Caribbean woman-child, domestic and limiting; little here supports the expansion of the self."[19] In affirmation of this point, Jamaica Kincaid in a recent interview explains how she tried to replicate their relationship: " 'Girl' is my mother's voice exactly over many years. There are two times that I talked in my life as a child, as a powerless person. Now I talk all the time."[20] At the very least, the social and moral commandments render answering back, let alone rebellion, a risk-taking business to the listening, provoked, effectively silenced daughter. At an even deeper level, in a perverse displacement, the mother is encouraging the daughter to live a version of her now hidden past sexual life. She goads her daughter into being on permanent guard, ready for any eventuality:

> Don't throw stones at blackbirds, because it might not be a blackbird at all; this is how to make a bread pudding; this is how to make donkona; this is how to make pepper pot; this is how to make a good medicine for a cold; this is how to make a good medicine to throw away a child before it even becomes a child; this is how to catch a fish; this is how to throw back a fish you don't like, and that way something bad won't fall on you; this is how to bully a man; this is how a man bullies you; this is how to love a man, and if this doesn't work there are other ways, and if they don't work don't feel too bad about giving up; this is how to spit up in the air if you feel like it; and this is how to move quick so that it doesn't fall on you. (p. 5)

Only by keeping her barriers high can the mother control external behavior. A bottled-up insecurity, even a sense of terror, lurks around the
edges of such injunctions. At the same time, the mother reminds the
daughter of familiar cultural practices — the injunction about the blackbird, for example, warns against accepting what lies on the surface.[21] The
blackbird's complexity also inscribes the importance of obeah in everyday life.

On the other hand, the entire section could be the daughter's own
internal monologue. What if the daughter is simply imagining this or-
acular, maternal discourse, extrapolating certain worries expressed by
the mother in day-to-day asides? What if the daughter is already aware of
temptation but worries about crossing her mother's path? Is she enunci-
ating her own worst fears and using her mother to project anxieties
about a perceived "lack"? Perhaps she plots disobedience and has re-
hearsed this revenge against the mother — a form of compensation or
expiation by the daughter. She is allowing her mother to speak her mind,
to read the daughter's thoughts and respond. As compensation for "bad
thoughts," she is constructing negative mother-daughter dialogues in
which she has to suppress any response.

At any rate, the implied narrator in "Girl" dialogizes many silences
on the daughter's part. The mother-daughter relationship appears to
be framed principally in terms of maternal-colonial power, mixed with
probable rage and frustration in the daughter. A polyphony of messages
fuses with conflicting reactions.

Three shorter references supplement the complexity of the mother-
daughter relationship and its embedding of colonialism. In them, different evocations of motherhood and resistance erupt. In its mystery
and private symbols, for example, the section named "At Last" invokes
a mother getting a chance to explain some troubling issues. She does
this through a displaced conversation in which territorial and emotional
spaces represented by a home and its yard signify speakers. A narrator
expresses anger at a pregnant mother for neglecting the eldest child,
presumably herself, pouring forth her jealousy in a tale of red ants. (Red
ants recur in several later texts.)

The debate between the home and the yard dramatically reenacts the
narrator's material and psychic lives. The confining house obliges the
narrator to listen and obey a list of her mother's dos and don'ts, remi-

niscent of the maternal commandments in "Girl." In this case, home emblematizes a restrictive maternality, life lived as a dominated person. Through the mother, this moody older child who feels jealousy toward new siblings begins to speak that jealousy and her sense of neglect: "We held hands once and were beautiful. But what followed? Sleepless night, oh, sleepless night. A baby was born on Thursday and was almost eaten, eyes first, by red ants, on Friday" ("At Last," p. 14). In the borderland of the yard, the narrator can cherish secrets and distance herself from circumstances that invalidate her. The yard signals spaciousness and seeming freedom. Her agony at (maternal) separation symbolically reverberates in her anguish about doors "tied so tight shut." The mother vehemently denies that the doors were even (ever) closed. In two subsequent and related exchanges, the speaker asks morbidly, even ominously, if "what passed between us" was "like a carcass? Did you feed on it . . . Or was it like a skeleton? Did you live on it?" (p. 15). Emotionally torn apart, she feels eaten alive and dead at the same time. She adds that "eggs boiled violently in that pot" and a coconut fiber mattress "made our skin raw," pointed allusions not only to poverty but to conceptions and births that plagued her life. Perhaps she hints at efforts to terminate pregnancies.[22] Additionally, with respect to political environment, British colonists tried to pick the carcass of Antiguan people clean and reduce a living culture to a skeleton. Eggs boil violently because sex for women can be perilous and birth in such a society is a dangerous engagement.

Second, In "What Have I Been Lately," the narrator muses scenarios aloud to voice herself into an indeterminate environment, both visionary and material. This meditation on infinite space links to her sense of loneliness, perhaps as compensation for the absent mother, perhaps a sign of the merger of two "mothers." The nature that surrounds her reminds her of that which never deserts her: "To love the *infinite* universe is to give a material meaning, an objective meaning, to the *infinity* of the love for a mother. To love a *solitary* place, when we are abandoned by everyone, is to compensate for a painful absence; it is a reminder for us of the one who never abandons."[23] Dreams of the past and future merge with the present. Another evocative monkey tale erupts where the monkey (the narrator) avenges itself against its enemy. In its first manifestation, the monkey does nothing, as if lying in wait, living up to its trickster image. In both cases, the narrator is an agent, but the point where the narrator stops and the monkey starts slips out of reach.[24] That monkey remains elusive as it does throughout Kincaid's texts, signifying simultaneously the ubiquity of resistance, noncomplicity, and mimicry. "At Last" also parodically reenacts itself as a self-conscious fiction: "In the covert form [of self-awareness], this process [of narcissistic texts] is internalized, actualized; such a text is self-reflective but not necessarily self-conscious."[25] What complicates the metafictional self-reflection is the powerful (and avowed) injection of intentionally refigured autobiographical moments.

A third section entitled "The Letter from Home" features an epistolary monologue, a subtle stylistic variant on "Girl" and "Holidays." "Letter" exemplifies Kincaid's preference to articulate concerns through a polyphonic speaker, often in dialogue. Starting softly with milking cows and churning butter, the prose moves rapidly to a greater order of intensity, antinomies, and surreal elements: crashing tree branches, hissing gas, incantatory images of lizards: "My heart beat loudly *thud! thud!*, tiny beads of water gathered on my nose, my hair went limp, my waist grew folds, I shed my skin; lips have trembled, tears have flowed, cheeks have puffed, stomachs have twisted with pain" (p. 37). Fantasy and realism, nurturance and death lie side by side in an uneasy union. Water appears in an elemental state. Sexual imagery abounds subtly and overtly: "My waist grew folds, I shed my skin." Once again she claims a sexual and important subjectivity, evoking distinctly anticolonial obeah practices in which priestesses shed skin, a developmental paradigm of sorts. Lizards echo penises, quickly fusing and separating.[26] A complex world emotes where identities shift and exchange themselves. Signs of the evolutionary process spell gradual but qualitative changes.

The challenge of the maternal-filial unit that peppers the text culminates in the section "My Mother." Both eulogy and matricidal desire, "My Mother" movingly recasts preoedipal bliss. The narrator opens with a near death-wish fantasy as she confesses the depth of her love: "Immediately on wishing my mother dead and seeing the pain it caused her, I was sorry and cried so many tears that all the earth around me was drenched. Standing before my mother, I begged her forgiveness, and I begged so earnestly that she took pity on me, kissing my face and placing my head on her bosom to rest. Placing her arms around me, she drew my head closer and closer to her bosom, until finally I suffocated. I lay on her bosom, breathless, for a time uncountable, until one day, for a reason she has kept to herself, she shook me out and stood me under a tree and I started to breathe again" (p. 53). She wants to control her mother and annihilate herself. In common teenage fashion, she wishes her mother dead and simultaneously longs for her love. She projects the perceived threat of maternal withdrawal as a threat to the mother herself at her own guilty hands.[27] She also represents the trickster monkey again in a different form. Images of suffocation and death signify certain damning realizations: Her excess denies room for growth, and even love is corrupted as a consequence. But after she interjects duplicity to signify distance, resentment wins out. Water symbolizes negation: "Between my mother and me now were the tears I had cried, and I gathered up some stones and banked them in so that they formed a small pond. The water in the pond was thick and black and poisonous, so that only unnameable invertebrates could live in it. My mother and I now watched each other carefully, always making sure to shower the other with words and deeds of love and affection" (p. 54). Slimy worms characterize the texture of their relationship that has literally sunk very low, into the wind. Water is now stagnant. Only mud (not a vibrant connection with and to the imagination) resides in the depths. This meditation continues with several lush fantasies that oscillate between the registers of love and hate. In one surreal cross-cultural episode that invokes an ancient Hindu myth, mother and daughter mesmerize each other and turn themselves into lizards: "Silently, she had instructed me to follow her example, and now I too traveled along on my white underbelly, my tongue darting and flickering in the hot air" (p. 55).[28] In a second vision, a grazing lamb — the innocent lamb symbolizing British imperialism? — inspires insight or self-revelation in the speaker: "The lamb is cross and miserable. So would I be, too, if I had to live [like colonizers?] in a climate not suited to my nature" (p. 57). After this, she digs an immense hole over which she constructs a beautiful house, a fatal trap for her mother to fall through. Instead the mother walks on water and easily evades death. The mother confounds boundaries just as colonizers survive in the face of hatred. The episode epitomizes childhood and colonizer, a continuum that encompasses peoples and their bipolar reactions. It also amounts to a death wish. But water acts atypically; its fluidity becomes a site of safety.[29]

These matricidal, anticolonial desires are indivisible from the protagonist's burning hatred — "I glowed and glowed again, red with anger" (p. 59). They also intimate emotional antipathy too — some kind of unfathomable, unfaceable sadness. At the biological level, the gap between hatred and sadness, however, underscores the intensity of the narrator's devotion, hinting at a dimension of insecurity. After powerful rejection, the narrator inevitably starts a self-barricading process to preserve personal intactness. In that sense, *At the Bottom of the River* explains conflicts faced by Kincaid's later, often similarly profiled narrators. Perhaps Kincaid's own personal agony erupts here. She has talked more than once about the differential treatment her biological parents gave her brothers almost from birth. As an only child for so long, Jamaica Kincaid expected that same undiluted level of affection and attention to continue. Her sense of emptiness as a child who emotionally feels neglected growing up fills in many fictive textual silences. At the same time the paradigm might be attached to the uphill struggle indigenous people wage against insensitive foreign forces.

At the end of "My Mother," as the protagonist approaches the jetty where she will leave her natal home for Britain, she rapidly becomes saturated in preoedipallike longing, her ego no longer concerned with its own intactness: "What peace came over me then, for I could not see where she left off and I began, or where I left off and she began. . . . As we walk through the rooms, we merge and separate, merge and separate; soon we shall enter the final stage of our evolution" (p. 60).[30] But no sooner has this fantasy begun than it explodes and flashes warning signals; it becomes a fairy tale that part of her craves to preserve, but its idyllic features are also corrupted by ominous signs: agitated motion and a lamb that emblematize a contaminating British colonialism and an imposed Christianity. It is as if the narrator tries to imagine a state of permanent harmony in which hostility insistently intervenes: "My mother and I live in a bower made from flowers whose petals are imperishable. There is the silvery blue of the sea, crisscrossed with sharp darts of light, there is the warm rain falling on the clumps of castor bush, there is the small lamb bounding across the pasture, there is the soft ground welcoming the soles of my pink feet. It is in this way my mother and I have lived for a long time now" (p. 61). This joyful vision of the sea echoes the world of Mrs. Do As You Would Be Done By in *The Water-*

Babies. Blue invokes transparency, the meshing of boundaries, a diaphanous veil. Next to white, blue is the color of the immateriality that the narrator seems to long for. But it represents only a vision, nothing more, and the proleptic presence of the usually beatific lamb, as well as sharp "darts," unexpected interventions, mark a rank uncertainty lurking beneath.

The accumulation of injuries that the narrator experiences in "Girl" and "My Mother" culminate in a meditation entitled "Blackness," about a foreboding yet comforting set of sensations that rehearse her inner and outer confusion. Symbolic blackness recalls the soot of Grimes's corruption that drenches vulnerable Tom. The two mothers coalesce in a brilliant fusion: "The blackness fills up a small room, a large field, an island, my own being. The blackness cannot bring me joy but often I am glad in it. The blackness cannot be separated from me but often I can stand outside it" (p. 46).

Coping with overwhelming emotion induces disintegration. First of all, the narrator lives with a mother — at one level biological — whom she hates and adores; the mother engenders the narrator's defiant, single-handed struggles at school against indoctrination. This mother is also the motherland. She represents (is) British postcolonial authority, an unmothering mother, one who does not nurture. The narrator is experiencing dislocation as if she were saying, "I can no longer say my own name. I can no longer point to myself and say 'I.'" "Blackness" involves linguistic alienation, feelings of loss and censorship that threaten to annihilate her: "First, then, I have been my individual self, carefully banishing randomness from my existence, then I am swallowed up in the blackness so that I am one with it" (p. 47). Trapped in signification that does not offer validation, she feels beaten down, dissolved almost. This feeling of impending erasure recapitulates an incident from "Holidays" that identifies a similar sense of disappearance: "How frightened I became once on looking down to see an oddly shaped, ash-colored object that I did not recognize at once to be a small part of my own foot" ("Blackness," p. 47). Now she has lost her voice in public, barely holding on to that hovering space in language where the prediscursive registers, where there are no borders constructed by the West to contain people. The narrator resorts — but only just — to semiotic babble.[31] Rhythmic harmonies and onomatopoetic reverberations pulsate in harmony. The narrator ponders her existence, rejoices in her power when she finds "I was not at one with myself and I felt myself separate." Immediately after she cuts into that private exultation by describing herself as a "brittle substance dashed and shattered, each separate part without knowledge of the other separate parts" (p. 48). Seesawing between numbness and vital awareness, between familiarity and strangeness affirms isolation but induces a sense of diverse vantage points that she can occupy simultaneously. The ensuing vision signals colonial devastation, the visionary narrator representing colonized people: "I dreamed of bands of men who walked aimlessly, their guns and cannons slackened at their sides, the chambers emptied of bullets and shells. They had fought in a field from time to time and from time to time they grew tired of it. They walked up the path that led to my house and as they walked they passed between the sun and the earth; as they passed between the sun and the earth they blotted out the daylight and night fell immediately and permanently. No longer could I see the blooming trefoils, their overpowering perfume a constant giddy delight to me" (pp. 48–49). The inner silence that immerses the narrator also protects her against hideous, frequent nightmares. Such an interiority offers something resembling a precolonial harmony — in Africa, say — where "the pastures are unfenced, the lions roam the continents, the continents are not separated" (p. 52).[32] The speaker's subjectivity is continually in flux. Although she calls it peace, this felt integrity is also a fragile edifice she has constructed in order to hold mental wolves at bay. Her vision of a wholesome erasure is also a self-obliteration: "Living in the silent voice, I am at last at peace. Living in the silent voice, I am at last erased" (p. 52).

In the end, where a mother describes a daughter, we review the familiar situation of "Girl" from an alternate site. By now this daughter acts catatonic, out of reach. The mother's discourse recalls Tom from *The Water-Babies* who is made transparent "when passing through a small beam of light" (p. 49). "She sees the child's cruelties — [she is, the mother says] pitiless to the hunchback boy." On a more endorsing note, the mother also understands that the child is enamored of "ancestral history" (p. 51).

This maternal narrator, then, pictures herself plurally to one who cannot decode it. It is as if the original daughterly narrator of "Girl" voices her mother into a more high-profiled existence to keep things fair, to give her mother a chance to tell "her side of the story." But unlike the mother in "Girl," she cannot pronounce judgment. Instead, she is sad for the daughter's seeming loss — or what would seem a loss — of the mother. She can only try to surmise what happened and fit the daughter's actions within a framework she can comprehend: "Having observed the many differing physical existences feed on each other, she is beyond despair or the spiritual vacuum. . . . My child rushes from death to death, so familiar a state is it to her" (p. 51).

On the other hand, at the end of the mother's musings, the narrator validates the mother's influence, almost as if the narrator were willing the mother to think positively: "Though I have summoned her into a fleeting existence, one that is perilous and subject to the violence of chance, she embraces time as it passes in numbing sameness, bearing in its wake a multitude of great sadness" (p. 51).

The last section, which bears the title of the volume, "At the Bottom of the River," conjures up a dream world. The narrator shares a vision of perilous terrain where power and antinomy are the order of the day. This metaphysical beauty has little or no meaning outside of human contact: "The stream . . . awaits the eye, the hand, the foot that shall then give all this a meaning" (p. 63). Once again, water will heal, will provide clarity, will function as a catalyst. The fluidity and motion of water underscore the elusiveness of identity that has beleaguered the narrator. She is at one with the ocean, where boundaries dissolve. Anton Ehrenzweig comments as follows, discussing the separation of self and other: "The London psycho-analysts, D. E. Winnicott and Marion Milner, have stressed the importance for a creative ego to be able to suspend the boundaries between self and not-self in order to become more at home in the world of reality where the objects and self are clearly held apart. The ego rhythm of differentiation and dedifferentiation constantly swings between these two poles and between the inside and outside worlds. So also does the spectator, now focusing on single gestalt patterns, now blotting out all conscious awareness."[33]

Fluidity also suggests that those committed to unitary thinking — a hallmark of colonizers — those for whom linearity and Western logic are guideposts to life, are incomplete by definition; they cannot fill in or articulate the primal scene. The narrator describes such an individual: "He cannot conceive of the union of opposites, or, for that matter, their very existence. He cannot conceive of flocks of birds in migratory flight, or that night will follow day and season follow season in a seemingly endless cycle, and the beauty and the pleasure and the purpose that might come from all this" (p. 63). A sense of fusion, even harmony that the narrator slid or escaped into and out of in "Blackness," "At Last," "What Have I Done Lately," and now "At the Bottom of the River" is unavailable to such a being. "At the Bottom" asserts that a focus on identity implies "neither the ontologically given and eternally determined stability of that identity, nor its uniqueness, its utterly irreducible character, its privileged status as something total and complete in and of itself."[34] This individual is an incomplete man who lives with undeveloped senses in a denatured world; he is spiritually dead in his interiority and contradictions; he "sits in nothing, this man" (p. 64).

To illuminate the amplitude of this fantasy, the narrator emphasizes those who cannot participate in the vision, those who cannot "see." The couple in question closely resembles the parents whom Kincaid discusses in interviews and characters who are like those parents fleshed out in later texts. Much is made of the carpenter (Kincaid's stepfather was a carpenter) who measures and sizes up the world. This man sees beauty and is sometimes joyful before he fells the oak and kills the cow. His narrow perspective fences him in.[35] Uncomprehending of a wider, all-embracing, nonbinary world, he "feels the futility . . . [and] a silence stretching out . . . its length and breadth and depth immeasurable. Nothing" (p. 68).

Functioning as a Cartesian cogito, this man surveys "a . . . last nail driven in just so." Anything he cannot pin down is outside his universe. His senses may be technically alive but that hardly matters for he is too absorbed in disintegration: "Tomorrow the oak will be felled, the trestle will break, the cow's hooves will be made into glue." He appreciates beauty but finds engagement ultimately impossible: "crossing and recrossing the threshold" between uncertainty and precision (p. 68).

The narrator has learned to reject rigid taxonomies and exacting litanies. But coming to this determination — rejecting "measurement," the totality of a certain weltanschauung — has not been easy: "How vainly I struggle against all this" (p. 68). At times, life not death intrudes on these meditations on mortality. Her mother's catechism of dos and don'ts in "Girl" cuts off the chance of response. Like the carpenter, the mother sizes things up and tries to be a God of sorts, leaving the narrator without power over these outside acts and utterances.

Having withdrawn from this world of measurement and betrayal, the speaker negotiates herself toward a new position where she can function more freely as a subject. The in-dwelling becomes trancelike and opens up into space. She begins to see through to the bottom of the river, to a primal condition in the world. The narrator longs to perpetuate that moment of clarity, that condition of original harmony. Water imagery suggests transition, too, in its evocation of simple youthful pleasures.

Thus Kincaid implies longing and unsureness in diverse ways. Her structure also affirms the indeterminacy implied in the poetics. It underlines her refusal to affix an "essential" meaning and offer comforting certainties. Repetitions, dreamlike and surreal sequences, trances, free association, fragments even, dominate the brief sections. Seeming nonsequiturs, ambiguities, doubled meanings, allusions, occasional typographic blanks and spaces add to the ethos of indeterminacy. Magic-realist yokings coupled with water imagery propel the protagonist toward writing. Delving the depths dredges up the narrator's unconscious, how she should and can create.

Here the narrator rejects all forms of truth and beauty, conventionally and Eurocentrically understood. She discerns multiplicity in all things. Hence how things are said to be is nothing more than that: one person's excluding discourse. In this plural world, "false are all appearances" (p. 69). She has learned that she must keep engaging in wholeness: for ontological preservation, she must eschew the disloyal, orthodox world that betrays those who seek peace and union. She tells of a creature like herself who was stung by a honeybee that she chased. The ecstatic pain and power of that sting symbolize her quest. That language of quest could also be a hearkening to and a search not only for her own voice and body but those of her mother too. The quest could be "an attempt to locate that 'internal,' the space of women's being, before it is filled with dread."[36] This creature has begun to know pain and pleasure and its affect in equal measure; it lives inside and outside itself and when it vanishes it leaves a glow. The narrator hints at self-reversibility. She can be inside and outside at once. The honeybee is also the site of creative association and play. Somewhat like an Indian runner, the narrator wants (and wants to be) this mystical experience.[37]

In this translike state, the speaker comes to know that union is the sine qua non of joy.[38] The bird who tries to kill the lowly worm is killed by the boy who can be protean if he chooses. If the worm resembles a form of human consciousness, then all that attack its integrity are in danger. Only those who let well alone, who live and let live and embrace diversity, dwell as whole beings in any space.

The narrator's disquisition ends with a radiant spectacle at the bottom of the river where the grass is a green "from which all other greens might come" (p. 76), where neither day nor night exists. There is a mystical sense that this "nature is never spent; there lives the dearest freshness deep down things."[39] This nigh-on perfect world is "not yet divided, not yet examined, not yet numbered, and not yet dead. I looked at this world as it revealed itself to me — how new, how new — and I longed to go there" (p. 78).

But this paradisiacal place also intersects ineluctably with a physical plane where the narrator discerns her own physicality while mystically glancing at herself. The vision becomes even more expansive and inclusive. Standing above land and sea, the narrator stoops down and touches the deepest bottom, an elemental place where life begins. This scene suggests a synthesis of the scientific transcendental arenas of the text. The battery of images around evolution, insects, vertebrates, and even the fusion and interchangeability of tenses culminate in this epiphanic moment. And sure enough, material thoughts continue to intervene, paralleling, partly dissolving these lucidly transcendent experiences. She thinks of the "smell of vanilla from the kitchen." Nonetheless, though appetite, smell, sight, and sound merge in a kinaesthetic union, her thoughts are temporarily still suspended, as it were, "conscious of nothing — not happiness, not contentment, and not the memory of night, which soon would come" (p. 80). She is "stripped away." This pared-down state might be something that can be articulated and conceived, — but it is still a condition not materially attainable; neither a recognizable human presence outside the imagination nor an inner sense of the world. At the moment of that insight, when that apparition realizes itself, the "awakening" assumes a physical form. Her withdrawal from the world of a measuring father-colonizer and a family-tending mother is complete — because through her exploration she has gradually staked a new position where she can comfortably stand. She ends by claiming a public voice, having constituted the conditions for doing so.

The "I" recognizes writing implements that connect her to "human endeavor" and empower her reentry into the world.[40] She locates herself on the continuum of all living and lighted things that have existed and continue to exist: "The lamp is lit. In the light of the lamp, I see some books, I see a chair, I see a table, I see a pen; I see a bowl of ripe fruit, a bottle of milk, a flute made of wood, the clothes that I will wear. And as I see these things in the light of the lamp, all perishable and transient, how bound up I know I am to all that is human endeavor, to all that is past and to all that shall be, to all that shall be lost and leave no trace. I claim these things then—mine—and now feel myself grow solid and complete" (p. 82). At that climactic moment when she apprehends the possibility of infinity, the "I" sounds herself (itself) into beauty, into the void, and into the world. The child-becoming narrator returns to one original source—mother's milk. She wants to write in white ink, with the pen and the milk, to recover that sense of union.[41] Put another way, the narrator simultaneously connects with art and life, embracing this newfound being, however partially. At this point she speaks and speaks tellingly: "My name [fills] up my mouth."

The variant meditations, each an entity in its own right, end with an identity claim, not as a resolution but as one way of vocalizing a vision, of culling fragments from a collective past. Jamaica Kincaid does not favor or intend any firm closure. To impose a synthesis is to be a carpenter, one who measures things and identifies a fixed, unmediated meaning. Nonetheless, the speaker does experience a revelation that propels her on a journey toward writing, toward articulation. She experiences a vocation of sorts through mystical means.

On the other hand, the epiphanic final section marks the entry of the narrator into art, into a world in which she senses she can function. She realizes that she cannot live without division. Dredging herself into externality and out of her interior, she emerges from the chrysalis that alone will complete the thorax. Out of this decision to individuate, art and a butterfly emerge. The possibility of drowning transforms into rebirth. Contradictions merge. Undertaking a quest—metonymic for coping with loss—she shapes a beginning where she can enter the symbolic order through cultural production. She has excavated the tools that will enable her to take a stand. Symbolizing the depths of the unconscious, the bottom of the ocean creatively baptises her into life and anticolonial opposition. Thus "At the Bottom of the River" investigates the making of an artist-activist and a myth. It traces the gradual discovery of conditions out of which writing can evolve and be put to political use. Conditions of colonialism create artists who battle that institution. A portrait of the artist emerges as an adolescent female whose repressed desires assume a healthier, counterhegemonic form of expression. With the lamp, the light, and a room of her own, the narrator marks her entry into discourse. The narrator refuses but also has to use the father's text to claim identity. Entry into language and art constitutes an original and striking victory over diverse mothers, "the (in)security of a childhood always begun anew."[42] Art and transcendent political vision supersede postcolonial contamination.

Each section of *At the Bottom of the River* is a discrete narrative about a child growing up in a world where psychological, physical, and political dominations seem the order of the day. Little escape exists outside the imagination. Collectively assembled yet chronologically unconnected, each section loosely features recurring thematic elements, many of them overlapping: a state of mind at a given time ("Holidays"); an apprehension of something that is massively compressed ("Girl"); plural versions of the same experience ("What Have"); a sense of ontological abyss ("Blackness"); desire and imagining ("My Mother"); vignettes of school and peers that disclose jealousy, fear, and despair ("Wingless"); an attempt to normalize experience while maintaining great distance through a deliberate surface account ("Letter from Home"); a playing-out of oppositions between an inner and outer world, a mother-self dyad ("At Last"); self-reconciliation, self-knowledge, and an entry into light ("At the Bottom of the River").

Operating within an economy of loss (of the mother, of primal love), the narrator embarks on a reconstitution of her world; she constructs more fluid boundaries. On the one hand, she articulates a world of beauty and preoedipal bonding where image and sweet sensation rule; throughout the ten sections, she probes how "the onset of puberty creates the essential dialectic of adolescence — new possibilities and new dangers" (p. 6). The individuation process that involves alternating cycles of rejecting the mother and longing for harmony unfolds in a painful way, chronologically disjointed, its form fragmented. The discontinuous parts of this process match the narrator's psychic fragmentation. Such discrete articulations oppose the linearity of traditional Western modes of narrative. Through metonym and memory, she calls up her prememory life. Craving both distance and intimacy, she lives in intense self-absorption, experiencing turmoil and a plummeting self-worth as she senses public and private rejection. Periodically she attempts to empower herself. In the river apparition, she claims herself, according to her own satisfaction. She envisions an adult life where she can be a recorder of community life.

Sexual difference plays a vital part in the formation of the narrator's identity. In this multiplicity and fluidity that is sometimes associated with the female body, textuality suggests or is, in part, corporeality.[43] A female unconscious voices itself through mobile representations of the body, through the thorax that briefly fascinates the narrator in "Holidays." What is a headless body? What produces it and how does objectification effect it? Does it symbolize a sense of objectification, of erasure? A father obsessed with exact measurement (the symbolic order, the law of the father) contrasts with a woman-child focused on absence and incompletion in a prediscursive order. The child lives in a world of feeling without shadow, a womb-enclosed state. She is forced to abandon "an attempt to locate that 'interval'; the space of women's language before it is filled with dread."[44]

Beyond that, "At the Bottom of the River" subtly challenges the mechanical separation often imbricated in gender (not biological) difference and female roles; such differentiation lies within the realm of the carpenter. In contrast to his fixed perspective, this protagonist swims into light and creativity, toward the lamp and the pen. In a sense, she transforms and transcends the girl in the opening section who is no longer the repressed term of an equation involving the domestic or the colonial family. Now she flouts the expected role of women in Antiguan society, an ideology that reduces females to ciphers. "At the Bottom of the River," then, is a series of negotiations through which the speaker navigates through and out of preoedipal, prelinguistic, unmediated love into a functioning life within the symbolic order that will facilitate a counterhegemonic position.

Jamaica Kincaid stated recently that having small children did not allow for the absolute immersion in meditations on unindividuated unity out of which *At the Bottom* emerges. Perhaps one thing she was referring to was a certain indecipherability that marks this book. An already acclaimed journalist, Kincaid recapitulates the traumas of childhood and adolescence as a female growing up in a poverty-stricken, now postcolonial island where her mother — read multiply — dominated her life. Within the insistent probing of this mother-daughter unit, the factors of poverty and imperial expropriation constantly affect the speaker's maturation. Others also loom large as she uneasily reckons with a number of questions: Who she was then, in the light of the person she has become and the persona she has created who facilitates this reconstruction. Can this "I" ever be fixed since it (she) seems to be dispersed everywhere without a "care."

How this apparently discontinuous narrative tells itself, offering different versions of the same event, hopping around, fusing fantasy and dreams with harsh material realities, is symptomatic of what the text tells. The occult, the esoteric, the regressive signify a center that is not holding.[45] The format of loosely connected segments introduces the idea of the arbitrariness of narrative and the complexity of colonial life. The reader is always aware of other options necessarily suppressed, choices temporarily vetoed. The symbolic order denies the "girl" a free place, so she ruptures it with the semiotic. Figuring deep-dyed poverty, night-soil men witness the phantasmagoric sight of a skinless woman who will drink her enemies' blood in secret and of Mr. Gishard, dead and reappearing. The night-soil men quietly come to pick up people's excrement because no sewage system exists — that is one thing — and the dead Mr. Gishard appears — that is another. Both are substantive, both important. Respectively they signal colonialism and its opposition in people's culture. Thus the narrator lives coincident existences in different spaces, mentally, physically, politically. The formation and claiming of identity that constitute *At the Bottom of the River* are born of now-irrecoverable conditions and origins. However inchoately, the imagination of the girl empowers her to see through and beyond to what might happen and to recuperate what has been submerged.[46]

To add an additional layering to the narrator's textural life, Jamaica Kincaid stated in an early interview that Bruno Schulz's surrealism and

Nadine Gordimer's suggestive tale of South African racism, "A Lion on the Freeway," influenced her writing at this time.[47] Their texts enhanced her apprehension of a universe she wanted to convey. But Kincaid puts her own personal stamp on these apprehensions. She blends obeah with dreams, introduces trancelike states, intertextualizes, and reinterprets fantasy.[48] She endows her narrator with a rich interiority. Wearing one face in public, another at home, the speaker is so terrified of being dissolved that she lets fear engorge her. But in her imagination, the narrator can be anywhere and do anything. By suggesting who and how she is becoming, she traces herself as a subject-in-process negotiating that central mother-daughter twosome. The narrator understands the world through obeah, through dreams, trance, and an acceptance of the fantastic that coexist side by side in Kincaid's unique version of magic realism. She combines this with an understanding of socially constructed mores and cause-effect relationships encapsulated in the linear thinking of the carpenter. This fusion of physical and metaphysical worlds, of personal and (post) colonial identities, characterizes Jamaica Kincaid's special vision.

In future writing, Jamaica Kincaid will introduce textual self-resonance, but at this point the reader cannot know that these experiences, this sensibility, and the crucial strategy of naming will continue in later texts. At a metafictional level, Kincaid invites the reader to ponder the separation between life and art and their interaction, how the narrator's everyday musings, her unsureness, constitute artistic expression.

Even within the texts themselves, some kind of narratival mirroring process operates. The speaker in one section seems to echo others: Some incidents and motifs reoccur. In "Blackness," the ill child hearkens back to the one whose mother instructs her. The reader is invited to consider possible ambiguities. Are these narrators the same or different? If they are the same, what does that signify? What multiple positions, both imagined and material, are possible? How do imagined ones get played out? Obeah then becomes critical because the text insists that all enactments be treated on the same plane of seriousness. Part child, part adolescent, the narrator comes to terms with a world that fuses fantasy, Eurocentric conceptions of the world, and day-to-day events.[49] She accepts these factors and considerations as separate and equally privileged modes of knowing.

Inextricably linked to the mother-daughter separation, colonialism insistently inflects the text. Coupled with the complicating of female experience, that imperial presence suggests its pervasive, quotidian intersection with gender relations. Only language and memory can conjure up the mother-daughter split. That is to say, although the lost biological mother is a major trope, at a different symbolic level outside womb and home, the lost mother also represents precolonial roots before the advent of a vicious surrogate colonial mother. Seemingly a solitary individual, the narrator emblematizes the colonized and joins herself globally to a school of oppositional thinking. Implicitly, Kincaid suggests that alternate explanations always exist. Thus the mystery and indeterminacy of the text further affirm the absurdity of linearity and fixed meaning. At the same time, Kincaid always insists that magic events do not altogether function with different laws but rather "weave a miraculous occurrence into a rigorously everyday reality."[50] In that sense, *At the Bottom of the River* is counterintuitive, a reverse articulation that deals with disputed epistemologies. Jamaica Kincaid denies complexity of meaning and unfixedness now; whether to believe that scenario of rescripted simplicity is another question. Neither its magical nor its factual elements deny the historicity of the text. Time constitutes a network of convergencies of time past, present, and imminent. From the start, the family to which Jamaica Kincaid constantly refers to is also the macrocolonized Antiguan family, the island population before 1967 and any form of independence. In that sense, all references to a mother allusively resonate with colonial as well as maternal signs.

Put another way, the variant narrators of *At the Bottom* speak internally and externally, exemplifying a personal marginality and an abiding sense of alienation that in the last section slides into epiphany. Nothing conforms to an everyday conception of time or space; the surreal world mingles interchangeably and equally with the world of material reality. Water suggests quotidian and historical fluidity, the constant transformation of events and experiences always in process. And precisely that easy fusion of fantasy, memory, and everyday life creates coherence. Thus a fluid investigative perspective alternates with intimations of postcolonial life and affirms a national cultural heritage. The plural narrator does not accept any demarcation between given fact and an intuited sense of her world. Claiming the rights of an omniscient storyteller, the speaker transforms (transcends) herself and her inner imaginings. Neither author, Elaine Potter Richardson, born in Antigua, nor the narrator who chronicles the events, nor the protagonist living and reliving certain experiences can live distinctly. The narrator reinstates local and personal history as global.

These overlapping speakers create a chorus of voices that sound throughout. Because memory is a primary textual cohesion and because the refraction of that memory is splintered, nothing is fixed, everything is in flux, even the motion toward the lamp and the pen at the end.

In her next text, *Annie John*, Jamaica Kincaid changes pace but retains some constants nonetheless. From a mystical probing of growing up, constructed as a set of fragmented though allied experiences, she moves to a less densely textured chronicle although the representation of living as a (divisive) diverse set of experiences remains.

ANNIE, GWEN, LILLY, PAM AND TULIP: NEW BEGINNINGS

According to Jamaica Kincaid, *Annie, Gwen, Lilly, Pam and Tulip* was originally written as a section of *At the Bottom of the River.*[51] It was later published on its own as a book. A limited edition appeared in 1986 and a trade edition in 1989, both richly illustrated by Eric Fischl.[52] *Annie, Gwen, Lilly, Pam and Tulip*'s close relationship to *At the Bottom* includes a shared sensibility and a locale of shifting languages, its vision preceding the later, idyllic vision of *At the Bottom*. It sketches the process that leads to a necessary transcendence. Additionally, it uses the names Annie and Gwen, which appear prominently in Jamaica Kincaid's next work, *Annie John*.

Thematically, *Annie, Gwen, Lilly, Pam and Tulip* diverges sharply from *At the Bottom*, with chronological time as a particular case in point. The five characters of the title live in a precolonial world where everything appears superficially perfect to Pam. But intimations of future catastrophe also abound in their apparently isolated world: Lilly is thirsty, Annie inclines to withdraw, Tulip seems perilously naive.

Annie, Gwen, Lilly, Pam and Tulip begins and ends with Pam as the speaker. At first, she describes her utopian surroundings, a world, as she later states, "free of envy, pestilence, or shattering pronouncements"

(p. 6, my pagination). She is "completely happy" as she observes the activities of her female companions, characterized by images of fertility and adolescent sexual yearnings. Imagining herself as "parched earth," Lilly rejoices in her "many existences"; Gwen traces "the evolution of a small mound, so interested is she in all that covers the earth's surface"; Tulip's mouth is "moist with excitement from some secret observation just made" (p. 1); Annie meditates "in her print dress covered with firemen carrying their ladders, arms flung wide apart" (p. 1). This eroticized discourse of thirstiness, breasts ("a small mound"), firemen to the rescue, and a "mouth moist with excitement" invokes ideas about sexual nurturance, coming-of-age, and reproduction. More ominously, it hints at the imposition of a motherland.

On another note, Pam's first statement is also freighted with ambiguity: "This is a perfect place prospering in greens, yellows," she announces, suggesting in the polyvoiced "prospering" the attractive economic potential of the place. Her language resonates with apprehensions about an interloper. The sluggish invertebrates she refers to evoke prehistory. Birds fly around in whose cries there is — presently at least — no terror. Spatiotemporal forces still maintain harmony. "Revelling in her many existences," Lilly conjures up a unity-in-diversity that is about to be torn apart by people who think and behave single-mindedly. In addition, if their "small place" is perfect, no colonial motherland yet exists. Neither division, dissent, nor radical domination has yet occurred.

Discursively, Kincaid seems to suggest the threatening presence of the imperial mission, in its various disguises. While (the flowering) Tulip passes the water (of survival) to Lilly, "two great monarchs are dancing" (p. 1). These royally named butterflies symbolize an impending intervention, although few could guess what their beautiful exterior inwardly signifies. Uncertain or unaware of the strangers' disposition, Tulip prefers to think the best, speculating that the butterflies are dancing "in affection and contentment, on Annie's head" (p. 1).

Annie's attire and Tulip's commentary on the insects are of a piece, ideologically. Outwardly graceful while bent on feeding from the (unsuspecting) flowers, the powerful creatures flutter importantly, even ominously — at least in nomenclature — over her four friends while Annie wears a dress that marks helplessness — a forced impotence — and destruction. Resuscitation and rescue also follow.

Annie's response signifies her claim to independence, a refusal to be duped. She declines to see either the monarchs, Lilly's desire, or Pam's state of nirvana. Instead, she moves unconsciously into a future state of "overwhelming blackness," sensing that this condition will become a "permanent and essential part of my nature" (p. 3).

The prepubescent Tulip points out the dual intensity of Lilly's ontological state: "Your whole being quiver[s] with excitement . . . you become a new and strange animal with whom I am not familiar" (p. 2). Images of ripeness, excitement, coming of age, of Lilly waiting for a downpour herald a transformative period. Her imagined state has become real. The disaster she predicts will be a brutal process, exercised by predators: "Whole cavalries of men off to a destiny newly arranged for them . . . I can feel myself bend and dip and rise up to meet the great pressures" (p. 2).

Following the dance of the monarchs, Pam hears voices "on the wind" that herald change and a new dispensation: "The words strike at me like pellets released from a slingshot; the voice moves swiftly in many different directions and I feel that it aims to disturb and conquer; I see that the voice . . . will put before me an ancient parable, the meaning of which I shall fail to grasp and so earn considerable scorn" (p. 3). Recognizing that her failure to comprehend the significance of this presence might result in suffering, Pam feels the weight of progress bearing down on her, the limits of her own importance, the finiteness of happiness. She extends a doubled response to the wind: Its encirclement of the people, though not yet tangible, suggests that usurpers are close by. Simultaneously, she becomes lost in woollike clouds, "only this minute just fleeced from lambs," soft sensations without boundaries. Who or what are the symbolic lambs, clouds, and wind that resound with multiple meanings, concurrently abetting and contesting one another? At one level, clouds are imposters that hide the wind's intention to destroy. They create illusions that fool the people. Metonymically, Pam and the people are lambs who have lost their way. Lambs are also fleeced, vulnerable and naked creatures, with a hovering suggestion of rape, some recent violation of a stolen innocence and virginity. Resistance is omnipresent, too, in the fact that the shorn lambs — admittedly a pitiable sight temporarily — can recover what has been expropriated — on the other hand, they may also be killed: No one, that is, "not even the least privileged among us, is ever entirely powerless over the messages that traverse and position him at the post of sender, addressee, or referent."[53]

In the conflicted triple imagery from nature to the clouds, the lambs, and the wind, the characters already feel the effect of the outside. Pam is lulled into believing she still lives in a "perfect place"; she has not yet faced the fact that her Eden is disappearing. She longs for a primal-parental return: "for our mother's lap and our father's lips after days of absence" (p. 4).

In Pam's multivalent dialogue, Gwen recognizes Pam's visionary powers to see through to a less perfect time. Ironically, though Gwen grasps Pam's prognosis, she herself refuses to see that "the horizon [is] clear and empty of anything foreign and dangerous" (p. 3).

Lilly understands that the magic has gone: "To me, now, the drops of water on the heart-shaped leaves are just that — something ordinary and without substance or meaning in my imaginary life" (p. 5). The wind is here to stay, less of a mystery, more of a harsh and understood presence, harbinger of daily tyranny. Predicting the original colonial encounter, Lilly observes that "the elements do battle and take sides between day and night" (p. 4). Fixing herself as marginal to the tumult, she recognizes that she has to remain inside too.

By contrast, Annie chooses to detach herself. Pursuing her campaign of self-reliance in the face of invasion, she splits infinitesimally. Perhaps she is a mimic person who shows different faces, dependent on circumstances. These roles represent the form of control that she devises for herself: "Living again solely inside my overwhelming blackness, I have divided myself — my physical quantity, that is — into millions of tiny particles, each distinct from the other, each the color of the sea in all its great length and breadth and depth, boiled down and reduced to a small pebble; each then burning, burning up to a white heat, a luminosity so intense, so blinding. . . . In this state, I live by forces I do not completely understand but to which I submit as if I have never known fear or doubt, and so now I believe myself eternal" (p. 5). Pam recognizes how resourceful Annie is living "in a world over which only she has complete dominion" (p. 6).

At the end Pam pronounces for all of them, but first mourns her own loss: "I see a time when I shall be damp and made to feel constantly uneasy, my edges curled like paper discarded, first to the cold night, then to the blazing sun; I see that this shall happen to me against my will and that I shall be powerless to reverse my misfortunes; I see this as I hear the voice on the wind, new and cold and strange and circling my perfect place" (p. 6). She clings to her original vision in the face of horror while Lilly, in turn, imagines, almost accepts vicariously out of community love, Pam's pain: "Her blood struggling as it courses through her veins, her arms crossed protectively over her heart and the small mounds that are her breasts" (p. 6).

Lilly, on the other hand, opts to meet the invading forces head-on; fierceness constitutes another kind of resistance to future disaster. Despite being scared, she wants to experience the reality of what is happening in order to taste life to the full. Lilly predicts a harsh cycle of events but cycles that end in death also regenerate: "My hopes and dreams first yellowed, then thoroughly tarnished, then dashed to smithereens like glass forcefully meeting a tiled floor; I mean to be first oval and glowing and then, in due course, withered and dry; I mean to have much passion and sorrow pile up on me like carts of coal just delivered and lying in a yard — so shall I know Who or What it is that made me" (p. 6). The nurturing, traditionally maternallike Tulip whose name marks a continuing harmony with nature, wants to reconcile their differences. She will endow the others with strength, comfort Gwen who will be bound to Pam "as echo to a cave," understanding the process they will have to endure, perhaps the only character who discerns that compromise is survival in the postinterventionist world. Tulip is the mother who represents and to some degree incorporates the community. She may see herself as inferior to the other four — "they are superior beings" — but she knows that she possesses survival tools. Kincaid leaves us in a contradictory space in the presence of speaking subjects who may disappear (as the Arawak people did), but who give one another a full identity for the time being.[54] They have no need of patronymics that signify possession and legitimacy: " 'Annie . . . ,' *said Tulip*. 'Pam . . . ,' *said Gwen*. 'Tulip . . . ,' *said Lilly*. 'Lilly . . . ,' *said Annie*. 'Gwen . . . ,' *said Pam*."[55] Naming one another in the final sentences, the five characters acknowledge their own existences and return to the origin of things. Tulip, it seems, will survive to tell their stories and keep memory alive.

Annie, Gwen, Lilly, Pam and Tulip, then, is set in precolonial times. Consequently, everyone is effectively a mother of those who came later.

The five characters are ancestors who both fear and yearn. They are about to be forcibly expelled from the garden because the knowledge they have gleaned of the outside implies their own destruction. The world before measurement also marks a world of transition where people are beginning to size things up. Childhood innocence is fast disappearing to be replaced by adolescence and coming of age. Alive at the dawn of historical events, the quintet come to know conflict and the danger of believing in perfection.

In their "wish for the comfort of our mother's lap and our father's lips" (p. 5), Pam and Gwen sense future division, a fracture of their paradisiacal unity. The island's inhabitants are growing up, wakening from bliss to the reality of cultural identity. Hence, Annie, Gwen, Lilly, Pam, and Tulip come to understand not only the importance of naming but the fact that naming in and of itself is not a tidy solution. Perhaps it signifies presence and endows identity, but it can dissolve neither aggressive interventions nor imperial power. The story resembles the clouds, lambs, winds, and withered dreams in that it prefigures references that have not yet arrived. Kincaid poses new conditions of possibilities that are somewhat life-imperilling but not terminally so. Nothing is immovable, everything is in motion. Offstage may seem remote, but its minatory presence is everywhere. Meanwhile, people function separately and in unison, their voices redolent of life, announcing perpetual action and counteraction.

Annie John: *Mother-Daughter–Christopher Columbus*

Chapter 2

She was an *obeah* woman, perhaps not on the Haitian scale — they are very different — but she did believe in spirits.—**Jamaica Kincaid, interview**

But the typical reality of someone like myself in a place like Antigua is that the political situation became so normal that we no longer noticed it. The better people were English and that was life. I can't say that I came from a culture that felt alienated from England — Europe. We were beyond alienation.

It was amazing that I could notice the politics the way I did. . . . I took notice of it in a personal way and I didn't place it within the context of political action. I almost made a style out of it.—**Jamaica Kincaid, interview**

IN *At the Bottom of the River,* her debut as a writer, Jamaica Kincaid examines a formative phase of the narrator's life, her own life fictionalized. Preferring to suggest rather than state explicitly, she gives nothing away. In the hypnotic vision that ends the text, she inchoately apprehends a life-art dyad that is inflected by a growing political understanding.

Kincaid's second work, *Annie John,* was written after she came to the United States from Antigua and was working for the *New Yorker.*[1] In *Annie John,* many of the personal and political elements in *At the Bottom* resurface in somewhat sharper outline.[2] The novel begins with a clear designation of age and thematic concerns: "For a short while during the year I was ten, I thought only people I did not know died" (p. 3). Divided into eight parts, the chapters as they appear in the text are entitled "Figures in the Distance," "The Circling Hand," "Gwen," "The Red Girl," "Columbus in Chains," "Somewhere, Belgium," "The Long Rain," and "A Walk to the Jetty."

In the first part, "Figures in the Distance," subterranean feelings of rejection translate into a fixation on death and funerals, perhaps Annie John's way of displacing and reconstituting the fear and emptiness she experiences.

She is ten, she proclaims, as she describes the family's temporary summerhouse on the outskirts of St. John's and her father's prowess in renovating and repairing their house. The father builds the new roof, a necessary structural extension to accommodate the growing family. The fact that, in short order, three brothers were born into the family where Jamaica Kincaid had been an only child for almost a decade, seems to inflect the text.

Annie John, then, starts with death, because death is what this nine-year-old feels when her house (and family) start expanding. For the child, this expansion demarcates something ominous, although she never refers directly to the cause. We know the cause only from autobiographical accounts: the shock of discovering how differently her parents intended to treat their male children compared to herself.[3] This intense personal pain, the sense of deprivation stemming from the law of the father, looms as the major trauma of her childhood.

Annie John's fixation on death intertwines with a keen awareness of her new responsibilities and her acceptance of obeah: "We were afraid of the dead because we never could tell when they might show up again" (p. 4). This imaging of obeah, indigenous people's culture versus an imposed Western bureaucracy and its dominative value system, stresses her egalitarian acceptance of material and supernatural realities; for Annie John, they are indistinguishable.

Furthermore, this early mention of obeah immediately though subtly signals Annie John's apprehension about colonial domination.[4] Obeah widened the gulf between slaves and slave owners and enabled slaves to maintain a measure of control over their lives. Annie John's commitment to cultural beliefs is one way of maintaining personal control that is linked to a larger historical context where people need to cope with an always fluid and death-dealing condition of life. This possibility also meshes with statements that Jamaica Kincaid recently made when she talked of unfathomable actions she committed that same year:

> When I was nine, I refused to stand up at the refrain of "God Save Our King. I hated Rule Britannia . . . I thought that we weren't Britons and that we were slaves.

Cudjoe: No one ever told you this — it was just instinctive?
Kincaid: No, no one ever told me that — well, my mother used to be
            an Anglophile.[5]

At the end of part one, the nine-year-old speaker manifests her ability
to act independently of her mother, to conceal what she feels; she seems
oblivious to a typical colonial intrusion at a funeral: "We sang a hymn —
"All Things Bright and Beautiful" (p. 11),[6] another echo of the protagonist's life in *At the Bottom of the River.*

Finally, Annie John stresses her easy ability to lie and the difficulty of
duping her mother. The language of the passage accentuates her guilt
and a certain surface unity amid deep division within the family. Water
once again makes its ambiguous mark: "When I got home, my mother
asked me for the fish. . . . Trying to think quickly, I said that when I got to
the market Mr. Earl told me that they hadn't gone to sea that day because
the sea was too rough. 'Oh?' said my mother, and uncovered a pan in
which were lying . . . an angelfish for my father, a kanya fish for my
mother, and a lady doctorfish for me — the special kind of fish each of us
liked" (p. 12).[7] Annie John tries to return the lie of her free existence
with ready lies about daily living, creating storm at every turn.

"The Circling Hand," elaborates on a crucial fact of Annie John's
existence: her love for her mother. She tells of many tender repetitive
moments growing up that intertextualize the ever-vigilant mother and
the seemingly passive daughter of "Girl." She offers numerous instances
of their mutual love: "She warned me not to play around the coal pot,
because I liked to sing to myself and dance around the fire. Two seconds
later, I fell into the hot coals, burning my elbows. My mother cried when
she saw that it wasn't serious, and now, as she told me about it, she
would kiss the little black patches of scars on my elbows." They often
took an everyday bath together, and special baths, too, steeped in herbs
that would ward away the women by whom Mr. John had children.
(Importantly, this father later turns out to be a stepfather.)[8] As in *At the
Bottom of the River,* water is purification. These women were "trying to
harm my mother and me by setting bad spirits on us" (p. 15). Sometimes, when they went shopping, "she would suddenly grab me and
wrap me up in her skirt and drag me along with her as if in a great hurry. I
would hear an angry voice saying angry things, and then, after we had
passed the angry voice, my mother would release me" (pp. 16–17). The

power of culture is part of everyday living. The child follows her mother around as she prepares mouth-watering meals and labors at immaculate washings. Water again facilitates life and even values; the mother tries to keep the house clean at numerous levels of the story. During lunch the parents talk endlessly as the child stares at her mother in adoration: "When my eyes rested on my father, I didn't think very much of the way he looked. But when my eyes rested on my mother, I found her beautiful. Her head looked as if it should be on a sixpence. What a beautiful long neck, and long plaited hair, which she pinned up around the crown of her head because when her hair hung down it made her too hot. Her nose was the shape of a flower on the brink of opening. Her mouth, moving up and down as she ate and talked at the same time, was such a beautiful mouth I could have looked at it forever if I had to and not mind" (pp. 18–19). Annie John's negative witnessing of her father establishes personal priorities and injects political overtones. It crops up in another section where the young girl's gaze on her mother is all-consuming, devoid of any detachment. She speaks of the perfumed baths they take in harmony together.[9] This kind of gaze craves merger; it is a gaze in synch with a mimicking life: "As she told me the stories, I sometimes sat at her side, leaning against her, or I would crouch on my knees behind her back and lean over her shoulder. . . . At times I would no longer hear what it was she was saying; I just liked to look at her mouth as it opened and closed over words, or as she laughed. How terrible it must be for all the people who had no one to love them and no one whom they loved so, I thought" (pp. 22–23).

In *Annie John,* Kincaid inflects the gradually seesawing and ultimately agonized mother-daughter relationship with commentary about growing up as a female dominated by colonizers and their allies who administer patriarchal dictates, the law of the father. This doubled reading of the mother-daughter relationship continues as Annie John discusses poverty, a fact of her life that underscores feelings of political and personal powerlessness. Why a hardworking family should be living in such dire circumstances is a question only indirectly answered. The legacy of colonialism constantly hovers over and around the text.

Annie John's father "would step outside to the little shed he had built for us as a bathroom, to quickly bathe in water that he had instructed my mother to leave outside overnight in the dew" (p. 12). At one level, we witness people with a strong sense of community and without luxury steadfastly surviving. At another level, the mother does what the father requests.[10] He has access to water and mobility; he receives priority treatment as head of the family and as icon of colonial power.[11] Simultaneously, the family's immersion in water marks their stability. Water with beautiful aromas spells a hydrotherapeutics that negates a stagnant colonialism. Water is vitality and an awakening of nerve centers.[12]

This emphasis on poverty among black Antiguans mingles with reservations about male power. The episode that accentuates their life at subsistence level is followed by another exposé of Annie John's necessary submission to patriarchal authority that crucially affects her daily existence. She utters prophetic words that zero in on and emphasize the speaker's trauma: "If I had been a boy, I would have gotten the same treatment, but since I was a girl, and on top of that went to school only with other girls, my mother would always add some hot water to my bathwater to take off the chill" (pp. 13–14). Annie John is identified with water — and with alienation and death. Her mother, moreover, adds fire to a cold water situation, rendering it more agreeable. The hot water suggests the mother's vigor and desire for her daughter; perhaps she wants her daughter to be even "warmer" than she was when she almost drowned en route from Dominica, an event foregrounded in the next section.

That section, entitled "Gwen," explains how Mrs. John left Dominica after quarreling with her father and was almost lost at sea. The appearance of her trunk records how her life is changing, but old desires remain: "She painted the trunk yellow and green outside, and she lined the inside with wallpaper that had a cream background with pink roses printed all over it" (p. 19).[13] The longing for (stereotypic) romance remains inside while symbols of sun and the outdoors predominate. Now Mrs. John's possessions are replaced in the trunk by all her daughter's baby clothes, every detail of her childhood down to "my first pair of earrings, a chain around my neck, and a pair of bracelets, all specially made of gold from British Guiana" (p. 20). The jewelry tellingly marks bondage and colonialism as well as efforts to "feminize" Annie John and connect her to her heritage. Chains and bracelets are historically laden artifacts among a formerly enslaved population. The former signify bondage while the latter can also aid in warding off such evil.

Contrasted with her mother's independence and departure from her natal Dominican home is her father's protected existence until tragedy strikes. His parents having abandoned him, he wakes up one day to discover that the grandmother he slept with is lying dead beside him: "Even though he was overcome with grief, he built her coffin and made sure she had a nice funeral. He never slept in that bed again, and shortly afterward he moved out of that house. He was eighteen years old then" (p. 23).

Annie John's mixed feelings continue to resonate. After a retelling of the trunk story for the umpteenth time, the three of them take tea together, with the child occasionally fetching food items for her mother: "Sometimes when I gave her the herbs, she might stoop down and kiss me on my lips and then on my neck. It was in such a paradise that I lived" (p. 25). But already the idea of paradise has been severely questioned. A key turning point surfaces when Annie John outgrows her clothes. She is horrified to learn that the mother has called an arbitrary halt to look-alike dresses. She equates the mother's clumsy efforts to separate with a personal abandonment: "You are getting too old for that. It's time you had your own clothes. You just cannot go around the rest of your life looking like a little me" (p. 26).

The break in the mother-child unit has begun, along with Annie John's sense of alienation. She does not even have the comfort of knowing she can always fall back on her family. Her fears are compounded when the mother tells her she is becoming a young lady and that they can no longer enjoy close family moments browsing through the childhood trunk. That particular recapitulation of their old togetherness belongs to the past. Annie John's mother counsels that life must go forward not backward. But instead, this new mandated relationship generates flux. Nurturing hatred, fearing abandonment, Annie John longs for a return to intimacy. She secretly harbors a notion of herself as a person so monstrous that her mother wants to be free of her. In another sense, Annie John displaces onto her mother antagonistic feelings of rejection, of a confused self-location that in turn engenders psychic fragmentation. Since her birth, she has lived in her mother's shadow, and now that she has to fend for herself in her own spotlight, she seeks shade. She assumes she cannot live up to her mother's level of competence. Put another way, since she can barely conceptualize, let alone accept, her mother's cultural construction, she ceaselessly tries to fashion a subjectivity in opposition. Meanwhile she internalizes all this turmoil.

Other implications of this serious and highly self-conscious mother-daughter separation come into play. Annie John craves to resemble her mother, but her mother knows that imitation is dangerous, that survival depends on a sense of individual autonomy.[14] She wants Annie John to stand on her own feet, to know when to add hot water and when not to. Little Annie John does not realize the full consequences of the rather abruptly tendered "lesson," or rather, she begins to understand and realizes how hard life will become now that she is alive to these reservations and stipulations. Especially hard to gauge is whether Annie John exaggerates; any mitigating circumstances or diverse ways that Mrs. John tried to alter the relationship can only be guessed at.

Annie John's affiliation is now symbolically linked with males and cultural practices. She leaves traditional feminine ways behind. She knows that opposition to a world of harmony concretely exists: "In the end, I got my dress with the men playing their pianos . . . but I was never able to wear my own dress or see my mother in hers without feeling bitterness and hatred, directed not so much toward my mother as toward, I suppose, life in general" (p. 26).

This process of maturation continues. Annie John is dispatched to various tutors to be coached in being a lady. She has to subject herself to social prescriptions and learn to be a well-behaved female. A hint of political savvy enters the text when Annie John describes her experiences with the piano teacher, "a shriveled-up old spinster from Lancashire, England, [who] soon asked me not to come back, since I seemed unable to resist eating from the bowl of plums she had placed on the piano purely for decoration" (p. 28). More lies to cover up ensue — why should she submit? — followed by further hurtful statements about separation from the mother: "Once, when showing me a way to store linen, she patted the folded sheets in place and said, 'Of course, in your own house you might choose another way.' That the day might actually come when we would live apart I had never believed. My throat hurt from the tears I held bottled up tight inside" (pp. 28–29).

Jamaica Kincaid specifically elaborates on Annie John's possible feelings, as if she were mediating a young response, authentic in its time and place: "At the time I didn't know I was thinking this, but now I realize that the convention of being this 'well-behaved child.' I just can't do it."[15] Jamaica Kincaid's candor about the "real life" level of Annie John's feelings of distance opens up new options. According to autobiographical evidence, the child's feelings were connected to the birth (by now) of her two brothers and the large difference their presence rendered in her life.

The incident marking drastic change and the need to recompartmentalize her life for the purposes of control is Annie John's transition to a new school and the chance discovery of her parents making love. The night before this happens, she fails to make her bed correctly: "In the center of my bedspread, my mother had embroidered a bowl overflowing with flowers and two lovebirds on either side of the bowl. I had placed the bedspread on my bed in a lopsided way so that the embroidery was not in the center of my bed, the way it should have been. My mother made a fuss about it" (pp. 29–30). For the mother, not just the disorder (that as a controlling person she clearly abhors) but the import of her relationship with her daughter and her daughter's future status are at stake here. Annie John refuses a smooth transition, even exacerbates their fracture and no longer — or at least only erratically — tries to please her mother: "I had lately become careless, she said, and I could only silently agree with her" (p. 30). Annie John politicizes the concept of the well-behaved child. Well-behaved for whom, the text mischievously asks?

When Annie John returns from church, she says in a rather odd turn of phrase, "My mother still seemed to hold the bedspread against me"; then she heads for Sunday School where she receives a merit certificate. On her return, when she finds her parents in bed, she states instantly that

> it didn't interest me what they were doing — only that my mother's hand was on the small of my father's back and that it was making a circular motion. But her hand! It was white and bony, as if it had long been dead and had been left out in the elements. It seemed not to be her hand, and yet it could only be her hand, so well did I know it. It went around and around in the same circular motion, and I looked at it as if I would never see anything else in my life again. If I were to forget everything else in the world, I could not forget her hand as it looked then. I could also make out that the sounds I had heard were her kissing my father's ears and his mouth and his face. I looked at them for I don't know how long. (pp. 30–31)

A chain of signifiers shifts dramatically from love to church (purity) to sexuality; it emphasizes the more general dislike, even contempt, Annie John is feeling about domestic changes. Sex symbolizes unpleasant disruption. Perhaps she realizes that her parents are behaving so that siblings (and more disruption) might be born; she thinks of death — her own death, metonymized in her mother's white and skeletal hand.

She displays a typically scared or embarrassed reaction. She rattles cutlery and ignores her mother when she appears, replying defensively when her mother asks her (also defensively and perhaps hurtfully) if she is "going to just stand there doing nothing all day?" (p. 31). With love for her mother apparently draining out of Annie John's body, she then thinks of food — of nurturance, of her womb relationship, of times when her mother would chew up hated carrots to make them more palatable for her daughter. She attempts to maintain a feeling of union but the rift is too wide.

That afternoon on a walk with her father, she refuses to hold his hand, "doing it in such a way that he would think I felt too big for that now" (p. 32). She masks and compensates for her anger and insecurity by designating proximity as her mother's privilege. Parental sexuality bothers the adolescent; her entry into adolescence and the foreign feelings this generates transforms the stirrers of these feelings into "alien parents."[16] Put another way, her father is helping to renegotiate family power relationships that directly favor the sons. Almost immediately, Annie John enters the new school and transfers her "overpowering feelings" to Gwen, mentioning nothing of this new love to her mother.

To compensate for a sense of maternal loss, Annie John desires membership in the school community: "My heart just longed for them to say something to me" (p. 34). Everything is new, she keeps saying, as if to affirm the fundamental break she already knows exists. When she marvels at her classmates' camaraderie, she uses her mother and their estrangement, the oedipal and biological ties that so hugely affect her, as her points of reference: "Except for me, no one seemed a stranger to anything or anyone. Hearing the way they greeted each other, I couldn't be sure they hadn't all come out of the same woman's belly, and at the same time, too. Looking at them, I was suddenly glad that because I had wanted to avoid an argument with my mother I had eaten all my breakfast, for now I surely would have fainted if I had been in any more weakened a condition" (p. 35).

Paralleling these thoughts is a seemingly constant awareness of colonial interventions in her life. Her gradual attempt to break from her mother and render her an other fuses with thoughts about the school headmistress; this woman represents colonial forces attempt to swallow up the people to perpetuate their moribund colonizing life: "She looked like a prune left out of its jar a long time . . . her throat would beat up and down as if a fish fresh out of water were caught inside" (p. 36). Pursuing the complex, even manichean poetics of water, Kincaid suggests that the headmistress pollutes all the natural qualities of water. Only a captured fish removed from its hydric environment will associate with her.

In a transfer from her biological mother to the (British) mother country, the motherland, in a gradual coalescing of these roles, Annie John discloses that her mother likes (identifies with) "English people," except for their hygiene habits. Her own mother had been the one described as having a white skull-like hand. With the dried-up prune metaphor linked tentatively to the skeletal hand, *Annie John* suggests a transference of maternality from the personal to the political. Less directly, she intertextualizes the maternal death wish felt by the protagonist in *At the Bottom of the River*.[17]

Elaborating on the colonial nature of the school, Annie John comments that, whether black or white, her teachers are named after well-known kings and a celebrated admiral of the fleet, ending pointedly and wittily with the name of a notorious old prison: Miss George, Miss Nelson, Miss Edwards, and Miss Newgate. To stress her conflict (even disgust) with the implications of these names — their historical and contemporary weight — she denotes the home teacher, Miss Nelson, reading "an elaborately illustrated edition of *The Tempest* (significantly Shakespeare's most overt play on colonialism) and discloses how glad she is to get rid of her old notebooks that sport Queen Victoria on the cover: "a wrinkled-up woman [another one] wearing a crown on her head and a neckful and armfuls of diamonds and pearls — their pages so coarse, as if they were made of cornmeal" (p. 40).

The troping of royalty is a familiar element in Kincaid's work. The name of Annie John's school — Princess Margaret — appals her; she also recalls a childhood incident with deep distaste when she awaited the arrival of Princess Elizabeth and Prince Philip (nicknamed the royal sweethearts in the 1950s), whom everyone was cheering. British royalty symbolizes a relationship and a status she rejects and is trapped in, another hideous parental immersion. When the students later read aloud their autobiographical essays composed that morning, Annie John displays an unstated debate between devotees of Antiguan national history and those identified with British colonial history; that is, she concretizes the debate between nationalism and colonialism. One pupil narrates her experiences on a Girl Guide jamboree, meeting "someone who millions of years ago had taken tea with Lady Baden-Powell";[18] another tells of going to Redondo, a nearby island (a rock in fact) and seeing booby birds tending their young (p. 41). The institution of Girl Guides and patriotism-loyalty-maternality links to Queen Victoria and the annual celebration of Empire Day in which Brownies (Annie John was one) and Girl Guides enthusiastically participate. Jamaica Kincaid sharply underscores these powerful signs of colonial indoctrination and entrenchment.

Again fusing twin laws of the mother country, and the father, Annie John discloses her entrancement (and titillation?) at the goings-on of female students: "No sooner were we back in our classroom than the girls were in each other's laps, arms wrapped around necks. After peeping over my shoulder left and right, I sat down in my seat and wondered what would become of me" (p. 37). She takes refuge and pride in her intelligence. She will soon disrupt the unison with which students respond to teachers, her sarcasm about their "barely visible curtsey" — a soft colonial symbol — noticeably apparent (p. 38).

Annie John's composition read aloud to her classmates concerns a holiday on Rat Island with her mother, who attends her daughter lovingly. Then the child despairs when she thinks her mother has disappeared. Annie John disguises the authentic situation — that she and her mother are presently quarreling and not likely to stop — with a fairy-tale conclusion. In this sense, Kincaid suggests that autobiography goes beyond real life into fiction.[19] Notably, the paradisiacal story involves water and simple childhood pleasures as if Annie John were not only retelling a favorite story but imagining, too, a return to primal, undifferentiated harmony.[20] The Rat Island scenario is a paradigm of Annie John's desire and a prolepsis of its impossibility. Insofar as the saltwater sea threatens Annie John's security, the Rat Island episode also serves as a metonym of the colonizing impulse from "across the sea." Unlike terrestrial water, it serves humankind less gently. Brilliantly indicating a correspondence between water and losing her mother, given that motherhood and the sea are sometimes metonymically connected, Kincaid indicates the intensity of the loss suffered by the child, "a metaphor of the oedipal crisis."[21]

Thus Rat Island represents Annie John's worst dread: to lose her mother which, in her present state of obsessive connectedness, is tantamount to losing herself, to dissolving into the very water. At this point, the moment of Annie John's grasp of self-identity and self-naming is far off. The mother, meanwhile, does what she needs to do for herself. She trusts (or wants) the daughter to stand on her feet; she might even be a little thoughtless in not bidding a friendly farewell to the child. But, paradoxically, it is precisely in the working out of this contradiction — she loses herself if she loses her mother and her mother's action instructs her in the importance of working things out on her own — that the protagonist learns who she is and claims herself. At the time, however, she bypasses buried feelings and quickly displaces her agony.[22] In a burst of woman identification — "just-sprung-up love" she terms it — she announces her desire to spend the rest of her life with her classmates. But quickly Gwen becomes the focus of these initially generalized feelings of love. Annie John becomes "best friends" with Gwen to the tune of youthful ecstasy (p. 47).

Annie John reveals a complex sense of identification and projection. She wants to harmonize with the other pupils, but she enjoys being smart and appointed monitor over them. Power engages her although she still rebels against it. She specifically sees her "old frail self" in another student to whom she is by turn kind and cruel. Most of all, she relishes notoriety "for doing forbidden things." She wants to be subversive, as if to compensate for traumatized feelings of abandonment and domination, both personal and political. In these matters she credits her unconscious with agency: "If sometimes I stood away from myself and took a look at who I had become, I couldn't be more surprised at what I saw" (p. 49). Giggling about growing breasts with her girlfriends "in a nook of some old tombstones," she says: "What perfection we found in each other, sitting on these tombstones of long dead people who had been the masters of our ancestors! Nothing in particular really troubled us except for the annoyance of a fly colliding with our lips, sticky from eating fruits" (p. 50). The sexual resonances in the vexing fly that bothers the young girls invokes "the behavior of slaveowners of old."

She rather pointedly follows this slave-owner episode with praise for Enid Blyton. In the chain of colonial signifiers, the name of Enid Blyton, a popular British writer of children's stories, insinuates something about Annie John's experiences as a black pupil in a society undergoing fundamental transition. Long before the writing of *Annie John,* controversy had arisen in Britain over Blyton's racist texts. In *Here Comes Noddy,* for example, three nasty "golliwogs" mug "poor, little" Noddy.[23] In 1977, Bob Dixon was one of many critics to object to Blyton's diehard racist characterizations.[24] Nonetheless, Blyton's texts were and had been a component of the literary repertoire of thousands of British children growing up in the thirties, forties, and fifties. This allusion reminds readers of typical forms of indoctrination of the colonized, of insistent metropolitan interventions in African-Caribbean culture.

Perhaps not coincidentally, Annie John then mentions another turning point—menstruation. Ironically, Miss Nelson revives her with smelling salts. The teacher whose name connotes imperial victory brings Annie John back to life. Annie John longs to suspend indefinitely the moment of her classmates' concern for her condition, a moment that contains another undercutting irony: "Nothing, nothing, [she desires] just sitting on our tombstones forever." Slave owners' tombstones are metamorphized into the place where the colonized gather to lend support and (logically) organize resistance (p. 53). Enemy tombstones ironically mark the site of ex-slaves' maturation.[25]

In a night-day contrast, the section "The Red Girl" follows "Gwen," as much a paradigm for Annie John's conflicts as a description of friends. For what the red girl induces in Annie John is outright disobedience and subversion of maternal desire; Annie John further cultivates duplicity and nearly gloats about her "expert stealing. . . . an innocent fact had become a specialty of mine" (p. 55). She treats the maternal relationship as a cat and mouse game, plotting something anew as soon as they act amicably toward each other.

Within one paragraph, Annie John transforms herself from someone who causes the girls at school to shape their mouths "into tiny 'o's" when she uses the impressive word *amber,* to a person (like them) who widens her eyes and does the same with her mouth when the red girl climbs a tree to win Annie John the ripe guava she wants. She nicknames this new friend for her hair color, like a "penny fresh from the mint." The Red Girl is new money, a transformed person in Annie John's eyes, like the individual Annie John wants to become: "For as she passed, in my mind's eye I could see her surrounded by flames, the house she lived in on fire, and she could not escape. I rescued her, and after that she followed me around worshipfully" (pp. 56–57). Annie John enjoys the fact that the Red Girl's world diametrically opposes the order and spotlessness that Annie John is used to. She smells "as if she had never taken a bath in her whole life" (p. 57). Not only does Annie John betray Gwen, finding her dull next to the Red Girl, she begins to collect and play skillfully at marbles — a game absolutely forbidden by her mother. "Perhaps it had stuck in my mind that once my mother said to me, 'I am so glad you are not one of those girls who like to play marbles,' and perhaps because I had to do exactly the opposite of whatever she desired of me, I now played and played at marbles in a way that I had never done anything" (p. 61).

Playing marbles is a self-directed apprenticeship at a time when she already loathes being apprenticed to a seamstress picked out by her mother.[26] Disobeying and withdrawing emotionally from her mother in a qualified revenge, a victory over maternal surveillance, she becomes an artist in her prowess at marbles and in her appreciation of their striking qualities: At one level, marbles represent embryos of the breasts she and her friends covet. Beautiful orbs of defiance, they proliferate, have to be concealed, are exchangeable, and always desirable. At another level, they resemble the stolen library books she hides, treasures that identify rebellion against constraining gender roles, a personal power gained by outwitting authority, and an obsession with knowledge that rivals her previous obsession with death. By secreting books and marbles, she breaks from the world of the adult community and builds an alternate way of discerning and doing. Declining to be a gracious object, a lady for the community to admire, or even mother's helper around the house, Annie John constructs herself against the cultural grain. She will not and cannot renounce desire and self-determination. She makes intricate excuses to meet the red girl and indulge in rituals of punching, crying, and kissing — thus simulating the inextricable pain-pleasure mix she finds in her public and private relationships: "And so wonderful we found it that, almost every time we met, pinching by her, followed by tears from me, followed by kisses from her were the order of the day" (p. 63). Further, she steals to buy seductive presents for this fascinating friend, thinking nothing of unlocking her parents' safe and removing money.

Hallmarks of poverty are evident as the mother searches for forbidden marbles. Household storage of Christmas cards, for example, is outside, under the house. She stashes stolen public library books there too, her only source for leisurely reading in a (presumably) bookless house.

The father's silence rings out as he hears her mother's explosive indictments when she suspects Annie John is playing marbles. It resembled "two [long] chapters from the Old Testament. . . . They talked about me as if I weren't there sitting in front of them, as if I had boarded a boat for South America without so much as a goodbye. I couldn't remember my mother's being so angry with me ever before" (p. 67). This wrath engendered in her mother seems to be the point, conscious or unconscious, of her naughtiness: the marbles, the meetings, the money-stealing. Since maternal attention is what she yearns for, she subversively copies the unconventional and mischievous Red Girl as deftly as she can.

In the end, to find out where the marbles are, the mother cunningly and transparently tries to elicit her daughter's sympathy by telling her a long story about a "dangerous, horrible black snake in a basket of figs on top of her mother's head." She appeals to the daughter's potential maturation, reminding her of sexual dangers they share as women. But her strategy fails.

Annie John's love for her mother, her conflation of the Red Girl with her mother (both throw stones), sings out loudest just before she dissolves this psychological ploy: "To have been the same age as someone so beautiful, someone who even then loved books, someone who threw stones at monkeys in the forest" (p. 70).[27] As the trickster in Caribbean culture, the monkey assumes many disguises. Here, as frequently happens, the monkey symbolizes aspects of several relationships: the protagonist's relationship with her mother and the mother's relationship to colonialism. Like the monkey, the narrator moves to avoid being struck. She ignored the advice she was given and adopted the new strategy of actively throwing back the stone. She strikes back, that is, trying to hurt as she had been hurt. But the separation she effects emotionally damages her. And even more ironically, the monkey avoids the stone only to end up mimicking the mother by throwing back a stone. The monkey "teaches" that no one should assume a familiar response to injustice. In the long run, however, the mother or daughter (monkey) leaves a permanent mark on the other.[28]

In an extreme identification with her mother, Annie John returns her mother to Annie John's own age: "Feeling such love and such pity for this girl [her mother in the snake story] standing in front of me, I was on the verge of giving to my mother my entire collection of marbles. She wanted them so badly. What could some marbles matter? A snake had sat on her head for miles as she walked home" (p. 70). Then she discerns her mother's "soft and treacherous" voice and summons her own brand of duplicity, denying the existence of the marbles, connoted as any number of things — babies, men, a new brother, and a new rejection.

Menstruation immediately follows, but with a designated chronological gap, the incident quickly swept away. She stops playing marbles, the Red Girl is sent to Anguilla, a northernmost island in the Leeward chain where Antigua lies. The Red Girl symbolically goes north to freedom as Annie John does at the end. Again she represents Annie John as Annie John wants herself to be — escaping, having adventures, eschewing conventionality. But the Red Girl's voyage cannot be idyllic. Like Annie John's life, it teems with tension and reversal. Annie John's dream about the friend's departure involves a boat splintering in the sea and drowning passengers, almost identical to an earlier story about her mother's departure from Dominica: A hurricane blew up and the boat was lost at sea for almost five days. By the time it got to Antigua, the boat was practically in splinters, and though two or three of the passengers were lost overboard, along with some of the cargo, my mother and her trunk were safe" (pp. 19–20). The difference in the stories resides in the fact that Annie John once again rescues the Red Girl and they live in a dubious state of happiness: "Together forever, I suppose, and fed on wild pigs and sea grapes. At night, we would sit on the sand and watch ships filled with people on a cruise steam by. We sent confusing signals to the ships, causing them to crash on some nearby rocks. How we laughed as their cries of joy turned to cries of sorrow" (p. 71). In consigning the Red Girl to sea in a dream, Annie John is shedding her past and her memories; she is also dissolving a part of herself (in problem-solving water) that gains pleasure and grief simultaneously from her disobedience.[29]

While Annie John is learning to cope with complex emotions, she is also identifying herself politically at school. The chapter entitled "Columbus in Chains" opens with a description of the sun shining as the "trade winds blow," winds named after colonial sea routes that Christopher Columbus helped chart. As added adumbration, the second paragraph opens with chockablock references to England, colonialism, and slavery. First, the Anglican bell strikes the hour, a constant colonial signal throughout the text. Second, Annie John's boasts of her school prize, "a copy of a book called *Roman Britain.*" Apparently this book is a customary school prize as well as an inside joke to anyone who stands outside colonial propaganda: After all, Romans colonized the British who are still attempting to interpellate Antiguans in imperial ideology. Third, she describes the minister's daughter, Ruth, who is a blonde dunce from England whom Annie John used to ridicule. When the English student Ruth has to wear the dunce's cap, Annie John remarks that she "looked like a girl attending a birthday part in *The Schoolgirl's Own Annual*" (p. 75), a book depicting jolly white girls, often up to high jinks and oblivious to the world outside themselves, a jabbing reminder of the conventional colonial paradigm of ignorance and neglect. Not uncoincidentally, the dunce cap is atypically coronet-shaped, and appears to Annie John's conflictual gaze—mocking yet sympathetic—as a regal crown, a synthesis of stupidity and power, as the teacher, Miss Edwards is: "When I first met her [Ruth], I used to walk her home and sing bad songs to her just to see her turn pink, as if I had spilled hot water all over her" (p. 73).

Annie John pities the ignorant Ruth—as alone in an "alien" country as her biblical counterpart—whose ancestors had done "terrible things." Worse still, Ruth's father had been a missionary in Africa. Annie John proclaims awareness not only of her own socially constructed role in the colonial paradigm but of her present indoctrination. She unmistakably regards her teacher as complicitous with British colonialism. Coldly ironic, she introduces Queen Victoria's very name: "Her ancestors had been the masters, while ours had been the slaves. She had such a lot to be ashamed of, and by being with us every day she was always being reminded. We could look everybody in the eye, for our ancestors had done nothing wrong except just sit somewhere, defenseless. Of course, sometimes, what with our teachers and our books, it was hard to tell on which side we really now belonged — with the masters or the slaves — for it was all history, it was all in the past, and everybody behaved differently now; all of us celebrated Queen Victoria's birthday, even though she had been dead a long time" (p. 76). After this calculated, colonially signed paragraph, Annie John describes the history lesson on *A History of the West Indies,* chronicling the colonizer's doctored version of Caribbean history, generally unchallenged by the students.[30] Annie John, on the other hand, refuses to be silenced and radiates awareness of cultural complicities and contradictions. When the teacher discovers that Annie John has mockingly defaced the history book picture of a manacled Columbus, she becomes enraged. Miss Edwards's hagiographical depiction of Columbus as a white, imperialist icon bears a second-cousin resemblance to Noddy, pompous racist protagonist of British children's fiction exported to Antigua; the legendary adulation accorded Blyton's characters resembles the reverence in which Columbus has been held for centuries.

Under the picture of a chained-up Columbus in the history text, Annie John has derisively written: "The Great Man Can No Longer Just Get Up and Go." Literally and metaphorically, she punctures-punctuates Anglo-Saxon historical "reality," attuned to the fact that the Italian adventurer and colonial agent of Spain symbolizes all those who have tried to limit and even dissolve the political and cultural life of Caribbean people.[31] She marks the text with an oppositional Caribbean history, writ large, impudent, provocative, and with deliberation. Once again she conflates the autobiographical with the fictional, the incident deriving from a remark — "the great man can't shit" — that Jamaica Kincaid's mother made about her grandfather.[32] Refusing to sound herself through a white middle-class imaginary, she ridicules a history lesson, neither authentic nor "all in the past" (p. 76), that teaches the date of Columbus's "discoveries." Since fictions in this culture, she has learned, are taught as facts, "and language has been rendered unprivileged by the imposition of the language of a colonizing power," she plays around with these "facts" and defaces white culture, or rather revises it to bring it more in line with historical authenticity.[33]

Additionally, by resisting these received imperial interpretations and a prescribed location, Annie John functions as the singular representative of historical maroons, slave rebels whose name derives from the

Spanish term *cimarron* — wild or untamed. She declines to be mentally manacled by Miss Edwards, whose name conjures up Edward VIII, an independent-minded king who recently abandoned a life of duty to a country bent on territorial acquisition. Later, the characterization of Miss Edwards as a "bellowing dragon" (to Annie John's knight, presumably) duly underscores the ethnocentric history lesson (p. 78).[34] Annie John battles Miss Edwards's defense of a holy ground that her pupil, proud of a lineage that includes slave insurrectionaries, rejects with disdain.

Annie John's defiance stems not only from the exercise of power as an adolescent teetering between childhood and adulthood but also from a calculated political rebellion that she attempts to name: Her resistance identifies lies about the colonial past, a distorted postcolonial present, and an unpredictable future. She disrupts the "veneer of family harmony"; she flouts the advantages of a traditional education.[35] Although she is doubly suppressed and branded as an autonomy-bent girl and, in the eyes of postcolonial gazers like Miss Edwards, encoded as an ignorant and presumptuous colonized object, she refuses obliteration in either sphere.

The episode's symbolic significance is encapsulated in the punishment the authoritarian Miss Edwards metes out to Annie John; the pupil is commanded to write out *Paradise Lost*.[36] Having located herself on the edge of naughtiness — nuanced opposition to imperialism — she has surrendered primal innocence. Paradise slips away as she recognizes its boundaries. We never learn what happens afterwards; this indeterminate closure underscores the multiple lost paradises marked by Columbus's Caribbean presence.

Not by chance, the Columbus incident is associated with an earlier escapade in Annie John's life. While Miss Edwards stares at Annie John's deliberate textual defacement, the student flashes back to memories of herself and her friends dancing "on the tombstones of people who had been buried there before slavery was abolished in 1833." There they would "sit and sing bad songs, use forbidden words, and of course, show each other various parts of our bodies. [Some] would walk up and down on the large tombstones showing off their legs" (pp. 80–81). Ringleader in these exploits, Annie John thus links Columbus and the white student's unforgotten, plantocratic forerunners to historical memory and her prideful reclamation of unnamed ancestors. The reverberation of these earlier audacious acts within her present situation recalls the narrator's ongoing struggle for personal freedom and political integrity. It stresses, too, the consistency and dialectic of subordination and rebellion.

Annie John relished defacing the picture of Columbus, whom she detests. Quickly, she mentally shifts images from Christopher Columbus to her grandfather, Pa Chess, from paternalistic colonialism to paternalistic domesticity, and her own mother's sardonic anger when she discovers that Pa Chess is ill. The fact that Annie John's mother mocks her own father's inability to have a bowel movement and hence be clogged up with waste metaphorically invokes Columbus's inner corruption from a colonized standpoint.[37] In a recent interview Jamaica Kincaid talked about that very linkage in response to a question about whether her "personalizing . . . enabled [Kincaid] to make the connection between Columbus and your grandfather. [She replied:] That's right. You see, I reduce everything to a domestic connection. It's all the great men who have been humbled. Finally."[38]

At the beginning of "Somewhere, Belgium," with its vague European title, Annie John suggests that five years have elapsed since her obsession with death and her condition of unhappiness. However, she also indirectly refers to prior sources of unhappiness, such as poverty and social constraint. Annie John's mother probably needed her — we infer — to help around the house. She poignantly describes her sadness: "My unhappiness was something deep inside me, and when I closed my eyes I could even see it. It sat somewhere — maybe in my belly, maybe in my heart; I could not exactly tell" (p. 85). She imagines a physical shape — she sees its size and feels its weight — to her pain, "a small black ball, all wrapped up in cobwebs . . . no bigger than a thimble, even though it weighed worlds" (p. 85).[39] As a major trickster in Caribbean culture, the spider easily deceives. What appears negatively to Annie John at the time later becomes a source of joy, a means of entry into the adult world, a sign of self-determining. Her only recourse is to gaze at herself and count her toes, as if to prove a condition of consciousness. One aspect of her unhappiness is the fact that she cannot do as she pleases, possibly a code phrase for balking at being asked to help around the house while she is not recognized as worthy in her own right.

Using the gendered language of sewing, she describes her oncoming depression. The ball of pain is no bigger than a thimble that "weighed worlds fastened deep inside me, the sun beating down on me. . . . [a] dark cloud that was like an envelope in which my mother and I were sealed" (pp. 86, 91). Her mother's sewing represents that abandonment, just as its visible complement — her realization of separation — was the episode in the fabric store when her mother said they could dress alike no longer. This girl constitutes the family's repressed term. She signifies the expected role of women in Antiguan society, the silent perpetuation of an ideology that reduces females to ciphers.

At this point, her relationship with her mother hits an all-time low; the mother is trying — Annie John is firmly convinced — to manipulate her daughter constantly, the adolescent's eye view permitting no mediation. Annie John even finds fault in words that many would see as her mother's efforts to please her: "We both noticed that now if she said that something I did reminded her of her own self at my age, I would try to do it a different way, or, failing that, do it in a way that she could not stomach. She returned the blow by admiring and praising everything that she suspected had special meaning for me" (p. 87). Annie John becomes overtly secretive, raising (to raise) her mother's suspicions; they are a couple with a bright public facade and in private, a hateful relationship: "No sooner were we alone, behind the fence, behind the closed door, than everything darkened. How to account for it I could not say. Something I could not name just came over us, and suddenly I had never loved anyone so or hated anyone so" (p. 88).

Like the insect in *At the Bottom of the River,* she feels "as if I had grown a new skin over the old skin and the new skin had a completely different set of nerve [never] endings" (p. 91). In dreams that her mother has taught her to take seriously, severe words reverberate through her head since her ominous dream matches her "real life" thoughts: "My mother would kill me if she got the chance. I would kill my mother if I had the courage" (p. 89). During this sorry state of affairs, she moves up to a class with dull older girls she despises, some of whom carry "mirrors in their schoolbags" (p. 90). Annie John carries no mirror because who she is still bewilders her.

Gwen has lost her magic for Annie John because of her conventionality — a "bundle of who said what and who did what"; orthodoxy deeply threatens Annie John, who is trying so desperately to find solutions that will balance her state of mind. She tightly cherishes the little control she does muster. The last straw is Gwen's enunciation of an inane and harmless hope that Annie John will marry her brother Rowan, symbolic of Annie John's desire to escape the law of the father.

Annie John's most frequent dream occurs in Belgium, where her favorite author, Charlotte Brontë, lived for a time. In identifying with *Jane Eyre,* with whom Annie John has one name (loosely) in common, Annie John betrays certain gaps in her insights about postcolonial Antigua. That young Antoinette Cosway (later Bertha Rochester and Jane Eyre's "rival") is a character—the madwoman in the attic—whose "type" would be historically well known in Antigua, remains unstated.[40] Annie John also seems to desire and identify with Charlotte Brontë herself, with whom she conflates Jane Eyre's status as an independent female, a solitary fearless subject who visits Brussels, a desirable cold place—the antithesis of Antigua, familiar, warm, and despised.

Annie John covets Brontë's and Eyre's collective voluntary exiles—Jane Eyre also "escapes" from Thornfield Hall—their ability to flout authority. She craves what appears to her as their self-constructed autonomy. In ironic reversal, Jane Eyre–Charlotte Brontë is the exotic outsider and feisty heroine whose gender painfully impedes her: Annie John's daydream includes wearing a protective skirt "down to my ankles" and carrying protective weapons, "a bag filled with books that at last I could understand" (p. 92). She longs for a trickster mode, a telling mark of an indigenous culture.

She takes to walking home alone, still without a mirror, but staring at her reflection among household goods that include "bolts of cloth, among Sunday hats and shoes, among men's and women's undergarments, among pots and pans, among brooms and household soap, among notebooks and pens and ink, among medicines for curing headache and medicines for curing colds" (p. 94).

Here Annie John fuses sex, domestic chores, respectability, her unstated desire to write, and most relevant to the present time, illness. Just as she projects herself into Jane Eyre, she compares herself to the lonely, exiled, phallic, and aggressive Lucifer: "He was standing on a black rock, all alone and naked. Everything around him was charred and black, as if a great fire had just roared through. His skin was course, and so were his features. His hair was made up of live snakes, and they were in a position to strike" (p. 94).

Her encounter with Mineu, a former companion and now a high school boy, loitering in the street with friends, illumines her paranoia. Mineu is a childhood friend with whom she stopped playing after he tricked her into sitting naked on top of a red ants' nest that stung "all over . . . in my private parts. His mother refused to admit that he had done something wrong, and my mother never spoke to her again" (p. 100).

She translates the schoolboys' mumbled, insecure remarks about her beauty into "malicious" comments, and launches into a fascinating account of old power relationships she acted out in games she formerly played with this boy. When, for example, they acted out a local scandal with Annie John the junior partner as usual, Mineu played "the murdered man and the murderer, going back and forth; the girlfriend we left silent" (p. 97). As the play-acting mother, Annie John weeps over the murderer's hanged body. But when a real-life disaster happens and Mineu cannot prise himself loose from a noose, Annie John remains stationary. She watches him strangle until his mother rescues him: "As all this happened, I just stood there and stared. I must have known that I should go and call for help, but I was unable to move. . . . Much was said about my not calling for help, and everybody wondered what would have happened if his mother hadn't been nearby" (pp. 98–99). Mineu's hanged body is a projection of authoritarian figures who try to dominate her. Annie John, meanwhile, is the silent female murderer who acts her traditional passive role as a nonagent, while his self-destructive agency plays itself out in material life.

When her mother later accuses Annie John of being a slut for talking to these boys, she loses herself in misery and a sense of degradation. Annie's mother wants to control her woman's body just as personal and political conditions in Dominica threatened to control the body of Annie John's mother. Ironies abound. Annie John's mother wants to protect Annie John from a situation she avoided. Once again, Kincaid intertextualizes *At the Bottom of the River* and its insistent references in "Girl" to the daughter being a "slut." Annie John continues the saga of a certain coming of age, a bildungsroman begun in *At the Bottom*.[41] She responds in kind, complaining about her mother's double standard, specifically her reasons for leaving Dominica after a huge quarrel with her father about whether she could live by herself: "The word 'slut' (in patois) was repeated over and over, until suddenly I felt as if I were drowning in a well but instead of the well being filled with water it was filled with the word 'slut,' and it was pouring in through my eyes, my ears, my nostrils, my mouth. As if to save myself, I turned to her and said, 'Well, like father like son, like mother like daughter'" (p. 102). Her mother's presumptive accusation threatens Annie John's fragile identity, her sense of "moral" equality; the word *slut* suffuses her senses. Once again, as in the two stories of the ocean and her illness, water marks betrayal. The seeming irrationality of the mother's charge suggests some overwhelming maternal fear connected to the mother's adolescent argument with her father. Perhaps the fear concerns sexual freedom—her subsequent departure from home and giving birth. In other words, Annie John's mother might be drawing on personal shame in this crucial incident. Such a hypothesis also explains why Annie John recollects this particular memory when she earlier finds her parents making love. A menacing sexuality becomes the womb's fluid, her body's fluid. She halts this frightening transformation with words to her mother that claim this charged sexuality as parental heritage. She pointedly embraces her father's sexual popularity and (possibly) her mother's shame. They hurt each other emotionally, then retreat to cope individually with the serious aspersions Annie John has cast: "At that, everything stopped. The whole earth fell silent. The two black things joined together in the middle of the room separated, hers going to her, mine coming back to me. I looked at my mother. She seemed tired and old and broken. Seeing that, I felt happy and sad at the same time. I soon decided that happy was better, and I was just about to enjoy this feeling when she said, 'Until this moment, in my whole life I knew without a doubt that, without any exception, I loved you best,' and then she turned her back and started again to prepare the green figs (bananas) for cooking" (pp. 102–3). Back comes a conflation of potent images: black things in transformation and conflict, recalling the fluid spider and figs signing femaleness, bonding, creativity, duplicity. Since up to now her mother has possessed and directed her life, Annie John now rejects that model and asks her carpenter stepfather for a new trunk. She no longer craves her old possessions, the symbols of identity contained in her mother's trunk that was safely transported from Dominica to be born anew into and with Annie John's baby world. Annie John wants to start fresh; she will be her own repository. The new trunk will only contain Annie John's life, not her mother's. Again the trunk functions symbolically as a terminal point: "I wanted only to see her lying dead, all withered and in a coffin at my feet" (p. 106). Again the death image links up with the ambiguity of maternalities.

In "The Long Rain," Annie John becomes severely ill. Feeling deprived of maternal care, she foregoes all sustenance, akin to maintaining self-sufficiency at all costs: She holds on, as it were, through denial. Yet her refusal affirms her impotence, keeps sexual growth at bay. She attracts hyperattentiveness as she becomes temporarily anorexic and incontinent.[42] Annie John negotiates a return to a preoedipal, infantile state, surrounded by fluid and imprisoned by the rain—the sound it made, she said, "pressed me down in my bed, bolted me down" (p. 109). More to the point, she lives symbolically alone in a house of people: "My mother and father, sometimes together, sometimes separately, stood at the foot of my bed and looked down at me. They spoke to each other. I couldn't hear what it was they said, but I could see the words leave their mouths" (p. 109).

En route to the doctor's, her father carries her on his back; when they return, her mother undresses her and puts her to bed. They handle her as if, she contentedly intones, "I were just born" (p. 113). Their words die at her feet and they cannot touch her as she refuses to be sited in the symbolic order. Annie John loses her hearing, taste, understanding, memory: "The words traveled through the air toward me, but just as they reached my ears they would fall to the floor, suddenly dead" (p. 109). Any sound she hears—synesthetically transformed—is also, paradoxically, a gaze. Even her senses become unfixed.

During this prolonged, cryptic illness, she experiences unfamiliar sensations after she becomes drenched in a seeming bed-wetting dream, at one level suggesting a lack of control, a freeing of the body. She finds herself in her father's lap and experiences a "funny," apparently sexual feeling: "I liked and was frightened of [it] at the same time. It dawned on me then that my father . . . slept in no clothes at all . . . I do not know why that lodged in my mind, but it did" (p. 113).

The illness represents a new present for she now talks about her desires as things of the past. It functioned as a crucible of sorts in which complexities were reduced to their simplest terms. Masturbatory fantasy and involuntary sexual arousal for her father coexist with a regression to infantilism, a reenactment of preoedipal immersion in amniotic fluid; water is again the primary signifier. By inscribing Annie John's psychic watershed in the title of the chapter, "The Long Rain," Kincaid provides a dense, elemental metaphor to represent the terrifying feelings that threaten to engulf Annie. Illness accentuates her longing for maternal attention. To put the case more forcibly, grief has engendered sickness because she equates separation with annihilation.

Through association, she highlights her Brownie troop of her child-hood, her role as a colonial leader of the First Division Troop in which she marches.[43] She describes her thoughts about being a Brownie as if to connect these experiences with a disturbing history but also with the realization of being used, of being someone's robot.

At the end of the episode she synthesizes various elements all con-nected to a British-colonial stranglehold on expropriated Caribbean land. When the Brownies begin, they assemble at the Methodist Church, raise the Union Jack, and swear an oath of loyalty "to our country, by which was meant England. For an hour and a half, we did all sorts of Brownie things; then we gathered again around the flagpole to lower the flag and swear allegiance" (p. 115). She ends with an ironic and pro-phetic (or self-fulfilled) reference to her mascot, an owl: "It was wished for us that as we grew old we would grow wise also" (p. 116). Her thoughts swirl as her mother's discourse infuses that of the Brownie while she looks down at them and at herself, presumably derisive about her antics as a loyal, colonial child-subject.

Sexuality, African-Caribbean politics and culture, unconditional pa-rental nurturance play their part during her illness, as if she were sorting out and prioritizing the elements of her life. Throughout her perilous psychodrama, she uses the time to meditate and analyze. Almost self-indulgently, she can freely destroy, abandon, or subvert what has irri-tated her. In another way, she purges herself as she pleases. During her illness she recapitulates a primordial scene in which water, womb-like, surrounds her and engages the undivided attention not only of her mother but also (unwomblike) of her father. This preoedipal merging encompasses a strange form of sexual difference, a means of bonding with both parents, a refusal to allow them as a pair to be separate from her as the one. A bizarre incident emblematically illumines her inner turmoil while recording her youthful and desperate efforts to chart the formation of an oppositional subjectivity.

In a fit of delirium, she washes old photographs that start intimidating her, notably one that "straighten[s] out the creases in Aunt Mary's veil . . . to remove the dirt from the front of my father's trousers. . . . My mother was on her hands and knees, trying to dry up the floor . . . even in my state I could see that [the photos] were completely ruined. None of the people in the wedding picture, except for me, had any face left. In the picture of my mother and father, I had erased them from the waist down" (p. 120).

Meaning slides metonymically from washing to a sexual sign; purity dissolves the possibility of birth. She then lays the soaked photographs to rest in a perfumed bed of talcum powder, a miniature erotic grotto, a people's ritual modeled on her grandmother, Ma Chess's beliefs. The performance of this purification-obliteration ritual drenches her nightgown and sheets. She has enveloped herself in a primal reprise, rubbing out faces that speak the life of family members. Immersion has become self-definition as she figuratively resites herself in the security of the womb. In and with this water, she can gain freedom. She creates a path to communication and love. Effacing her father's sexuality, she can reclaim oneness with her mother. This revocation, however, can never occur because she already exists in the symbolic order.

She continues: "In the picture of me wearing my confirmation dress, I had erased all of myself except for my shoes" (p. 120). These specific shoes identity a tense altercation between Annie John and her mother. For the ceremony in which she would be received as an adult into the Methodist church, she selected shoes pronounced too risqué by her mother; they sported cut-out sides that exposed the flesh of Annie John's foot, marks of the virginity that her mother sought to protect. In her mother's eyes, she embraces what her mother wards off at all costs: the potential of being sexually active, a slut in her mother's term. Thus, she operates in a state of nonclosure, of confusion even. Her public, religious induction acknowledges imminent adulthood while the reversion to infantilism that characterizes her sickness signals a refusal of that very acknowledgment. So in the photos, her shoes emphatically remain.

Finally, the mother does obeisance as Annie John washes away any possibility of more babies. Yet she both reserves and receives the right to her own sexuality, keeping visible in the picture only the shoes her mother had deemed too sexually bold for her confirmation. Thus she confirms herself according to her own sexual (as it were) dictates.

Annie John becomes the center of the universe; the fishermen deliver fish and inquire kindly after her. At this point, another odd break occurs in the text. When her parent's friend Mr. Nigel, the fisherman, visits her sickbed and laughs at a remark she makes, that laughter spontaneously threatens to engulf her. This complex eruption signals that a gap is opening up: Abject passivity and even degradation are transforming into their opposite, a moment of liberation, her laughter a ridiculing of what she feels they have done to her. She is dissolving her trancelike state through connection with the everyday world of sight and smell.[44] She is opening herself up to new possibilities where what has been repressed can begin to dissolve. The invitation to laugh back at and with the fisherman secures relief; a vital safety valve opens up that she has never located. This feeling of self-disappearance is accompanied by memories of Mr. Nigel's domestic happiness. Desperately, she leaps on him, fells him, and pours out thoughts that crowd her head. Then her grandmother—an obeah woman and a Carib Indian—travels from Dominica and sleeps at the foot of her bed. She hears and recalls the old childhood stories her mother no longer wishes to recount.

At night, she barely functions; in the daytime she is an infant in the symbolic order: "I would lie on my side, curled up like a little comma, and Ma Chess would lie next to me, curled up like a bigger comma, into which I fit. In the daytime, while my mother attended my father, keeping him company as he ate, Ma Chess fed me my food, coaxing me to take mouthful after mouthful. She bathed me and changed my clothes and sheets and did all the things that my mother used to do" (p. 126).

Annie John has transformed herself into a sign of language without voice. This and her grandmother's obeah practices locate her in a historically perilous border area between speech and magic.[45] Note, too, since obeah functioned as a source of deep contention between slaves and slave owners, Annie John is recovering by means of insurrectionary tools against the likes of schoolteacher Miss Edwards. Obeah frequently functioned as an important African cultural practice that politically bonded the slaves. Via her grandmother, Annie John embraces a form of cultural syncretism. She accepts the intervention of a pre-Columbian world by embracing her Carib Indian grandmother, part of the identity she has fought for; she accords ancestral status to Amerindians, an "ancestral presence" to Ma Chess.[46] Ma Chess's success also affirms African cultural practice and counters paternal disapproval of obeah. In this section Alexander John is again associated with Western practices, with buying an English felt hat annually. Ma Chess represents not only family ties but Annie John's (and Jamaica Kincaid's) cultural rituals and roots and traditional consultation with diviners or conjurers. Ma Chess relates to indigenous people and to African religious leaders of old, one of whose main tasks was healing the sick, dealing with "illness, disease, and misfortune." In traditional African beliefs

> conjurers were portrayed as individuals who, in curing illness, combined their knowledge of the medicinal properties of plants, herbs, roots, barks, animal substances, and so forth with mysticism. In addition, they were revered as individuals whose mystical power made them adept at ferreting out both the mystical causes of illness and the human agents. . . . In most conjure tales, narrators concentrated on the mysterious illnesses and diseases that individual members of the community experienced and the miraculous cures effected by conjurers in these instances. At the same time, individuals learned from these narratives the consequences of being the victim of conjuration and those that awaited individuals who abused this power. As in this tale, the actions of conjurers to affect a cure were sometimes pictured as being as devastating to the original perpetrators as their actions had been on the victim.[47]

On this reading, a highly inflected maternality is one associated with original anticolonial intervention and metonymized as Annie John's heartless mother from Annie John's point of view; the doubled mother is the one who ultimately suffers Annie John's abandonment and by extension, political victory.[48]

After this, the illness mysteriously vanishes, coinciding with the cessation of the rain. In her first trip outside, Annie John establishes her reemergence into the symbolic order in a highly coded passage that hovers between death and life through water imagery:

> The sounds I heard didn't pass through me, forming a giant, angry funnel. The things I saw stayed in their places. My mother sat me

down under a tree, and I watched a boy she had paid sixpence climb
up a coconut tree to get me some coconuts. My mother looked at my
pinched, washed-out face and said: "Poor Little Miss, you look so
sad." Just at that moment, I was not feeling sad at all. I was feeling
how much I never wanted to see a boy climb a coconut tree again . . .
how much I never wanted to see the sun shine day in, day out again,
how much I never wanted to see my mother bent over a pot cooking
me something that she felt would do me good when I ate it, how
much I never wanted to feel her long, bony fingers against my cheek
again, how much I never wanted to hear her voice in my ear again,
how much I longed to be in a place where nobody knew a thing about
me and liked me for just that reason, how much the whole world into
which I was born had become an unbearable burden and I wished I
could reduce it to some small thing that I could hold underwater until
it died. (pp. 127–28)

Through physical illness, Annie John has navigated to a place where she
knows what she needs to do for herself. She now knows that she can start
over, without feeling stifled. She transcends a shying from independence, fully aware that dependence is killing her slowly. Having exter-
nalized her distaste for the fantasy and hypocrisy of her world, she re-
commences a slow, lopsided dance into adulthood, into a version of
psychic and physical health. She has to abandon the deathlike sight of
her mother's hand; she has to drain (out) her old world. In order to
live — she apprehends — she will have to abandon the island to dispel its
power over her. It is as if she continues with a vision of the world,
differently conceived but still fragmented: "For if an immediate vision is
possible and must be sought, then it is necessarily accompanied by visionary constructions that are imperfect . . . fragmentary, schematic . . .
Truth can only be partially spoken. And it is enough to begin."[49]

Her return to school signposts her reinforced, dual position in the
world as insider and outsider. As if play-acting, she dresses quaintly,
beating an inward retreat, while enjoying lavish attention through ec-
centric behavior; ontologically dislocated, she buttons up her developing person to hide the mismatch of her physical, cultural, and psychic
subjectivities. With this self-imposed outsider status, Annie John rejects
maternal definition, or rather refashions a sense of personal pride in her
own terms.

Self-dramatizingly, she compares the weather to her own condition as if weather constituted an authentic index and she wielded that kind of power. Although the rain that has fallen for three months during her illness has symbolically destroyed her mother's garden and fruit trees, they are restored. Her father too, puts in a new foundation and continues building. If is as if the new world order allows Annie John to leave. She will grow and build and be a foundation elsewhere. Everything has changed and is recommencing, most of all Annie John.

Upon her return to school Annie John becomes the focus of attention, finessing her absence so skillfully that students wish (or she thinks they wish) that they had also been ill. By removing herself dramatically to meditate on the contradiction of her situation, she is associated with a form of "studiation."[50] She is now at peace, having made some decisions in her (acquired) regressive state. She no longer filters everything through "a giant, angry funnel" (p. 127).

"A Walk to the Jetty" designates her fresh start, the illness of the "Long Rain" apparently cured. She has (she might imagine) dissolved her liminality and moved to a higher place.[51] At the signal of the Anglican church bell — a common colonial reminder — the family activities begin. These range from donning obeah-treated garments to hair grooming. After her metamorphosis following rain and resolution, a postlapsarian Annie John walks to the jetty with her parents. This time the topos of water represents purification of a different sort. Literally (at the jetty-*jeté*), she will throw herself into deliberate departure. Having gained a form of freedom, of temporary transcendent agency, she waves good-bye and sails for cold London.

She is also, then, always in two places at once. Although she refuses to recognize the fact, her life continues in Antigua even when she leaves, if only through parental and community discourse. She remains part of that life whether she writes to her parents or not. In this final section, Annie tries to come to terms with the problems she has faced throughout her recital. She relishes distance in all senses. There will be no more establishment Anglican bell tolling her to plural duties, no more Brownies or Girl Guides, no more swearing mindless allegiance to the Union Jack. She is content to be internally divided, thinking private odious thoughts and smiling gratefully: "Passing through most of the years of my life" (p. 138) as the threesome walks to the jetty. Once again she recapitulates her past life even though she talks of it as a "dust heap."

She feels the need to affirm it to herself, commit it to memory, store it up like money in the bank for a future occasion.

She began with death and she ends by noting that for thirteen of her seventeen years she has lived in a room that was an extension of the house, built because more room was needed after the birth of siblings who are the silent text of Annie John. Connected to the extension is the unspoken element of poverty that she is glad to be rid of. Its presence permeates the last chapter. On their daughter's last day in town, these parents walk with her for half an hour to the jetty—no cab for this family—and then, presumably, walk back. Since her father is thirty-five years older than her mother and she is seventeen, he is sixty-five at the very least and probably older. Indirectly, she also returns to the sexuality she was angry and curious about. She will not marry, she scoffs at the final breakfast table, certainly not an old man whom she would have to wait on hand and foot. Annie John is now the betrayer at this last supper, refusing conformity, flouting family orders; she is the new Judas in an ultimate role reversal. Gwen is a silly goose to be contemplating married life. Somewhat mysteriously at that festive breakfast, she compares her father metonymically (though his teeth) to a horse and her mother (through her chewing) to a donkey.

Annie John is leaving things—her whole life, she thinks—behind. Her vanity, her unaffected childishness mix silently and easily as she recounts old times. On that last walk, she treasures old stories of love— when she shopped by herself for the first time; of duty—when she worked for the seamstress; and points of opposition—when she ate the sweet potatoes that were supposed to cure her friend's mumps. These reminiscences enable a rounding out of Annie John's character, its presence through space, time, and place. The flashback provides some context for Annie John's current project: a young woman confronting diverse pressures and claiming agency for herself.[52]

Her complex internality represented in the values and attitudes of Gwen and the Red Girl still exist side by side unresolved. She recalls her "Gwen side" affectionately, when she first walked alone and brought threepence worth of camphor, eucalyptus, and oil for her mother, when she was enthralled with a porcelain spotted dog outside a store, and especially when she dresses for her journey in the neat clothes ironed by her mother that have folk medicine pinned on them. She hates it but she does it for the last time, for old times' sake. Good-byes are the order of the day.

Her "Red Girl" side is there, too, in the seething, hateful denunciation of this "dust heap" of her life. She thinks in childish ways: She can leave her old life behind in the backyard and it can be dropped off in the community dump. She is sick of attention, of the fact that all her furniture has been made by her father and most of her clothes by her mother. Nothing belongs to or emanates from Annie John herself. Internally she is vowing vengeance, with no sense of her mother's exigent condition of life. She wants to be rid of senseless rules, of endless chores, of repetition, and feelings of nothingness. Her mother's fussiness is alluded to several ways: her systematic visits to the public library and her deep involvement in a book about boiling milk to purify it; in her checking Annie John's bag for its contents; in instructions and notes she hands to ship person-. nel about looking after her daughter.

Annie John takes grim pleasure in thinking she has pierced the veil of her mother's hypocrisy. She talks as if she had her mother's number, as if her mother's life were a series of calculations to trick her daughter. Her insecurity, her inner emptiness causes her to suspect her mother's affections. Unconsciously certain that she is worthless, she acts somewhat paranoid. She loathes her mother passionately and adores the mother she grew up with, the mother she followed and watched adoringly. She dwells in perpetual conflict.

The first words spoken in this chapter of incantatory farewells — "My Name is Annie John" — underwrite a longing to find herself. She seems unaware that her subjectivity is already constructed in certain ways and that these multiple "selves" are part of who she is.[53] For the time being, she covets an authentic identity, refusing to face the fact that one has already developed. So much of her early discussion centers on identity and naming. She watches her name emblazoned on her trunk before she falls asleep and her address fluctuates between England and Antigua. Her name is the first phrase that enters her mind as she wakens. Her self-consciousness or awareness of self—the soldiers in her mental army—keep her in formation: "They [her name] stayed there, lined up one behind the other, marching up and down, for I don't know how long" (p. 130).

But this naming, this attempt to claim agency, this structure she de-

scribes of who she is and what her life is about stems from the frail grasp
she maintains on who she is and what she will become. She is a characteristic adolescent, risk-taking and willful, yet filled with fear at the very
thought of it. The experience of leaving verges on the mystical: "I didn't
feel my feet touch ground, I didn't even feel my own body — I just saw
these places as if they were hanging in the air, not having top or bottom,
and as if I had gone in and out of them all in the same moment. . . . We
then arrived at the jetty" (p. 143).

In the end, she returns to the water imagery she has dwelt on throughout to discuss and envision moments of merger; most of these discussions of water have centered on her mother, multiplicitously conceived:
when she swam at Rat Island with her mother, when she looked out to
sea with the Red Girl, when she defaced the merchant adventurer Columbus and longed to go to Belgium, but most directly, when she was ill
during the rain and lay bedridden and endlessly drenched.[54]

The familiar hollow space inside her threatens to lurch up; she will
slip through the cracks at the dock; she will disappear into the water and
merge with the eels: "My heart now beat fast, and no matter how hard I
tried, I couldn't keep my mouth from falling open and my nostrils from
spreading to the ends of my face. My old fear of slipping between the
boards of the jetty and falling into the dark-green water where the dark-
green eels lived came over me" (p. 143). But a different effect from the
water comes over her at the very end: "I went back to my cabin and lay
down on my berth. Everything trembled as if it had a spring at its very
center. I could hear the small waves lap-lapping around the ship. They
made an unexpected sound, as if a vessel filled with liquid had been
placed on its side and now was slowly emptying out" (p. 148).

Annie John is now her own witness; her intense relationships still
exist but she is ready to embark. She is the vessel leaving old parts and
places, emptying out to let new experience fill her up. Her mother cannot take her words away, for she is taking them with her. All the water
that threatens to separate her from her mother and drown her — amniotic fluid — is being released.[55] In popular parlance, the water is breaking
and she is slowly being born anew. Once and for all, clear-headed and
articulate, she rejects preoedipal union, the imaginary. Water may have
been the feminine element and reflect the comforting security of the
womb, but all that has changed. Now she empowers herself by doing the

opposite — dredging her interior to let the water out. In the ocean, on the ship, the speaking subject will be moving to a place where she can fuse readily in a different world. She is poised for that new day. Yet the ambivalence that has eaten away at her never completely dissolves. And it still resonates at the heart of Kincaid's next novel, *Lucy* (1990), set twenty years later.

The careful building of Annie John's narrative through association complements the form: Following no consistent chronology, the sections track the narrator's circuitous coming to terms with her environment and this final exit. Through cumulative impressions and anecdotes governed by an informing intelligence, Annie John has faced down narcissistic colonial myths, refused colonial absorption. She declined to negotiate her birthright.[56] "Free is how you is from the start, an' when it look different you got to move, just move, an' when you movin' say that it is a natural freedom that make you move."[57] Annie John, then, continues the quest of a similar narrator in *At the Bottom of the River* for personal-political identity. Kincaid writes a discontinuous coming-of-age chronicle from a feminine and a feminist point of view. At the same time, culture, class, and racial differences are equally important influences.[58]

Jamaica Kincaid writes *Annie John* fifteen years after she came to the United States and after Antigua becomes independent. In several interviews, Kincaid invites readers to equate Annie John with herself.[59] Annie John is one of Jamaica Kincaid's avatars. That autobiographical factor, however, is made much more explicit in her next publication, entitled *A Small Place*. In this text Kincaid decides — it seems — to speak in her own voice. In *Annie John,* by contrast, the autobiographical and the fictional seamlessly interconnect, rendering the text constantly open, fluid, yet speculative. Perhaps forcing to the surface submerged anger at her colonized place helped provoke *A Small Place,* a polemic against British colonialism. Jamaica Kincaid's own view of what *Annie John* is about allows for its own potent silences that erupt in *A Small Place*.[60] "Well, it's a mask — she's not really hardhearted. She really wants to break down and be taken back in, but there's a parting place. She says she remembers that she's been told: 'Once you start to do something, you have to see it through,' and so she's got to see this thing through. But it's a hardness that has no substance, really, and if I were to continue to write this character — which I won't — you would see how the hardness is easily broken. She becomes enough of a woman to start imposing hardnesses on other people, but it's not a real hardness."[61] Kincaid continually crosses and recrosses the borderline between autobiography and fiction while maintaining distance. She constructs a narrator who, like Scheherazade, continually weaves a narrative for, as Jamaica Kincaid has remarked, she wrote to save her life.

At first sight, *A Small Place* seems unique, generically distinct from *Annie John*. On closer inspection, *A Small Place* is a transcendence, a near-distillation of a major though quiet aspect of *Annie John* that is already hinted at in *At the Bottom of the River*. It presents another dimension of Jamaica Kincaid's life, a more explicitly political one. It fills some gaps in *Annie John* even as it offers new vistas. It throws a bright light on the ongoing saga that illumines some of the mystery in earlier texts as well as the path this complex, composite narrator continues to travel. This is not to suggest Kincaid's texts are all deliberately linked by look-alike narrators. Far from it. But it is to say that the fictive-autobiographical dimension insistently punctuates the texts thus far and that this narrator was at least technically and in nomenclature distanced from Jamaica Kincaid. In *A Small Place,* the unnamed narrator is nonfictional and less personally embroiled. Kincaid needs this new narrator, in a sense, to make the implied resistance in *At the Bottom of the River* and *Annie John* unequivocal.

A Small Place: *Counterknowledge with a Vengeance*

Chapter 3

I can never believe that the history of the West Indies happened the way it did. . . . The wreck and the ruin and the greed. It's almost on a monumental scale.—**Jamaica Kincaid, interview**

I say that by delaying the achievement of self-government . . . a terrible damage was inflicted upon us. In reality, our people were miseducated, our political consciousness was twisted and broken. Far from being guided to independence by the 1960s . . . for forty years the imperialist governments poisoned and corrupted that sense of self-confidence and political dynamic needed for any people about to embark on the uncharted seas of independence and nationhood. We are still without that self-confidence and that dynamic today. We lack them because for the last half-century, we were deprived of making the Caribbean people what our history and achievements had made possible and for which we were ready. That then is my conclusion. They have not educated, they have mis-educated us, stood in our way, piled burdens on our backs. —**C. L. R. James,** *The Making of the Caribbean People*

In the battle a people recognizes itself again.—**Frantz Fanon**

✪ IN MANY WAYS, *A Small Place,* Jamaica Kincaid's first virtually un-mediated, anticolonial polemic, provides an important gloss and elab-oration on the early texts: *At The Bottom of the River,* which presents a visionary view of childhood, and *Annie John,* where she sketches an unsettling journey into adolescence that ends with Annie John sailing away, supposedly for the United Kingdom.

Jamaica Kincaid wrote *A Small Place* in the United States during the late 1980s, after returning from her first trip to Antigua following her departure in 1966 and a subsequent twenty-year voluntary exile. While she was growing up in Antigua from 1949 to 1966, the country was governed by legislative councils appointed by the British governor. A year after Kincaid left Antigua in 1967, the island gained associate status, a term and formula developed by the British government for colonized countries in transition to independence. This status involved ongoing British "protection." In 1981 under the leadership of Prime Minister Vere Cornwall Bird, Antigua became self-governing.[1]

What Jamaica Kincaid witnessed when she returned in the 1980s deeply displeased her: "I spent all the time I had been away from the West Indies and from my mother building some kind of 'literary monument' to it [Antigua], and it was interesting that when I got back it had changed so radically. I was shocked that it had changed for the worse."[2] By this admission, her earlier works commemorated a certain period in her native land which ensuing history exploded. Consequently, *A Small Place* marks a radical departure from *At the Bottom* and *Annie John*. This time the speaker (Kincaid, it seems, in her own voice, as a self-identifying speaker) knows she belongs to this place — Antigua is her point of origin — yet she feels alienated from the island for different reasons from those that impelled her to leave.[3] In that sense, the first three works form an uneven and discontinuous trilogy about Jamaica Kincaid's life over four decades. They constitute the critical early elements in an ongoing bildungsroman.

A Small Place searingly indicts Antigua's past and present governments, both incorporated British colonial and black Antiguan self-rule, for a glaring imbalance of power that silences the majority of the population. In variant formulations, this excoriation of historical and contemporary corruption simultaneously glosses *At the Bottom* and *Annie John*. *A Small Place* grounds these earlier fictional-autobiographical texts by explaining the cultural situation of Antigua and Antiguan response.

In *A Small Place* the speaker is concerned for her native land, not herself. Although telling vestiges remain of the fictional narrators in *At the Bottom of the River* and *Annie John,* the perspective has pointedly shifted. Most notably, this later voice is boldly denunciatory. She is affronted that the black Antiguan, postindependence government, instead of working on the people's behalf, takes economic advantage of the population; in the wake of its British counterpart, the government constructs and maintains that notorious colonial hallmark an uninformed populace, or perhaps better put, a populace who become so inured to manipulation that people come to accept it as a given of daily life.

On a macrolevel, *A Small Place* constitutes another way of rendering imperialism and its spoils, offering an updated representation of Antigua's history. It locates itself on a cultural-political continuum alongside such distinguished earlier condemnations of colonialism and postcolonialism as Aimé Césaire's *Return to My Native Land* and Frantz Fanon's *Black Skin, White Masks.*[4]

A Small Place is divided into four sections with several subsections. In the first section, the speaker discusses tourism and the reaction of black Antiguans to tourists. In the second, the speaker deplores what has happened in Antigua since self-rule was proclaimed in 1981; she queries why the Antiguan government mimics the metropolitan government in its policies of exploitation and domination. The third section, almost half the text, attacks the present government from a number of directions and indicts British colonialism and its shameful legacy. *A Small Place* ends with a discussion of the people presently living in Antigua, who, the speaker claims, have no sense of time or context. This ending doubles as a near-direct address to Antigua and Antiguans.

The principal elements of the text are synthesized in the opening section on tourism, where Kincaid sketches past and present inequities and their relative contexts. These range from the devastating history inherited from the British, the present government's continuation of economic expropriation of people's labor and sociocultural oppression, to the willingness of people to tolerate and even assimilate such a palpably unjust state of affairs. But despite implying the need for action, the narrator offers no blueprint beyond exposure and a quiet subtextual message: "The next step is up to you."

More specifically, the opening section describes the role tourism plays and the relationship of tourists to native Antiguans. Kincaid uses tourism as a template for the history of Antigua under colonialism; representing the legacy of colonialism, tourism sets up and underscores historical power relations and their continuance. In exposing tourism's nefarious, centuries-old point of origin, Kincaid aims indirectly to subvert the dominant paradigm of power as it presently exists on the cusp of the nineteen-nineties.

Narrated by a speaker identified biographically in the text several times as Kincaid herself, *A Small Place* charges representative tourists with certain responsibilities: They must acquire an informed context about the country they choose to visit, think about their role as visitors in that culture, comprehend what they are doing there, and know why they have come. Tourists should ask themselves, Is my presence welcome? Is the country built on tourism because the country the tourist hails from (or a politically like-minded country) has left Antigua precious few economic options? Are the people sick of this situation but deprived of other choices? Refusing to allow tourists to be divorced from their historical context, Jamaica Kincaid does not accept the old colonial dictum: I want service for my money. Instead, she turns the matter into a situation that demands self-reflection. Why am I here? Why do the indigenous people scarcely ever visit my country, enjoy pleasant holidays, and spend money freely?

Otherwise, if tourists travel mindlessly to Third World countries where the standard of living is pitifully low and think about how they can enjoy (profit) themselves, pay as little as possible for goods and services, bargain down shopkeepers and street vendors, they are "ugly" human beings who are indulging in hollow pleasures. Tourists, in a word, are morally culpable; they are accountable for their actions. Kincaid proceeds to mock the condescending discourse of unconsciously racist tourists who view local inhabitants as delightful objects of their gaze and for their consumption: "You look at things they can do with a piece of ordinary cloth, the things they fashion out of cheap, vulgarly colored (to you) twine, the way they squat down over a hole they have made in the ground, the hole itself is something to marvel at, and since you are being an ugly person this ugly but joyful thought will swell inside you: their ancestors were not clever in the way yours were and not ruthless in the way yours were, for then would it not be you who would be in harmony with nature and backwards in that charming way" (pp. 16–17). Kincaid's rhetorical ploy is to have this speaker (herself, or someone who shares many of her views) address potential tourists to Antigua. As an informed Antiguan citizen, the speaker imaginatively predicts the visit and the tourists' vast ignorance, but she goes well beyond that stage of condemnation. She spells out what is (might be) going on behind the facade of a sunny tropical isle. *A Small Place* is much more than a wake-up call for tourists. It indicts those who foster hierarchies and make such a corrupt form of tourism possible.

Jamaica Kincaid's opening *if* carries a weighty suggestion — more obvious in retrospect: "If you go to Antigua as a tourist, this is what you will see" (p. 3). This particular kind of tourist is the epitome of human callousness, no better than slave owners of old. (Kincaid leaves open the possibility, admittedly minute, that informed, courteous tourists exist who treat black Antiguans on a respectful egalitarian basis or at least understand the historical situation and act appropriately.) The conditional verbs focus her point aptly: "You may be the sort of tourist who would wonder why a Prime Minister would want an airport named after him — why not a school, why not a hospital" (p. 3). The hypothesis establishes that this sort of single, homogenized, representative tourist (probably most tourists) would not ask such troubling political questions. They are, after all, on holiday, and the quality of Antiguan life does not concern them.

By the end of this imagined scenario when the tourist is exclaiming about Antigua's beauty, Kincaid has already laid bare the mordant irony of her discourse because this enthusiastic tourist relishes the fact that Antigua is less green and therefore sunnier than other islands. The fact that the lack of green signifies that the population suffers from severe water shortage never crosses such a tourist's mind. All that matters to this tourist (white, racist, ugly, understood) is that the sun shines during the vacation, regardless of the implications of drought.

The narrator follows this with a direct comparison between the differential treatment at St. John's airport accorded returning black Antiguans as opposed to white tourists. Tourists are oblivious to these distinctions, to what is going on around them. They think only of reaching their destination with maximum efficiency. A typical tourist, in fact, relishes going through the customs line as rapidly as possible. The speaker intensifies this portrayal with another cynical description, this time of a ride on bad roads in a noisy but expensive Japanese-made taxi that was built to use nonleaded gasoline and is now filled with leaded gasoline. The speaker impresses on the reader not only that the tourist — who supposedly resembles the reader — will not notice the problem but also, and more to the point, that the driver is ignorant of this pernicious situation. Later, the tourist learns that a few roads were specially paved for Queen

Elizabeth II's visit to Antigua in 1985 (p. 12). The driver, besides, will be living in inferior accommodation — a shack along the road, perhaps — well below the standard of his car.

This leads into Kincaid's (or the speaker's) direct attack on the current government: Loans are available for cars but not for houses, because government ministers own the two major Antiguan car dealerships, "in part or outright" (p. 7).[5] Vignettes of Pigott's School and Holberton Hospital in St. John's follow, the former resembling latrines in a sea of dust, the latter a sight that should alarm any tourist since "no actual Antiguan trusts" the medical treatment received there. All the government ministers fly to New York for medical treatment.

Kincaid proceeds associatively. As part of her guided tour, she touches on the fact that "you couldn't just go to the library and borrow some [books]. Antigua used to have a splendid library, but in The Earthquake . . . the library building was damaged. This was in 1974, and soon after that a sign was placed on the front of the building saying, THIS BUILDING WAS DAMAGED IN THE EARTHQUAKE OF 1974, REPAIRS ARE PENDING. The sign hangs there . . . more than a decade later . . . a splendid old sign from colonial times" (pp. 8–9). After she outlines the condition of the library, she flashes to the fact that the Antiguan government gained independence from Britain just after the earthquake. People, she comments, thank a "British God" for this.[6] The speaker subtly scorns this worship of a colonial deity and speciously warns the tourist not to think of the confusion this practice generates. Instead the tourist — still homogenized, coded as male, and even more baldly ridiculed — is reminded that he has bought a new book on economic history that distorts metropolitan-periphery relationships since the tourist, anyway, prefers to see local circumstances in an inauthentic light (p. 9).

The revisions or falsifications of histories that attract tourists — she goes on to remark dryly — downplay and even dissolve the role of slavery in British profiteering and emphasize the supposedly fortunate acquisitions of local Antiguans. Wristwatches like the narrator's, she reminds readers, are not prizes: "Not only did we have to suffer the unspeakableness of slavery, but the satisfaction to be had from bogus colonial trumpeting to colonized people — 'We made you bastards rich' — is taken away" (p. 10). Yet this history of manifest exploitation should not, the narrator asserts ironically, spoil the tourist's holiday after so many "hard and cold and dark and long days . . . spent working" (p. 4). At one level, the narrator recognizes the humanity of less-than-affluent tourists who pinch pennies and save up all year round for their vacations.

The author-projecting speaker then fulminates against a certain Syrian merchant family who came to Antigua and started off selling dry goods door to door and now owns a sizable area of the land. Antiguans, she pronounces decisively, "hate them." When the tourist arrives at the hotel, the narrator cheekily mimics touristlike appreciation of the other's culture: "Oh, what beauty! Oh, what beauty!" and the tourist's conventionally narcissistic view of how he or she will look on the beach. This commentary marks the only time when the speaker has a tourist speak directly: "You don't like me?" is the tourist's amazed response to the very idea that local community members might not like a tourist presence, regardless of its financial boost to the island.

The speaker's comment on the contents of the ocean is calculated to nauseate anyone and certainly every tourist. Water apparently merges with human waste in the ocean; the sea has become a danger to people's health. At this point, the night-soil men of *At the Bottom of the River* intersect with the tourists. The Caribbean, in that sense, is cursed by colonial practices — for there is no sewage system — and so the night-soil men, through no fault of their own, are employed in a job that results in the East Caribbean being polluted with excrement and urine: "You must not wonder what exactly happened to the contents of your lavatory when you flushed it. You must not wonder where your bathwater went when you pulled the stopper. You must not wonder what happened when you brushed your teeth. Oh, it might all end up in the water you are thinking of taking a swim in; the contents of your lavatory might, just might, graze gently against your ankle as you wade carefree in the water, for you see, in Antigua, there is no proper sewage-disposal system" (pp. 13–14).[7] The delicious food anticipated by the tourist is similarly derided: "The pollution of the Mediterranean parallels colonial intervention." Beyond that, impure water is connected to obeah practices: "It is an opportunity for a curse; it receives a maleficent thought naturally. The moral axiom of absolute purity, destroyed forever by one pernicious thought, is perfectly symbolized by water that has lost a little of its limpidity and its freshness."[8] During these revelations, the narrator quietly reminds tourists (who are presumably ooh-ing and aah-ing about the beauty of the Caribbean) that they might be shocked to learn that millions of manacled Africans died crossing the Atlantic Ocean — specifically on the middle passage — as they journeyed to enslavement. This information links to the section on waste disposal in which Kincaid elides sewage with African deaths; in this way the speaker underlines the metonymic shift from tourists to colonizers. The ocean has room for all that. Just as the colonizers could dispense with anxiety at death, so, she cynically stresses, sewage (what the colonizers thought of the Africans) will dissolve into the Caribbean.

Kincaid continues with myriad asides, laced with frontal assaults on tourist indifference to the black population; she splatters the reader with a battery of hideous information about deterioration and the mismanagement and foul practices being executed all over the island. Those asides frequently introduce vital information that propels her associatively in diverse directions. Asides also suggest multiple expansions of the power relationships she is outlining and the importance of the marginalized. The fact that fundamental information is located in asides is a way of privileging the marginalized themselves, often rhetorically relegated by the government as "human asides."

Resuming the theme of tourist ignorance and thoughtlessness, the speaker insists that the actions of tourists turn them into a temporary human subspecies. Though they might be "whole" back home, that designation is artificial since tourists are ill-equipped to examine themselves psychologically in any sophisticated way. They are intent on the business of pleasure that absorbs so much energy and cancels their awareness of those around them. They have to be self-absorbed — ironically — to afford expensive Caribbean vacations. Tourists are oblivious to the fact that they are "visiting heaps of death and ruin" (p. 16). The reverse is even true. They claim inspiration from the sights and wax eloquent about the harmony of the people. In duplicitous tourist lingo, harmony connotes backwardness. Consciously or not, Anglo-Saxon tourists radiate a sense of superiority in Third World countries.

Kincaid's condemnation is absolute and unsparing, her revenge to let the tourist know how much Antiguans despise their behavior: "An ugly thing, that is what you are when you become a tourist, an ugly, empty thing, a stupid thing, a piece of rubbish pausing here and there to gaze at this and taste that, and it will never occur to you that the people who inhabit the place in which you have just paused cannot stand you, that behind their closed doors they laugh at your strangeness (you do not look the way they look)" (p. 17).

Tourists at second remove parallel the present government that perpetuates metropolitan corruption. Like their colonial forerunners and their ancestors, they view Antiguans as "other people who are in unison with nature and backward in that charming way" (p. 17). According to this commentary, tourism becomes a quasi-masochistic act, since tourists are spending every day and night in the company of people who despise their presence, a no-win situation for both sides.

Singled out as an individual not as part of "a mass," the tourist is defined by acquisition, either of personal experiences divorced from the people or by material possessions: "a person at home in your own house (and all its nice house things), with its nice back yard (and its nice backyard things), at home on your street, your church, in community activities, your job, at home with your family, your relatives, your friends — you are a whole person" (pp. 15–16). This ordinary person turned contemptible tourist whose life is defined by objects possessed never takes a good ontological look inside. The tourist is "not well equipped" to do so, and besides, it would ruin the holiday. Nonetheless, Kincaid states, the tourist does have some idea — a "slightly funny feeling you have from time to time about exploitation, oppression, domination" (p. 10) — of his or her role in maintaining metropolitan hegemony. The tourist consumes the history of Antigua, we learn, from a colonial analysis of economic history that distorts the ravages wreaked by First World interventions and obfuscates the modern capitalist mode of exploitation" (pp. 9–10).

In a pragmatic sense, Kincaid intends to turn tourists away from Antigua. She spells out facts that the tourist industry suppresses. Her polyvoiced discourse both derides tourists and indicts the government. The graphic commentary about the lack of an adequate sewage system and the need for tourists to consider, when they are swimming in the ocean, where the contents of their toilets vanished to, indicts both contemporary European gullibility and old and new corruption. Citizens are also invited to consider the quality of social services.

The other half of this dialectic — the black Antiguans who are being treated as servants by the tourists — are spoken of in mixed tones. On the one hand, Kincaid insists on the ignorance of such people as taxi-drivers. (Whether taxi-drivers are so uninformed is another story.) They do not factor insofar as government ministers bankroll the Japanese cars and hence profit from a monopoly and do not care how it affects the drivers.

On the other hand, black Antiguans know full well how exploited they are by tourists and dislike them accordingly. But they do not seem to connect their enmity toward tourists with the conditions of their lives, the show they put on for white tourists and the poverty they are obliged to endure. At the end, Kincaid reminds readers of the obvious: Most people are too poor to go anywhere and envy those who can. It is this poverty of colonized people that anchors her investigation in *A Small Place*. Kincaid recapitulates the point most completely in the final section.

The harsh guided tour of Antigua over, Kincaid remarks that a world of something exists in this, but "I can't go into it right now." The choice of prints for the British paperback edition of *A Small Place*—both on the cover and in the inside pages—further affirms Kincaid's subversion of a single-minded way—the tourist's, the government's—of looking at things. The cover depicts groups of well-clad black Antiguans working collectively in an orderly fashion for the master who surveys his plantation from the Great House. No visible overseer is present. Preceding the first page, however, the same picture appears in reverse. Nothing is stationary. The people now walk in the opposite direction. The Master's House has been reconstructed. The negative photo of idealized slavers has been flopped technically and metaphorically. The "world of something" is the consequence of metropolitan domination of an island population. The speaker tenders as a reason that the tourist is an "ugly human being." It is the same reason she offers in the next section when she discusses First World fussing about went wrong with the "empire": "I can say to them," she emphatically states, "what went wrong: they should never have left their home, their precious England" (p. 24).

In other words, tourists act insensitively because their behavior is a logical extension of preemancipation and preindependence colonial behavior. It replicates the notion that people's labor exists for maximum exploitation. Like colonists of old, tourists should enjoy the island to the fullest extent and get "their money's worth." Tourism is a modern version of colonialism; it is domination's new, lucrative face.

In short, Kincaid is arguing that tourists are constructed in capitalist, postcolonialist ideology. They buy a racist image of a "sunny isle," a mythology, in Roland Barthes's terms, not only because the island is not sunny, metaphorically speaking, but because their lives are unfulfilled yet they think of themselves as "entitled."[9] Despite occasional squeamishness about the obvious, they would prefer to look with "ignorant eyes" at the devastation of history and call it quaint and unusual. They have been taught to feel superior to a historically dominated population, so they do. Thus they keep the box of their own internal and external reality tight shut. Because of their ideological entrapment, they are incapable of understanding that it is they themselves, the tourists, who are out of step with the environment:

> Being ordinary is already so taxing, and being ordinary takes all you have out of you, and though the words "I must get away" do not actually pass across your lips, you make a leap from being that nice blob just sitting like a boob in your amniotic sac of the modern experience to being a person visiting heaps of death and ruin and feeling alive and inspired at the sight of it; to being a person lying on some faraway beach, your stilled body stinking and glistening in the sand, looking like something first forgotten, then remembered, then not important enough to go back for; to being a person marvelling at the harmony (ordinarily, what you would say is the backwardness) and the union these other people (and they are other people) have with nature. (p. 16)

Kincaid begins the next section by pointing out that the Antigua now enjoyed by tourists is not the Antigua she grew up in. That bygone Antigua is her next subject.

The second section begins tongue-in-cheek. The Antigua that Jamaica Kincaid knew no longer exists. But, she continues, addressing the same representative tourist, "let me tell you of the Antigua that I used to know" (p. 24). For the time being, that is, she maintains an overt (artificial) separation between present tourists and past English colonizers. The English are "they," the tourists are still "you" — the addressee — even though on the second page she pointedly designates the crime of imperialism as one of "leaving home" — the same "crime" with which tourists were earlier charged. The gap that she opens between tourists and colonizers is temporarily preserved.

With that tantalizing analogy that yokes the target of the polemic to the addressee, Kincaid proceeds to lambaste the English colonizers. While proclaiming that her identity is tied to England's history, Kincaid relegates the colonizer to the status of other — an objectified, totalized mass that has perpetrated three centuries of cruelty on an innocent island population. The tables are turning.

The Englishness that she unsparingly displays is characteristic of metropolitan behavior, of how the center of power acts toward the margins: the perpetuation of bigotry and violence, cultural deprivation, and the silencing of the people.

The speaker foregrounds a trio that she finds particularly reprehensible; the Barclay banking brothers, who were originally slaveholders, along with a racist refugee doctor from the Nazis who insists on his black patients being scrubbed before he sees them; and an Irish headmistress of a girls' school who not so subtly secured the exclusion of black children for a long time by accepting only girls born to legally married parents. In an intertextual reference to the concept of slut in *At the Bottom of the River* and *Annie John*, Kincaid indicts the headmistress of an Antiguan private girls' school hired through the colonial office, who "only in my lifetime [Kincaid's] began to accept girls who were born outside a marriage; in Antigua it never dawned on anyone that this was a way of keeping black children out of this school" (p. 29). When the school, run through the colonial office, finally accepted black pupils, the headmistress specifically reprimanded them for behaving like "monkeys just out of trees."[10] This bigoted triumvirate represent and partially control Antiguan economics, health, and education.

Another target is the people at the Mill Reef Club, a private, originally segregated club for rich North Americans who masquerade as philanthropists in the good old-fashioned colonial tradition. Part of black Antiguan history (ironically conceptualized by the speaker) is reciting the name of the first Antiguan black who ate a sandwich and played golf there. As an act of liberation, this naming matters. On the one side are the Mill Reef Club members denounced by the people as "pigs living in that sty" (p. 28); on the other side is the commitment to memory of an unjust history, another form of resistance. With these asides about knowing the enemy and the importance of historical memory, Kincaid refutes her own assertion that black Antiguans' perceptions of metropolitan misrule are "not political."

Antiguan people may refrain from designating the headmistress, the doctor, and the club members as racists — they may prefer such white-washing adjectives as "ill-mannered," "crazy," and "puzzling," respectively — but that language designates the coded language of "others," people inferior to oneself; it constitutes a nuanced rhetorical assault by those customarily assumed to be the inferior others. The relativist language of "ill-mannered" bespeaks the political language of a subjugated people. It constitutes a polite discourse of opposition that presses the realization of prejudice while downplaying the powerlessness and frustration involved (p. 34).

This question of language lies at the root of Kincaid's polemic. Even though the only language available is the colonizers', it can be used to subvert the British and their allies who not only attempted to eradicate the people's original language by separating slaves from the same area of Africa but also tried to suppress articulation in general, obliterate the point of view of the colonized, and outlaw literacy.

Kincaid affirms her commitment to language as an instrument of change even though her dissent has to be articulated in the colonizer's mandated language. She affirms its power but, more critically, the need to contextualize it. Individuals themselves do not determine meaning.[11] Sharing the discourse of colonists on the terrain of language, all four — the colonizer, the tourist, the speaker, and the people — mean different things by the same words and interpret them plurally.

Hence the defeat of the colonizer at one level. Despite a systematic, protracted attempt to deprive millions of their native land, their beliefs, and free expression, the island's original inhabitants still kept their beliefs alive and expressed ideas and feelings in the "language of the criminal [the English]." Most importantly, the chronicler stresses the relativity of meaning:

> When I say to the criminal, "This is wrong, this is wrong, this is wrong," or, "This deed is bad, and this other deed is bad, and this one is also very, very bad," the criminal understands the word "wrong" in this way: It is wrong when "he" doesn't get his fair share of profits from the crime just committed; he understands the world "bad" in this way: a fellow criminal betrayed a trust. That must be why, when I say, "I am filled with rage," the criminal says, "But why?" And when I blow things up and make life generally unlivable for the criminal (is

my life not unlivable, too?) the criminal is shocked, surprised. But nothing can erase my rage — not an apology, not a large sum of money, not the death of the criminal — for this wrong can never be made right, and only the impossible can make me still. (p. 32)

This indoctrination in the colonizers' language and meaning is matched by an educational system deliberately devised to exalt and maintain a pro-colonial vantage point, deftly evident in Antigua's post-independence motto: "A People to Mold. A Nation to Build." Knowing that schools and libraries are colonial tools, sites of propaganda, Kincaid turns that smugness on its head with *A Small Place*.

Furthermore, by introducing contemporary, let-sleeping-dogs-lie objections — all that happened a long time ago — she shows how these objections reflect on objectors and their fears. Those who aim to silence her are conspirators or accessories, persistently covering up their anxiety.

Most importantly, since the "you," or addressee, of the polemic is the one taking exception, she begins to narrow the gap between tourist and colonizer. Tourists in this diatribe against colonialism are not merely apologists for an imperial past; rhetorically they become — or they are — the same people who committed genocide in the Third World. Quietly but devastatingly, the speaker indicts and brings them together through the trope of staying at home: "You murdered people. You imprisoned people. You robbed people. You opened your own banks and you put our money in them. The accounts were in your name. The banks were in your name. There must have been some good people among you, but they stayed home. And that is the point. That is why they are good. They stayed home" (p. 35).

In exposing the imperial system, Jamaica Kincaid revises the dominant paradigm in which a metropolitan center extracts wealth from a colonized land at the margins of the system. Instead, Britain occupies the moral and ethical periphery, its tourists, slaveholders, headmistresses, and bankers all of an ideological piece.

The narrator ends by chafing at the old chestnut that colonizers brought progress to the uncivilized. Instead she privileges those earlier precolonial African civilizations and recasts the headmistress's aspersions — "stop behaving like monkeys." She goes on: "Even if I really came from people who were living like monkeys in trees, it was better to be that than what happened to me, what I became after I met you"

(p. 37).[13] Ironically, colonizers now are the unnamed, untamed others, inscriptions usually attached to the colonized. This continual familiarity toward the colonizer as "you" prevents the reader from thinking of Antigua's oppressors as a cold invisible institution. It personalizes, almost corporealizes exploitation.

The permanent damage that systematic colonialism inflicted on the land and the people fostered yet more damage in its wake. It caused the corruption of subsequent administrations under self-rule. Without education and skills, without undistorted historical narrative, the people were vulnerable to abuse; conditions were ripe for corruption. Self-deluded Britons could then consider their regime enlightened and falsify history accordingly. Oppositional critics like herself, however, lived to tell a different tale.

The third section reiterates the earlier opening forms of address to the tourist but with a sharp departure in focus: "And so you can imagine how I felt when, one day, in Antigua, standing on Market Street, looking up one way and down the other, I asked myself: 'Is the Antigua I see before me, self-ruled, a worse place than what it was when it was dominated by the bad-minded English and all the bad-minded things they brought with them?" (p. 41). Jamaica Kincaid feels "bitterness and shame" as she launches into the scandal of contemporary Antigua: "The government is for sale; anybody from anywhere can come to Antigua and for a sum of money can get what he wants" (p. 47).

In Kincaid's case, one of the major questions along those lines concerns the library — touched on very briefly in her opening "guided tour" in the taxi from the airport — and why it has not yet been repaired. She is exploring the consequences of postemancipationist rule by an elected government of black Antiguans. Has the Western presence, the covert text queries, damaged the country irreversibly? The library finely exemplifies what has happened. Despite the distortions the library offered people in the name of facts, it also offered a peaceful pleasant place for people to visit when the narrator was growing up; it occupied an assured cultural presence. Now its deterioration allows a racist clubwoman to be smug, display her power, and humiliate black citizens.

A great deal of the discussion in *A Small Place* centers directly or indirectly on the library, key symbol of colonial misrule and disservice. In the course of her investigation, Kincaid has been cobbling together complex narratives about tourists, British colonists, and now the present government. Through the library, she illuminates one crucial aspect of their interconnectedness.

She cautions tourists not to think of the damaged library and by extension suggests what it contains: "You have brought your own books with you, and among them is one of those new books about economic history, one of those books explaining how the West (meaning Europe and North America after its conquest and settlement by Europeans) got rich" (p. 9). The tourist already believes the distortions anyway, signifying extensive, ongoing colonial control.

She pointedly indicates the library's geographical location on Lower High Street, where government business and banking is administered and executed (p. 25). She explains that colonists made a point of building schools and libraries wherever they expropriated land: "You made sure to build a school, a library (yes, and in both of these places you distorted or erased my history and glorified your own)" (p. 36).

Having established the mythological content of the library and its key role in controlling people through institutionalized misinformation, Kincaid outlines what has happened to the library under self-rule. Standing at the temporary library on Market Street, she notes that the building was damaged in the earthquake in 1974. Why then, she inquires, has the library not been repaired or rebuilt in over a decade?[13] She hearkens back in loving tones to pleasant experiences in the library. Simultaneously, she introduces a mordant, now cynical adult appraisal, as if she were laughing wryly at how she was duped: "The beauty of us sitting there like communicants at an altar, taking in, again and again, the fairy tale of how we met you, your right to do the things you did, how beautiful you were, are, and always will be" (p. 42). She savors the irony of a colonial propaganda tool that simultaneously afforded her relief and felicity. The inefficiency of young librarians sets her off on a secondary train of thought about postcolonial education and its treacherous consequences. She censures this new generation of black Antiguans who speak English as if it were a "sixth language" and seem almost illiterate (p. 43). Whether the contempt might be a denial of inner sadness is hard to decipher.

The Mill Reef Club is again presented as a negative presence as she reexplicates the relativity of discourse, how people react differently to the same experiences: "The people at the Mill Reef Club love the old Antigua, I love the old Antigua. Without question, we don't have the same old Antigua in mind" (p. 44).[14] In this discussion, Jamaica Kincaid quietly offers an apology for stealing library books, a fact mentioned in *Annie John*. By explaining her theft in the face of the librarian's vigilant gaze, she accentuates her aberration. She further explains how she had read all the children's books by the time she was nine and then had to use her mother's library card. The narrator offers a sense of her life as a nine-year-old when her first brother was born and she felt estranged from her mother. This memory ties her negative feelings about separation to the cultural separation she now experiences and the double anger she feels: toward a government that systematically perpetuates malice and toward people who accept it supinely. Throughout *A Small Place*, she weaves this doubled dislike.

The narrator goes on to talk about how this beloved old library is now being pressed into service as headquarters for a carnival troupe; it is filled with costumes for "angels from the realm," the troupe's name. Alluding silently to an incident in *Annie John* where Annie John has to write out *Paradise Lost* as a punishment, this narrator softly intones: "Some of the costumes were for angels before the Fall, some of the costumes were for angels after the Fall; the ones representing After the Fall were the best" (pp. 46–47). Is she, then, one of these angels after the Fall? The narrator underscores the notion of lost innocence, of a young child who grows up in a paradise — or so she thinks — only to realize that more than one abandonment lurks around the corner. In this way Kincaid invokes earlier events and connects different aspects of her life to cultural realities.

These allusions to *Annie John* and the importance the protagonist attaches to library books highlight Annie's earlier opposition to the librarian whom she attempted to outwit. Her comment that the chief librarian tried to ensure that she did not "walk out with books held tightly between my legs (what a trick, I thought)" puts another twist on that situation (*A Small Place*, p. 46). Whereas she now sees the librarian as zestless, formerly that very librarian had been proud of her job and happy to uphold government-dictated standards against erring school children. In one sense, the librarian was little more than a lackey, squashing a budding resistance to government neglect. The librarian's suspicion that connected the hiding of the books to a sexual place hints at some fear of a clandestine reproduction, of taboo alliances between people and culture.[15]

Following her postlapsarian scenario, the speaker of *A Small Place* describes a Mill Reef Club member who exclaims how she encourages "her girls"—meaning black Antiguan women "not unlike me," Kincaid adds—to use the library. Of course, the clubwoman is happy to feed procolonial pap to black employees whom she wants at her beck and call. This conversation reminds the speaker that "a foreigner who is also a convicted criminal was financing the development." It leads her to seek out the minister of culture (who is in Trinidad watching cricket) to interrogate him about the library. She reasons that her inability to meet with that minister is for the best because he and her mother had quarreled during a past political campaign when her mother worked as an activist for the opposition. Pasting up posters outside the house of the minister of culture, her mother forthrightly responded to the Minister's remark— "What is *she* doing here?"—with a clever rejoinder: "I may be a she, but I am a good she. Not someone who steals stamps from Redonda" (p. 50).[16] Thus the narrator (Jamaica Kincaid) and her mother, at different levels, challenge the clubwoman, a white colonial representative who gloats at governmental corruption instigated by black Antiguan males; it vindicates or at least palliates British misrule.[17] *A Small Place* is a weapon for social change that privileges black women as agents of change and loci of contradictions. Kincaid questions the implied sexual ideology that denotes women as silent human beings as she assumes the role of oppositional critic who produces counterhegemonic knowledge.[18]

Jamaica Kincaid's own vengeance against the clubwoman looms in the future, when *A Small Place* is published. For the time being, the clubwoman goes about her business, oblivious as in days of old to insurrection before her very eyes. Kincaid's mother fights directly for an opposition leader who vows to stem corruption and get Antigua on a better regional and international footing. Together, Kincaid and her mother suggest a reinterpretation of Antigua's motto of independence: "A People to Mold. A Nation to Build." Kincaid's poignant regret that the government robbed her of the chance to reply to this clubwoman has a statute of limitations that is running out.

The mother's retort to the minister about a governmental scandal over postage stamps also challenges the subsequent three-page narrative about Antiguan people. "In a small place," it begins, "people cultivate small events." The narrator hints that people do not see the implications of their geographical locale, or the "larger picture" (p. 52). People in a small place do not site their actions on any continuum: "When the future, bearing its own events, arrives, its ancestry is then traced in a trancelike retrospect, at the end of which, their mouths and eyes wide with their astonishment, the people in a small place reveal themselves to be like children being shown the secrets of a magic trick" (p. 54). Everything remains something of a mystery. Events become everyday matters and everyday matters are events. No longer an event, this public library plaque (plague) has now been incorporated into everyday life. And to say this—to say something is an event—strips it of historical particularity; it makes it a "thing" happening on the outside. These things wash across the Antiguan landscape and the people—unlike people in the United States, for example, outraged over President Nixon's lies—do not demonstrate about the main public library remaining in disrepair for seventeen years. In a word, the speaker indicts Antiguan people for hyperpassivity.

This homogenizing of the people lies on a continuum with the collectivized designation of "tourists" and "natives." Tourists are also small, passive people who are molded according to governmental specification; they constitute a new critical mass subsequent to the institutionalization of postcolonial society. Like Antiguan people, tourists do not always recognize the larger context. "They can have no interest in the exact, or in completeness" (p. 53).

What Kincaid hopes to do with *A Small Place,* however, is alert both communities at once. Mischievously (since tourism is a major industry but needs a more appropriate formulation), she wants to outlaw Antigua as a desirable holiday hideaway. Second and more importantly, she wants to alert people about the need to act. So she takes upon herself the role of the people's advocate. The fact that Jamaica Kincaid became persona non grata after the publication of *A Small Place*—reviewed positively in Antigua's one radical newspaper, *Outlet*—positively indicates some influence the text has effected.[19] Kincaid herself speaks of it this way: "Yes. I thought [writing *A Small Place*] was a turning point in me. I wrote with a kind of recklessness in that book. I didn't know what I would say ahead of time. Once I wrote it I felt very radicalized by it. I would have just thought of myself as a liberal person until I wrote it, and now I feel that liberal is as far right as I can go. . . . I've really come to love anger. And I liked it even more when a lot of reviewers said it's so angry."[20]

After her diatribe against the library and the lassitude or gullibility of the people, Kincaid launches into a third attack, this time against Antigua's present government under the leadership of Prime Minister Oliver Vere Cornwall Bird. His very long tenure as prime minister — she discloses — was founded on a series of felonious activities. Kincaid queries how and why this bureaucracy was able to establish political dominion over the native population out of whose ranks they rose. Unlike British colonizers, they could not blame problems on race that had formerly functioned as a signifier of difference. Class and colonialism have become the master signifiers instead.

Folk mythology that developed around Prime Minister Vere Bird's meteoric rise involved his embezzlement of funds and then tossing the books into a furnace when he was caught. This relatively well publicized event in Antigua is in turn linked to the expulsion of an apparently honest leadership from the Antigua Trades and Labour Union and the resumption or restabilization of Bird's regime; the prime minister's brand of dishonesty replaces the old colonial venalities: new ways with new forms, the narrative suggests, but the same old tricks. She compares Prime Minister Vere Bird to Africans who sold their people into slavery: "The men who rule Antigua came to power in open, free elections. In accounts of the capture and enslavement of black people almost no slave ever mentions who captured and delivered him or her to the European master" (p. 55).

The fact that the people have a doubled view of Vere Bird — sometimes as George Washington and on other occasions as Jackie Pressor, head of the Teamsters who served time for expropriation of union funds — raises provocative questions that suggest byzantine shenanigans. Granted, Pressor was feathering his own nest; but, suggests the narrator, Washington also fought a colonial revolution that inevitably doubled as a self-interested movement. People fight for individual rights as well as a collective independence: "Attempts to conceptualize social agency, the ways people [could] mobilize to act both individually and collectively."[21]

The speaker most deplores how black Antiguans react in the face of corruption. She deplores the fact that during twenty years of self-rule, the people have persistently voted for the same tainted government with a one-year gap when George Thomson was elected. The continuing complicity of the people in this regime amazes her most. The popular Hotel Training school is one example of inertness and silent coercion since it amounts to little more than a scheme to train "good servants, how to be a good nobody, which is what a servant is. In Antigua, people cannot see a relationship between their obsession with slavery and emancipation and their celebration of the Hotel Training School. . . . people cannot see a relationship between their obsession with slavery and emancipation and the fact that they are governed by corrupt men, or that these corrupt men have given their country away to corrupt foreigners" (p. 55).

Good hotels mean happy tourists and yet another wheel within wheels comes full circle. Vere Bird's brand of leadership does not appropriately take the needs of Antiguan people into account. Instead, mimicking British colonists, Prime Minister Vere Cornwall Bird treats Antiguans as individuals who merit a hospital no sane person will voluntarily step foot in.

As if to explain such moral contamination, the speaker suggests that the government learned its lesson well from former Prime Minister George Thomson, who lasted only a year before he was obliged to step down on charges of corruption. A fiercely mounted and handsomely bankrolled opposition facilitated Thomson's downfall.[22] Thomson ended up as an out-of-work party leader driving a taxi, a fate no government member relished. But more to the point, government ministers crave membership, or at least recognition, in the Western world. With green cards in hand, they are ready to go (run) at a moment's notice.

Kincaid cites many examples of postcolonial mimicking maneuvers: For one thing, the air waves, as well as electric, telephone, and cable TV services, are owned by the government, the last by the prime minister's son. This effectively means — with specific and limited exception — that no antigovernment commentary is tolerated. The establishment media allot no time to political dissension except to denounce it; no free speech of any sort exists on the air waves. Other ministers buy businesses that the government then patronizes. A Syrian national who lends substantial sums of money to the government owns a large Japanese car dealership that holds the monopoly on government vehicles. Ministers are involved in drug trafficking; they share profits in the offshore banks, in popularity second only to tourism and gambling. The prime minister's friends own a notorious house of prostitution.[23]

The list of illegal and debased activities is so long and indeterminate that the disappearance of eleven million French dollars slotted for local development scarcely seems egregious. Most heinously, the government permitted the distribution of food contaminated by radiation; it does business with and sends ammunition to the government of South Africa; it declines to investigate cold-blooded murder when their vested interests are involved. These crimes are matters of public record.

Additionally, the present prime minister acts as if he were running a family business: his sons are in charge of heavily bankrolled ministries, Treasury, Tourism, and Public works. Jamaica Kincaid ends the section ominously, by asserting that the parallel with Haiti and the Duvalier family is not lost on people, nor is the emergence as well as the demise of Maurice Bishop, a different kind of Caribbean leader.

In these unrelenting anecdotes of state malpractice, Kincaid establishes a crucially absent counterknowledge about Antigua; she constructs a new genealogy of events. Uncompromising and incensed, she returns blow by rhetorical blow for bureaucratic assaults against the rights of the people, heavily implying that Vere Bird perpetuates British colonialism in a different way. She exposes nefarious global and internecine networks. In direct refutation of the duplicitous colonialist mode, she spares no one and tells a seemingly unvarnished account. Old mythologies are laid to rest. Unlike former English rulers and the present government, she disdains camouflage and cover up. Her counterhegemonic text destabilizes the colonial and postcolonial texts in the neglected public library.

In so doing, she spells out that people still have choices, although they might not easily spot them. More bluntly, Kincaid acknowledges that the people are prevented from discerning that any power conceivably lies in their hands. As she recently remarked, "We had better health and education under colonialism."[24] On the other hand, as she has also recently spelled out, England's formative influence and the colonial values it imposed are monumental.[25] She suggests that Vere Bird and Maurice

Bishop are not the only (representative) choices — a collective will also exists that can be called into play. She wants Antiguans to realize that the situation is less all-or-nothing than it seems. People do not have to sit around hoping for leaders; just as signally, they have to stop acting like tour guides, advertising their own degradation. They can do it (for) themselves, they can expropriate power. She urges black Antiguans to notice the correspondences between themselves and tourists, for people have become insensitive to their own needs. In a sense, they have had their desires ground out of them. Accepting what the government says, their inaction effectively maintains existing power relations. One way or another, they have to cut off this sick relationship with (as) tourists.

She wants tourists to return to history and draw contemporary parallels to what they see. Colonialism starts with invasion from the First World, with indigenous people as pawns in that expansion. These conditions create a sense of ahistoricity in the people who are invaded; and they stop looking at things in context.

Jamaica Kincaid's own departure from Antigua and her role as external observer who is simultaneously an insider are never problematized. How much of her anger is compensation for the privilege she gains from living in the United States and being part of that very North America whose colonial practices have played havoc with Antiguan people remains unclear? Unreserved in her condemnation, she might be using an all-out frontal attack to veil any privilege she gains from being a voluntary expatriate. On a more positive note, while she wants people to assume responsibility for their actions, possibly her departure from Antigua and her status as an expatriate are acts and conditions she invites the population to consider embracing. She wants people to face up to the near-surreal deformations Antigua has undergone.

Kincaid is also explaining Antiguans to the rest of the world because few Antiguans will read her book; thus, *At the Bottom of the River* constitutes a postcolonial political message. As noted, after Kincaid's departure from Antigua following the publication of *A Small Place,* she was declared persona non grata by the Vere Bird government and simultaneously denounced by governmental newspapers. The attempt to repress her voice was as successful as the attempt to repress her mother's.

The short, final section unpacks the tension of the first three sections rather differently. It opens with a panegyric to the beauty of Antigua, so perfect it is almost unreal. The salience of Pam's speeches in *Annie, Gwen, Lilly, Pam and Tulip* becomes clearer. In that sense, *A Small Place* continues the earlier work as bildungsroman. In that unreality lies opposition and resistance at work. It is so much larger than life — "Antigua is too beautiful" — that the sweet smell of lilies nauseates. The unreality is countered by parched grass, malnourished cows, and destitute people. An exercise in relational politics, *A Small Place* ends on a cacophonous note. That beauty is a prison, and in a Woolfian echo, Kincaid poses how differently life looks from the locked-in vantage point compared to the locked-out perspective.[26] Nothing — at least in terms of physical terrain — seems to have changed.

Politically, Kincaid argues that all masters are ignoble and all subjugated people are exalted, but that status, such as it is, disappears at independence. What is left on both sides are human beings. *A Small Place* is counterknowledge with a vengeance. Out of love and anger, Jamaica Kincaid pleads with Antiguans to reclaim agency and extirpate corruption. Her polemic dissolves all colonial and postcolonial attempts to stifle the voice of the people, to make "no tongue" the unspoken motto of a bogus independence.

She rejects the English and their present government's efforts to circulate a master narrative about Antigua; she demolishes their efforts to present a single way of telling the island's history. Demonstrating that Prime Minister Vere Bird's power is not a mandate for univocality, she dissolves his authoritarian regime, his false regime of truth, his venture to establish a black Antiguan bureaucracy that reworks old metropolitan ideas in order to co-opt and dominate the people who voted them into power. Her aim is to demonstrate to the people that they are not constituted as free agents, that they have been conned (as Kincaid's punningly named "Condrington" family manipulated slaves) into acceptance.[27]

Indirectly, the speaker contends that the continued subordination of Antiguans is the result of passivity. People highlight the oligarchal perspective by not rising up against the government. They do it (by) themselves. The present top-heavy hegemonic control of Antiguan society, she stresses, is not a "natural" situation, even though the government tries to present the dynamic of power as "the way things are." On the contrary, she suggests it is a government for the government against the people.

The people act as tour guides; they prefer not to demonstrate against the government's refusal to pass on postcolonial advantages to the general populace. They shy from exposé. They hope only for a new leader. Functioning like colonizers of old, tourists keep the old game going. Similarly, Vere Bird's administration acts like countless past English administrators. Tourists mutter about "natives" who inevitably despise the tourists; the government tries to maintain itself and act with impunity, insecure about opponents inside and outside the regime.[28] Vere Bird is George Washington and Lester Pressor. He treats Antiguans as the objectified (colonized) — a homogenized "they" whose only recourse when sick is a dirty, badly staffed hospital (pp. 7–8). The people are also children being fooled by a deceitful magician who learned from a world-class master, even though at one point they voted an opposition leader to power (pp. 57, 69). They celebrate Queen Victoria's birthday without taking cognizance of the fact she is dead.[29] Colonial ideology has distorted reality and served ruling-class interests. By not resisting this sufficiently, people have made themselves even riper for exploitation. They remain, in Bharati Mukherjee's words in another context, "true to the essentially damaged, ego-deficient, post-colonial psyche."[31] Kincaid does concede, however, that people remain largely unaware of their exploitation. Nonetheless, black Antiguan identity is not, as Vere Bird's actions and behavior suggest, monolithic and simple. Instead, Kincaid contends, environment and historical circumstances shape Antiguan identity. Thus in diverse ways Kincaid calls for change. She explains how ways of seeing and acting are relative to what people are told to believe and what people assimilate.

In *A Small Place*, Kincaid registers a subversive form of postcolonial cultural and psychic representation in which the author-speaker-citizen is also an intense participant in Antiguan affairs. With her confrontational style, she challenges hypocrisy and disperses the pernicious, postcolonial gaze. Simultaneously, she prises open creative possibilities for a new syncretic order, a new epistemological reading of a critical historical era, usually coded as the transition from British colonialism to national independence.

Hence *A Small Place* configures a dynamic interaction among plural vantage points, all dominated by and mediated through the narrator. A multicultural chorus with a fluid range, *A Small Place* invokes agitators as wide-ranging as C. L. R. James, Frantz Fanon, Walter Rodney, Aimé Césaire, Virginia Woolf, Nadine Gordimer, Annie Drew, and Selwyn Cudjoe.[31] Jamaica Kincaid weaves an allusive international quilt of discursive and activist opposition.

Deftly fashioned yet deceptively simple technical strategies enhance this complicated matrix of meaning. The intricate problematizing of the addressee and the speaker, the peppering of the text with parentheses and irony in various guises are favored devices. So are provocative rhetorical questions — Do you remember Liberty Weekend? (p. 49). What is a culture anyway? (p. 49). Where do all these stamps come from? (p. 5). One of her most striking plays in language occurs in a section on the government, where she refers to the English Codrington family (who settled Barbados and imported and sold slaves) as the Condrington family. The added *n* stresses "con" and hence their dishonest colonial role (p. 51).[32] In a witty twist to the idea that discourse is determined by the political stance that the person assumes, in this case their role in the colonial struggle, she effectively argues that "words . . . change [not only] their meaning [but their spelling too!] according to the positions from which they are used."[33]

Her own place, what is more, is complex. As an expatriate Antiguan, Jamaica Kincaid has one foot inside the island and the other in the United States. She has also recently been banned from returning. The library, however, is a crucial signifier since the cultural silence rendered by corrupt historical mandates complicates her goals and status as a counterhegemonic critic. Thus she renders *A Small Place* the site of conflicting discourses, that of the speaker, the author, and the shifting addressee. Exposing three hundred years of paternalistic governments, Kincaid refuses the position of the oppressed and promotes a discourse of liberation and authenticity that colonists have sought to deny and suppress. She fractures their spurious truth claims. She may be an expatriate living a form of psychologically and politically induced exile in North America, but she is also, as the head librarian states, an Antiguan "returning to Antigua after a long absence" (p. 44).

Lacking an easy point of access into Antiguan history and culture, Kincaid produces and presents a cultural polemic that irrefutably demonstrates how social conditions determine human consciousness.[34] With *A Small Place,* she has ceased to inoculate herself against the personal agony of her youth. The "I" now occupies multiple locations while appearing to remain intact: She and the third-person speaker feel at liberty to hang dirty linen in public; she calls racists by their name; she rejects the gentility of good manners, of subterfuge and cover-up; she will not be a loyal subject (object). The "I" slips around and outside itself, especially in the biographical anecdotes. At these times, the omnipresence of the narrator's life, and her mother's, sounds loudly. To put it another way, Kincaid has more overtly "given birth" to herself in a wider global context. She heralds her own as well as an Antiguan independence that is richer and more authentic than "flag" independence.

With *A Small Place,* Jamaica Kincaid offers new forms of representation, new vantage points to offset Vere Bird's invention of a false unity, of a totalized Antiguan nation. She envisages or at least allows for the possibility — though dim yet — of a new order emerging; resistant Antiguans will reflect the old passivity and become agents of their own destinies, like Kincaid herself. She underscores the fact that the government knows its number could be up. Another failure of postcolonial indigenous nationalism leaves open the option of new leadership, innovative ideas. Colonial mimicry can come to an end; it is not necessarily a pessimistic picture.[35] Her polemic is a form of collective self-identification and self-actualization in which she tries to mirror Antiguans as they are and as they can be — to themselves. Here you are, she says, warts and all — and this is why. Hence her careful explication of why Antiguans are temporarily entrenched in such self-defeating positions. But the crucial covert message attacks Vere Bird's hegemony; it is, she insists ominously, culturally produced and therefore always reversible.

A Small Place, then, exposes these forms of social construction, how people play roles mapped out for them that they encode as natural. Kincaid conflates two sets of people — first, the tourist and the English, second, Antiguans and tourists, then teases them apart. Similarly, she conflates the English and the postcolonial administrations but keeps their identities very tightly interwoven and often coincident. Kincaid tries to unravel how "the widespread depoliticization and effective subordination of the populace [take place]."[36] All addressees possess a heterogenous subjectivity in a wider, polysemic world than Vere Bird's tightly controlled "nation."

In the end, too, though somewhat elusively, the mother-daughter bonding that she so desperately sought in earlier texts comes into focus quite concretely. Jamaica Kincaid's values and her mother's are woven closely together as pieces of one whole cloth. The crucial incident concerning Redonda postage stamps and islandwide corruption in the mother's acerbic rejoinder to the minister elide inextricably into the overall exposé of *A Small Place,* postcolonial settlement dissolving on foundations that temporarily scaffolded the dream of empire.[37]

Even though Kincaid talks sarcastically about her mother's actions — "It so happens that in Antigua my mother is fairly notorious for her political opinions. She is almost painfully frank, quite unable to keep any thoughts she has about anything — and she has many thoughts on almost everything — to herself" (p. 49) — she still replicates her mother's acts. As a people's recorder, she defends her mother and publicizes her heroism as part of a revolutionary history. Together they are guerrilla fighters, an under- and overground resistance for a new dispensation that will include the excluded. Embedded in their tactics is a knowledge of past atrocities, a certainty about the degradation of master-slave relations. In conjunction with the efforts of native people, they will destabilize, fracture, and eventually uproot authoritarian male rule. Mother and daughter function in dual chronologies, the colonial and the postcolonial. Another hidden chronology also seems to lurk in the coincidence of Jamaica Kincaid's arrival in the United States just as protests about the Vietnam war and imperialism reached a peak. Jamaica Kincaid and her mother represent black Antiguan activists inside and outside the country who are ready for a new day.

In *A Small Place,* Jamaica Kincaid proffers a telling clue to the reading of her earlier as well as her later texts. The reportorial historical voice provides a new necessary next step to the semiautobiographical voice in this untraditionally ongoing bildungsroman. The polemic permits us to read Annie John's turmoil as adolescent confusion that often sprang from what she felt but could not name — insecurity as well as repulsion and fury at being treated as a latter-day colonial subject. But this is not to deny the complexity of the reader's position in the trap of fiction-exposé: We move through various stages of identifying with Annie John to viewing Annie John "off in the distance more," an interpellated subject in realpolitik. We witness a number of intersecting textualities, "the process of producing [texts] through the transformation of other texts,"[38] that help to explain a dominative, often invisible postcolonial world order, the "planned epistemic violence of imperialism."[39] *Annie John,* then, foretells the mature, radical politic of *A Small Place.* At one level, *A Small Place* is *Annie John,* part two, as well as an increment to the evolving bildungsroman of a female African-Caribbean speaker-protagonist. Kincaid's disclosures validate Annie John's faintly felt sense of being indoctrinated and condescended to. Earlier disquiet becomes withering sarcasm. In yet one more sense, Annie John also problematizes *A Small Place,* enables us to see that no last word exists. Together they help to reconceptualize contemporary definitions of female sexuality, motherhood, and race-gender intersections through the gaze of an African-Caribbean woman.[40] "A full literary reinscription cannot easily flourish in the imperialist fracture or discontinuity, covered over by an alien legal system masquerading as Law as such, an alien ideology established as only Truth, and a set of human sciences busy establishing the 'native' as self-consolidating other."[41] She shows her fictional and nonfictional texts alike as "determined by the social conditions within which they were produced but also as cultural artifacts which shape the social conditions they enter."[42]

In her own voice, Kincaid explains her distancing from and her love for her mother. At a symbolic level, she thoroughly enmeshes her metaphorical mother, emblematic of the despised colonizer, with a biological mother who embarrasses her but is, after all, the mother she loves. This explicit intervention in *A Small Place* of doubled maternal images intertextualizes the pervasive maternal relationship that permeates the collective texts. In Jamaica Kincaid's own words: "In my first two books, I used to think I was writing about my mother and myself. Later I began to see that I was writing about the relationship between the powerful and the powerless."[43] Despite a range of narrators — the young girl in *At the Bottom of the River* and *Annie John,* the narrator (Jamaica Kincaid) in *A Small Place* and afterwards, Lucy herself, and the colonized representative in "Ovando") — these narrators are not clearly distinct. She is simultaneously exiled and at home.[44]

Kincaid negotiates a new view of Antigua that foregrounds customarily excluded Antiguans by introducing them into the first three sections and rendering them the focus of the concluding section. In doing so, she already implies provisional answers. As a black, part Amerindian

Antiguan herself, Jamaica Kincaid's own responses to Antigua are integral to that location. Both narrator and speaker, Kincaid is included in the discussions and excluded by virtue of her observer's gaze; she is participant and outsider. She peoples the world of *A Small Place* with transhistorical antagonists: a corrupt British colonial government and a similarly corrupt Antiguan government, an invented history, and tourists transformed into morally culpable beings versus the Antiguan people and a very angry speaker. *A Small Place* is a different kind of "travel book."[45]

Weaving a quilt of missing and implied texts, folding in her biological with her colonial mother, the speaker draws on all the library books and newspapers that affirm British colonialism and calls for new readings: *A Small Place* is one such decolonized cultural production. She invites renunciation of the easy route to living that abandons challenge. Beyond that, she calls for the people to act. Inviting their creativity to come into play, she provides her own forecast and affirms the dignity of the people that can never be usurped: "Of course, the whole thing is, once you cease to be a master, once you throw off your master's yoke, you are no longer human rubbish, you are just a human being, and all the things that adds up to. So, too, with the slaves. Once they are no longer slaves, once they are free, they are no longer noble and exalted; they are just human beings" (p. 81).

Once everyone is demythologized, dedemonized, and deidealized, only human beings remain — on an equal footing. Antiguans are now the equal of these earlier colonists who violently disrupted their way of life. In a brilliant ironic twist, Kincaid further suggests that the English come up from rubbish to become human beings; they pulled themselves up from being masters. Native Antiguans, by contrast, are moving in an opposite direction, descending from being noble to being human beings. In point of fact, the text silently suggests, Antiguans are going up from a state of slavery to exercising full human rights.

Lucy: *A New Site*

Chapter 4

As I go on writing, I feel less and less interested in the approval of the First World, and I never had the approval of the world I came from, so now I don't know where I am. I've exiled myself yet again.—**Jamaica Kincaid, interview**

[The third scenario] is the scene where this new thing [cultural positionality] is worked out, and the difficulty we are having is the difficulty of that discourse emerging.—**Stuart Hall**

✦ JAMAICA KINCAID'S first post-Antiguan novel, *Lucy* (1990), whose title character travels from Antigua to the United States contributes to Kincaid's ongoing fictional semiautobiographical saga.[1] In the earlier novel and polemic, *Annie John* and *A Small Place*, Kincaid produces a "strategic formation"; in a limited way, the texts "acquire mass, density, and referential power among themselves and thereafter in the culture at large."[2] They construct themselves as a counterdiscourse to the dominant culture. As an African-Caribbean writer, that is, Kincaid has the capacity and often does speak to and from the position of the other. Not only does she specify confrontations along class-race-gender axes, she also unmasks "the results of those distortions internalized within our consciousness of ourselves and one another."[3] In *Lucy*, Kincaid pursues these concerns somewhat further. Casting aside adolescence, Lucy tells her own story while doubling as a representative of black Antiguans, a willing recorder of the island's oral narrative; she rescripts familiar thematics as well as exploring new ones. *Lucy* takes place in Manhattan during the 1960s just before Antigua's attainment of partial independence from Britain in 1967. *At the Bottom of the River* and *Annie John* were set in Antigua during the 1950s and 1960s, while *A Small Place* jumped forward to the 1980s. Nonetheless, *Lucy* contributes another layer to Kincaid's bildungsroman, reverting back in time to the end of *Annie John* when seventeen-year-old Annie sails for Britain about 1967. The protagonists, however, are quite separate in name, although their Caribbean sensibilities and undaunted commitment to unmasking hypocrisy still match.

Gender continues as a paramount issue. In *At the Bottom* and *Annie John,* the mother and daughter act out a highly charged relationship. In *Lucy* they intermittently enact a smaller version of the same. As in *A Small Place,* the image of the mother-child dyad in *Lucy* also encompasses a colonizing motherland as well as a biological maternality. Gender issues are tied to the colonial imperative. Lucy's voluntary exile in Manhattan calls for a reconfiguration. Early childhood, a feature of *At the Bottom,* reemerges, along with Annie John's coming to terms with growing up female in a colonized world. Migration, announced at the end of *Annie John,* is a solution to her difficulties; it becomes one of Lucy's crucial realities.

This time the narrator is a black Antiguan female not more than twenty years old who is bent on independence; she craves control of her life within the means at her disposal. Beginning with the day she arrives in New York from the Caribbean and retires to bed to avoid further stimuli, she is determined to be an agent rather than a passive receiver. Unlike the protagonists of other texts, she is surrounded almost exclusively by white people, not only in her immediate household but also within their circle of friends.

As an expatriate residing in the United States and assuming diverse roles, Lucy has to cope with metropolitan colonizing strategies toward herself as a British "subject."[4] She has to negotiate her way through differing representations of power within the three-child household, first with the husband, Lewis, a middle-aged lawyer; and second with the wife, Mariah, a rich but emotionally dominated and somewhat naive white woman from a distinguished Michigan family who initially thinks the world lies at her feet. Worth noting, too, is the fact that Kincaid uses no patronymic for Lewis and Mariah in a telling reminder of the erasure of African names. (Consequently, "the family" tends to get discursively and deliberately homogenized.) Successfully navigating through the couple's interpersonal complexities, Lucy witnesses Lewis's extramarital relationship with Dinah, Mariah's best friend.

More specifically, as an indictment of the colonizing project, *Lucy* directly follows *A Small Place*. In the latter, the speaker argues that people still act as a subordinated population in their postcolonial situation. They have little sense of the past, present, and future and treat everything casually, as it comes along. Ad hoc is their informal motto, a rough guideline for daily living. This ahistorical attitude corrupts people by dissolving or eliminating class divisions and the capacity to analyze. Alive to nuance, changing moods, and events, Lucy herself adopts a more explicitly counterhegemonic stance after biding her time. She grounds whatever she sees in an alternative vision.

Thus, despite one reviewer's complaints that Jamaica Kincaid is "dissociat[ing] herself from blacks in *Lucy*," Lucy's cultural awareness is abundantly evident.[5] She employs a strategy of cultural reversal. The novel complements *A Small Place* by revealing how the political legatees of residual colonial culture live their lives and think about their cultural place. Kincaid dramatizes authoritarian treatment of those regarded as native others. Lucy is simultaneously fetishized and condescended to in a revamped form of old power relations between the colonizer and the colonized. Beyond received imperial familiarity and fantasy, her employers and their friends try to homogenize difference and subsume it within their jurisdiction. They pretend that the power dynamic between the haves and the have-nots does not dominate everyday life.

The maid is more open. Attuned to an intraclass pecking order, she tries to make Lucy feel stupid and worthless, charging her with speaking as if she were calcified: "She said that I spoke like a nun, I walked like one also, and that everything about me was so pious that it made her feel at once sick to her stomach and sick with pity just to look at me. And so, perhaps giving way to the latter feeling, she said that we should dance, even though she was quite sure I didn't know how" (p. 11). Lucy displays pride in her origins, responding to the album of three insincere but "beautiful" white singers whom the maid favors by energetically singing a calypso: "about a girl who ran away to Port-of-Spain, Trinidad, and had a good time, with no regrets" (p. 12). In the face of racist stereotypes, she claims herself and her history.[6]

Lucy may occupy the maid's room, "a box in which cargo traveling a long way should be shipped," as she describes it, but adds: "I was not cargo" (p. 7). From the start, consciously or not, Lucy sets out to undermine metropolitan control and assert her right to contest. At the end of the opening chapter, Lucy matches as well as copes with Lewis's patronizing discourse about her cultural credentials: "It was at dinner one night not long after I began to live with them that they began to call me the Visitor. They said I seemed not to be a part of things, as if I didn't live in their house with them, as if they weren't like a family to me, as if I were just passing through. . . . Had I never seen anyone put a forkful of French-cut green beans in his mouth before? This made Mariah laugh, but . . . I didn't laugh, though, and Lewis looked at me, concern on his face. He said, 'Poor Visitor, poor Visitor,' over and over, a sympathetic tone to his voice" (pp. 13–14).

Lewis's supercilious commiseration is capitalized, indicating what he perceives as an important identifying category. As her employer he arbitrarily empowers himself to objectify her. As if to underscore his point, he glosses his description with a tale of monkeys: "He told me a story about an uncle he had who had gone to Canada and raised monkeys, and of how after a while the uncle loved monkeys so much and was so used to being around them that he found actual human beings hard to take" (p. 14).[7] Lucy then tells him a dream she had about Lewis chasing a naked Lucy around the house. After Lucy's dream, Lewis makes a "clucking noise," mumbling "Poor, poor visitor" repeatedly, while Mariah comments: "Dr. Freud for Visitor, and I wondered why she said that, for I did not know who Dr. Freud was" (p. 15).[8] Lucy is still unaware of her complex social and psychosexual reality. She has not begun to analyze her situation. Lewis and Mariah encode the dream as sexual, not colonial, betraying their ethnocentrism. They understand their interaction with Lucy only in Western terms. Lewis's imperial role, Mariah's complicitous encouragement, Lucy's resistance are beyond their conceptualization. I shall return to the monkey theme later.

A less mediated representative of the dominant discourse, Mariah's friend Dinah scarcely pretends; on meeting Lucy, she claims her social status as the "natural" course of things, the very issue against which Kincaid fulminated in *A Small Place*. The transposed narrator of *A Small Place* is now talking, in miniature, to a wealthy tourist:

> So you are from the islands? [says Dinah].
> I don't know why [Lucy responds] but the way she said it made a
> fury rise up in me. . . . And I was going to say it in a voice that I hoped
> would make her feel like a piece of nothing, which was the way she
> had made me feel in the first place. (p. 56)

Lucy wants to disrupt Dinah's colonial language but, for the time being,
cannot and will not face an altercation and its aftermath.

The section on Mariah articulates Lucy's continuing discord—albeit
more muted than in *Annie John*—with her biological mother. It begins
with Mariah's reaction to the weather, then continues with an incident
concerning daffodils as a colonial trope, followed by Lucy's indignity at
her mother's scolding about the dangers of the New York subway. Mariah discerns no connection between Lucy's anger at being forced to recite Wordsworth's "The Daffodils" as a form of ruling-class indoctrination and her mother's symbolic warning about the dangers awaiting an
African-Caribbean woman in the New York metropolis. Nonetheless,
Mariah's excitement at the weather and the sight of daffodils perplexes
Lucy: "How do you get to be that way," she inquires. She cannot fathom
how a windy day can make one person more agitated than someone
facing, say, a daily drought. What causes such priorities? Is it simply that
some lives are lived at a trivialized, even perilously self-indulgent level?
Could it be guilt or compensation? Later when the paper-thin surface of
Mariah's life cracks, Lucy implicitly receives her answer(s).

Kincaid packs a cluster of yellow images on the pages surrounding the
two incidents. Yellow represents domination—nothing but a facade of
beauty that masks decay, a mirage of power. Mariah is one of the "six
yellow-haired heads of various sizes [that] were bunched as if they were a
bouquet of flowers tied together by an unseen string" (p. 12). Members
of the family, from the point of view of colonized people, are indistinguishable; they live in a kitchen in different shades of (jaundiced?)
yellow where Mariah "with her pale-yellow skin and yellow hair, stood
still in this almost celestial light, and she looked glossed, no blemish or
mark of any kind on her cheek or anywhere else" (p. 27). Mariah's
unblemished, Euroidealized face connects to a later incident concerning
Lucy's mother and a gashed face. Yellow is dryness, a sun that yields
drought as a permanent condition. In a recent essay, "The Biography of a

Dress," that appeared after this manuscript was finished, Jamaica Kincaid provides further illuminating commentary on the color yellow, linking it with painful childhood memories of her mother that interact with pernicious colonial signs.[9] Yellow is the jaundiced marker of white cultural identity.

The second appearance of the daffodils involves Mariah's unilateral decision that Lucy should look at "hosts of golden daffodils." She brushes off earlier knowledge that Lucy was forced to recite "The Daffodils" growing up and hated to do so.[10] Mariah, that is, responds predictably. She ignores Lucy's feelings and insists that she look at the daffodils and admire their beauty. Mariah's motives remain unclear. Lucy, however, responds violently: "I wanted to kill them. I wished that I had an enormous scythe; I would just walk down the path, dragging it alongside me, and I would cut these flowers down at the place where they emerged from the ground" (p. 29).

As her employer, Mariah forces Lucy's gaze on the daffodils through trickery, just as Lucy was forced to recite the poem: "Now, look at this" (p. 29). Lucy is confronted with a sense of doubled colonial aggression — first, she is coerced into dealing with Mariah's gentle but insidious dialectic of conquest — "[She] took me to a garden, a place she described as among her favorites in the world. She covered my eyes with a handkerchief, and then, holding me by the hand, she walked me to a spot in a clearing" (p. 28). Then Lucy is forced — virtually — to gaze on the very daffodils themselves: "They looked like something to eat and something to wear at the same time; they looked beautiful; they looked simple, as if made to erase a complicated and unnecessary idea. I did not know what these flowers were, and so it was a mystery to me why I wanted to kill them. Just like that" (p. 29).

Even when Lucy displays her anger at the first mention of the daffodils, Mariah's response is almost culpably naive: " 'I told it to her with such an amount of anger. . . . Mariah reached out to me and, rubbing her hand against my cheek, said, 'What a history you have.' I thought there was a little bit of envy [note that Lucy spots no condescension] in her voice, and I said, 'You are welcome to it if you like' " (pp. 18–19). In a later incident, this envy receives a face when Mariah claims her kinship with Lucy, presumably in an effort to receive absolution. She craves to identify with oppression so much that she boasts about her "Indian blood" (p. 40). In an undisguised autobiographical moment, Kincaid as Lucy does not hide her contempt: "Why claim a thing like that? I myself had Indian blood in me. My grandmother is a Carib Indian. That makes me one-quarter Carib Indian" (p. 40). She mulls over the implications of Mariah's assertion: "Underneath everything I could swear she says it as if she were announcing her possession of a trophy" (p. 40). Mariah desires forgiveness for colonial complicity, but Lucy cannot countenance Mariah's efforts to rewrite history. In her efforts to cancel the past and reposition Lucy, Mariah contributes to and continues the totalizing narrative of old colonial relations. Lucy inquires sarcastically: "How do you get to be the sort of victor who can claim to be the vanquished also?" (p. 41). Lucy has trouble coming to terms with people who trivialize life-and-death matters; in her eyes, they live superficial lives. Her assessment of Mariah temporarily enables her to nurture a pyrrhic victory: "It was hollow, my triumph, I could feel that, But I held on to it just the same" (p. 41). Her elation is empty because she cannot separate her growing affection for Mariah — often imaged as Lucy's biological mother — from her growing distaste for Mariah's reactionary though understated behavior.

Lucy's seemingly inexplicable feeling echoes something Jamaica Kincaid once said in an interview. The fact that Lucy soon afterwards narrates a tale to Mariah about her hatred of the word *dominion* confirms certain ideas: "I feel that, in particular, my own history is so much about dominion; in fact we were called 'the dominion,' and all the colonies were 'the dominions.' "[11] Lucy's disgust at imperial expropriation of colonized peoples' cultures into that of the colonizer is being displaced onto the daffodils that represent the past and present of Lucy's life. More specifically, after Lucy excuses her dislike of the daffodils on the grounds that "where she saw beautiful flowers I saw sorrow and bitterness" (p. 30), a related incident takes place a few pages later. As if to underscore her colonizing power under the guise of benevolence, Mariah informs Lucy that en route to Michigan, she wants Lucy to share one of her favorite experiences: "spending the night on a train and waking up to breakfast on the train as it moved through freshly plowed fields" (p. 28). The significance of the daffodils and the fields is lost on Mariah, but when that sight finally comes, Lucy veils her powerful reactions — she experiences a moment of insight as if to say: the boss must not know what the insurrectionary is thinking.

This vision of plowed fields illumines another basic troping of colonialism. It represents Mariah's ignorance of Lucy's history and the power of Lucy's historical memory. Once again, Mariah's blithe ethnocentric attitudes enable her to find joy in something that marks cultural atrocity for Lucy's ancestors. In her ignorance, Mariah recalls the tourist in *A Small Place,* but this time Lucy only suggests its implications. In the dining car, furthermore, the diners resemble Mariah's relatives, while the people waiting on them strike Lucy as resembling herself. On closer inspection, Lucy decides the employees are less familiar and more supine than she at first thought: "My relatives always gave backchat" (p. 32). Mariah's telling obliviousness to this racist scenario sharply contrasts with Lucy's outrage, which perplexes her employer. The text searingly illumines Lucy's anticolonial fury that had earlier so bewildered Mariah.

Once at Lake Michigan, Mariah excitedly draws Lewis and the children into her holiday projects; she tries to force them to share her love and enthusiasm: "She said, 'Taa-daah! Trout!' and made a big sweep with her hands, holding the fish up in the light, so that rainbow-like colors shone on their scales. She sang out, 'I will make you fishers of men,' and danced around me. After she stopped, she said, 'Aren't they beautiful? Gus and I went out in my old boat — my very, very old boat — and we caught them. My fish. This is supper. Let's go feed the minions'" (p. 37). The word *minions* reminds Lucy of Antigua being a dominion "of someplace else." By contrast, it also recalls San Domingo, where the first successful antislavery revolution took place in 1791. Jamaica Kincaid herself states the point another way: "As I go on writing, I feel less and less interested in the approval of the First World, and I never had the approval of the world I came from, so now I don't know where I am. I've exiled myself yet again."[12] Inspired by the trout scene, Lucy tells Mariah a quaint childhood tale about eagerly asking her mother how the fishes were cooked during the miracle of the loaves and fishes. This complex imbrication of imperial culture, Christianity, and Mariah's pointed boast and allegory about historical expansionism — "I will make you fishers of men" — elicits from Lucy a response similar to the one she tendered to the family maid. She cancels out Mariah's subtle claiming of a missionary

role (to convert Lucy to her values?). Proudly invoking cultural difference, she ties Mariah's action regarding the trout to her mother's beautiful and frequent cooking of fish. Lucy also knows that Mariah remains
(irresponsibly?) clueless about the consequences of growing up in a
British "dominion," code word and not-so-subtle euphemism for hegemony over land-peasant ancestors.[13] But although Lucy underscores
ideological divisions, Mariah cannot comprehend that Lucy's experience
of the world induces an oppositional understanding and sites her in a
different place.

Intertwining sexuality, colonial recognitions, and gender relations,
fish and fishermen resonate throughout Kincaid's texts. In this scene
with Mariah, fishing bears a reverse symbolism — instead of being emblematic of Antiguan culture, it switches to a New Testament tropology
involving the apostolic succession and Jesus' famous miracle. Lucy reverses the anticolonial metonymic chain established principally in *Annie
John,* but also in *At the Bottom of the River* and *A Small Place.* By introducing the colonizing gaze (chain) on the same subjects, she highlights the
clandestine method of colonizers to remake societies in their own image.
Lucy exposes the suppressed in this pernicious system.

Mariah's psychical complexity is further exposed during an episode
typifying another colonial reversal. Vanishing marshlands preoccupy the
ecology-minded Mariah, symbolically as well as literally. Things are no
longer what they were in her family or in her Michigan environment.
Lucy laughs to herself at this self-delusory activity that prevents Mariah
and women of her class from facing global evils they helped to create and
maintain. Mariah and her affluent friends can burn with anger at the
destruction of the ecological system while Mariah employs someone
whose people suffer drought and chronic deprivation all year round.
Lucy (Kincaid) only hints at the massive ironies involved. Mariah's preoccupation with marshlands, with mud and viscosity, underscores her
distance from moral purity.

The rape of the people as well as the land is an old colonial signifier.
Now in one of its (almost) postcolonial transformations, these expropri-
ations distress the colonizers themselves. Moreover, colonial agents do
not recognize their own inconsistencies because they mystify their profit
from the rape of the land, an evasion constitutive of a colonial mentality.
Lewis and his class-allied peers buy stock and invest in corporations that

cut down rain forests, turning natural acres into development areas. For all Mariah knows, they could be buying timber and mining stock. Kincaid deftly inserts a question by the child Louisa to suggest this complex of issues while the mise en scène simultaneously reinscribes Lucy's old negative relationship with her mother: "[Mariah] moaned against this vanishing idyll [when marshland flourished] so loudly that Louisa, who was just at the age where if you are a girl you turn against your mother, 'Well, what used to be here before this house we are living in was built?' It was a question I had wanted to ask, but I couldn't bear to see the hurt such a question would bring to Mariah's face" (p. 72). Louisa displays Mariah's involvement in metropolitan power just as Kincaid's multiple protagonists charge their "mother" with favoring sons or complicity in the law of the father. Ironically, a dual maternality marks colonial-patriarchal power.

With no comprehension of context, Mariah yearns for days gone by. She seems oblivious to the impact of these days on Lucy and her formerly enslaved ancestors. Environmental reform as a master signifier is another form of control. Acquiring a more discriminating knowledge of the present has helped Lucy recover and understand her past. That knowledge has subverted her fantasy of otherness regarding Mariah and Lewis. From this point on, no one can extinguish certain radical possibilities that she begins to envisage. Inevitably and unwittingly, Lewis, Mariah, and their peers constitute themselves in misrecognitions.

Thus Mariah shifts her representation of the Great Lake that parallels the marshlands as Michigan's water sign. After several descriptions of a cool beautiful lake where they play every afternoon, Lucy finally reverses her judgments as she bids farewell to the lake: "I would not miss the lake; it stank anyway, and the fish that lived in it were dying from living in it" (p. 81). Immediately afterwards she describes the moon "in a shroud." Females can be eclipsed. Then she speaks of maturation — her defloration at nineteen when blood spilled on a white towel. In another rhetorical trick, she states that she was not then a virgin: "When I saw how much it mattered to him to be the first boy I had been with, I could not give him such a hold over me" (p. 83). Lucy has contemplated the lake differently before she apprehended the nature of her surroundings; but material reality overtakes her. "The lake or pool or stagnant water stops us near its bank. It says to our will: you shall go not further; you should go back to looking at distant things, at the beyond."[14]

In chapter 4, entitled, "Cold Heart," gender, colonialism, and ethnocentric attitudes more obviously start intertwining. Her employers' marriage is disintegrating as Lucy starts to heal herself psychologically while piercing through white liberal sham. Early on, as Lucy watches the entire family happily going out to dinner, she sees through them as an open window: "I was looking at ruins, and I knew it right then. The actual fall of this Rome I hoped not to be around to see" (p. 88). Lucy is coming to terms with naiveté and trickery; they lie side by side at night and collectively though diversely exploit her daily and exploit the Caribbean transhistorically; that growing realization has altered her view of a situation she originally desired — from a safe distance in Antigua. She has become hard-nosed.

In recent interviews, Jamaica Kincaid talks of the fatuity of imperial history books that she devours. Her mention of Rome recalls the proscription of paganism (involved in how people like Dinah, Mariah's supposed friend, regard Lucy), the rioting of Thessalonica, say (islanders, formerly slaves, are expected to "misbehave"), and invasion of indigenous people's land in the name of civilization. One irony of the metaphor citing early Roman invaders lies in the fact that Vandals (often a code name for native peoples) overran Rome. Alaric and Genseric sacked Rome in A.D. 410 and A.D. 455 respectively. Lucy's metaphorical density in "the fall of this Rome," its hybridity, encapsulates not only the family's disintegration but its colonizing aspect and Lucy's role as the marginalized servant who is not colonized, who refuses at many levels to mimic or participate. "The Roman empire fell because its social structure . . . was founded . . . on slavery."[15]

This allusive complexity is compounded when Mariah encourages Lucy to study Paul Gauguin, the postimpressionist painter who doubled as a successful half-commission man on the Stock Exchange and left his country to live in Papeete. Lucy's white employer praises an expatriate Frenchman's depiction of Tahiti, which Anglo-Saxon Mariah assumes is virtually synonymous and interchangeable with Antigua. Lucy's dry comment about gender and class difference also uproots well-known tales of Gauguin's sexual activity that ended in his death: "Of course his life could be found in the pages of a book; I had just begun to notice that the lives of men always are. He was shown to be a man rebelling against an established order he had found corrupt; and even though he was doomed to defeat — he died an early death — he had the perfume of the hero about him. I was not a man; I was a young woman from the fringes of the world, and when I left my home I had wrapped around my shoulders the mantle of a servant" (p. 95).[16]

With the best intentions, Mariah introduces Lucy to a painter whose canvases are peopled (Mariah thinks) by women like Lucy. In Lucy's conception, Paul Gauguin could be seen as a white cultural interventionist in Tahiti who became famous for painting his version of an ethnocentric gaze. Mariah's incapacity to understand Lucy's ire reaffirms the psychological damage and economic exploitation that Mariah's ignorance perpetuates.

Having identified herself as someone living on the borders of the household, Lucy goes on to admire the marginalization of artists she meets at a party she goes to with her "bad" friend Peggy. At one level, they are aesthetically connected; at another, they separate, just as Lucy separates from Gauguin. When the party's host Paul fetishizes her hair and treats her as an exotic object — he views Lucy from a vantage point that incorporates Gauguin's gaze — everyone at the party rapidly understands that she now occupies a role marked out by Paul: "It was understood that when everyone left, I would not leave with them" (p. 100).[17] To what extent she is a willing partner and goes along (and why not?) with being singled out by the host is left up in the air. Lucy — the implication goes — reverses their gaze and lets the drama play itself out. She draws together the sexual-intertextual dimension of Gauguin's behavior toward Tahitian women by inserting an old sexually based tale from her past at this point, told to her by a childhood Antiguan acquaintance named Myrna. It concerns the death of a fisherman and Myrna's reaction to it: "She told me that she had not been crying for Mr. Thomas at all — she had been crying for herself. She said that she used to meet Mr. Thomas . . . under a breadfruit tree that was near her latrine . . . at the back of her house, and she would stand in the dark, fully clothed but without her panties, and he would put his middle finger up inside her. . . . She and Mr. Thomas never spoke about it; . . . she said that she had not decided exactly what she was going to do with the money yet, but whatever it would be, she did not yet have enough" (pp. 104–05). The vulnerable child succumbs and even secretly enjoys Mr. Thomas's physical abuse. He makes her feel special and she could use the money. Perhaps the fisherman allows himself to think that the child is willing. She does, after all, wait and hope for him (and mourns his death). Lucy responds to the tale by being overcome with jealousy because the fisherman, Mr. Thomas, had singled out a "picky-haired girl" and not herself for "such an extraordinary thing."[18] The last thing Lucy wants is to be ordinary.

The tale underscores Lucy's former frustrations and her mixed judgment; it alludes to *At the Bottom* and *Annie John* in Lucy's related longings to break out of orthodox roles, if necessary at her own expense. Through the association of Mr. Thomas's hands with Paul's hands at the party as he rummages in a fish tank for a starfish-shaped rhinestone earring, Lucy connects sex, secrecy, oral narrative, and male-female relations. Paul represents a fake miniature version of Mr. Thomas, groping in a tank for a symbol of bourgeois living that emulates items of authentic tropical beauty. He fishes for a fake starfish that glitters, perhaps Lucy herself in a touch of self-mockery.

Thus Kincaid symbolically hints at Lucy's confused status by depicting her as an attractive but artificial starfish, an ornament that no longer belongs in the sea. The starfish is out of its element in a plastic world, no longer (in a sense) itself. This episode also foregrounds an important incident—almost a turning point—with a fisherman in *Annie John*. By supplementing Annie John's perceptions, we can reconsider her already-known vulnerability. Through reintroducing the same or a similar incident in different texts, Kincaid invites us to read them anew. Replaying them, as it were (and playing with the reader) to see what we "get" this time, she explodes the old hermeneutics of reading (con)texts from a single point of view, as well as the idea that texts, once written, have a fixed, graspable meaning.[19]

Concretely, in the chapter entitled "The Long Rain" in *Annie John*, when Annie John lies ill and Mr. Nigel, the fisherman, comes to wish her "a quick recovery," Annie John thinks to herself how much "he reminded me of my father. He was quiet and thoughtful in the same way, and he liked being a fisherman the way my father liked being a carpenter. As I was thinking of how much he reminded me of my father, the words 'You are just like Mr. John' came out of my mouth" (p. 121). Mr. Nigel's laughter "sucked up all the air" to such an extent that a hyperventilating Annie John hallucinates. She recalls her grandfather's death just after cursing God, the union of Mr. Nigel and Mr. Earl, the closely bonded fishermen, and the "barren, slightly crippled, Miss Catherine" who shared their lives. She, in turn, reminds Annie John of her Aunt Mary, decried by Annie John's mother as an "interfering idiot" (p. 122–23). These visions propel the invalided Annie John to leap out of bed so forcefully that she knocks Mr. Nigel to the ground and then compulsively chats to him about the tales concerning relatives that she has just connected.

This episode resonates with Myrna's story to Lucy about Mr. Thomas's sexual activities in the alley with her. Since Annie John sometimes fudges the facts, a reconsideration of what she knew when she threw herself upon Mr. Nigel seems in order. In *Lucy*, Mr. Thomas views her as a small, vulnerable child with a forbidding mother (pp. 108–9). By contrast, Myrna is a child with a "wicked stepmother" for a mother — another alter ego, perhaps a designation both Annie John and Lucy could relate to: "Though she lived in the house across from me, we were not friends, but our families shared the same fishermen, Mr. Thomas and Mr. Matthew, and she and I would often stand together under a tree, shading ourselves from the hot sun, waiting for them to return from sea with that day's catch" (p. 102).

This incident enables the reader to reconceptualize Annie John's lunge toward Mr. Nigel when he comes to pay his respects to the sick child. But if Mr. Nigel and Mr. Thomas fit the same relationship within the community in *Annie John* and *Lucy*, then Mr. Nigel, like Annie John herself, is retrospectively much more complicated. By refashioning such events, Kincaid stresses the perils of attaching fixed meaning to her fictions. In this case, Myrna's tale of an abusive, economically prompted encounter could be constitutive of Annie John's (or even Lucy's) sexual fantasy world. The episode, furthermore, links the race-class-gender axis.

Lastly, the gaze of the fisherman when he sees Annie John lying ill no longer remains unmediated; proleptically he is now refigured as a more complex figure in *Annie John*. Here are the intertwining elements of a bildungsroman at work. Myrna, who surreptitiously engaged with him in the alley, encapsulates Annie John's mother's definition of slut.[20] Is

Myrna a projection, we wonder, or just someone Lucy–Annie John desires to be? Both protagonists yearn to disobey maternal injunctions about acting as a slut. Not only does Lucy wish she could have been the very slut (in her mother's terms) that Myrna was, she rejoices in the fact that her sexual behavior would dismay her mother. This in turn eroticizes Annie John's catapult leap toward Mr. Nigel, immediately followed by verbal intimacy. Lucy dons the trappings of a fake starfish even more, as it glitters, promises, represents something it is not, immersed and even degenerating in the wrong environment.

That scene of Lucy's conflicted ontological status signals her growing resentment at being trapped. It heralds an ethical cleansing on Lucy's part: "I began to feel like a dog on a leash, a long leash but a leash all the same" (p. 110). Almost no compensation exists: "I was living in a home, though, and it was not my own" (p. 112).

A message from Antigua, however, marks a drastic change in Lucy's life. Lucy's mother sends a letter about the death of her father, its arrival coinciding with Lucy's newfound knowledge of Myrna's secret life. Although the letter is marked urgent, Lucy does not open it and responds to the inner strife it generates — over motherhood, sexuality, identity? — by buying a camera. As a functional metaphor, the camera works well. It is a tool for Lucy who is tired of other peoples' expectations about her and demands being made upon her. As far as she can, Lucy makes it her business to reject any expropriation of her subjectivity that she does not choose to give away. In that sense, the camera's gaze is empowering because it sets up distances and defines a distinct place and space for the gazer.

The camera proffers the illusion at least that material reality can be controlled when Lucy refuses to allow room for her mother's gaze across the Caribbean and the Pacific. Through her purchase, she dissolves the possibility of mutuality, or even reciprocity — that old, favored capitalist mode of exchange. Instead she reverses that gaze by gazing unrestrictedly herself. Scopic discoveries substitute for unpleasant visual images from her memory. Besides, with a camera, memories can be rearranged, boundaries can be fudged, photos can tell a lie and cover things up. Perhaps more to the point, photos can even the score. With a camera, a barricade is always present.

To augment her self-assertion, Lucy embarks on an almost immediate chance sexual relationship with the Panamanian man who sold her the camera, yet a somewhat familiar person — as opposed to her host family, say — from the island of Martinique. When Philip sells Lucy a camera, he qualifies as a coconspirator of sorts, a mysterious other who somewhat resembles Lucy. Her quest for self-completion results in their brief affair that assists her efforts to reverse the maternal gaze.

Finally, Lucy reacts to her father's death with a railing letter to her mother: "I said that she had acted like a saint, but that since I was living in this real world I had really wanted just a mother" (p. 127). Lucy opts to be her own person, to claim her sexuality as and if she pleases, to fly in the face of colonialism's desire to control "the natives," a desire that Annie John's–Lucy's mother mimics. In rejecting the injunctions that open *At the Bottom of the River* and continue in *Annie John,* Lucy articulates a resistance to colonialism. She has come to hate her biological mother, she says, although this pronouncement is persistently undercut by professions of love. What she has come to hate, perhaps more importantly, is the colonizing project that seeks to contain her. She will not be part of that imperial imperative while recognizing the trauma of separation (from both the biological and colonial mothers) that her act will entail. Her father's death frees her from speaking the patriarchal language of subjugation and accepting its terms. She jumps out of her time frame and anticipates or fashions a self-independence. Thus she substitutes an emergent postcolonial code of her own that derives from the very law of the father that she is contesting. Life as a slut is life lived freely.

The renegotiation of this old conflict reaches a climax after another potent intervention. The same Paul whose white hand dived (like Mr. Thomas's) for a fake starfish now proudly shows Lucy around the countryside, pointing out an old mansionlike plantation as a landmark to be admired. Paul identifies with the spirit of adventure in any man who crosses "the great seas, not only to find riches, he said, but to feel free, and this search for freedom was part of the whole human situation." He scarcely notices the dead animals around them, killed by fast cars now littering the highway. Lucy vehemently reacts, refusing any longer to speak the patriarchal language of oppression: "I tried to put a light note in my voice as I said, 'On their way to freedom, some people find riches, some people find death,' but I did not succeed" (p. 129).

After Lucy tells Mariah about her trip with Paul, Mariah connects Lucy's anger to feelings about her mother. As Lucy is coming to (re)create herself, so Mariah probes newfound psychological depths in herself, as if in a healthy mimicking gesture. Lucy confesses how angry she felt when she learned of her mother's plans for her male siblings' future education and professional careers. She confides that a "sword" pierced her heart: "To myself I [Lucy] then began to call her [Annie John's mother] Mrs. Judas, and I began to plan a separation from her that even then I suspected would never be complete" (pp. 130–31).

Lucy acts as if she wants to throw off two massive weights at once: the gendered, personal burden of knowing how her family favored her brothers that is inextricably fused with the burden of living as a female in a colonized country. Given Jamaica Kincaid's sense of the interrelationship between fiction and autobiography, here and elsewhere in *Lucy,* Kincaid significantly glosses Annie John's preoccupation with death or with sibling usurpation. Lucy finds both forms of authority treacherous; they are a pair of Mrs. Judases. The collection of birth and postbirth memories that follows underscores the fusion of the two mothers that underpins Lucy's life: Colonized Antigua meshes with her home life in a scenario that flaunts the colors of the Union Jack: "the color of six o'clock in the evening sky on the day I went to call the midwife to assist my mother in the birth of my first brother; the white of the chemise that my mother embroidered for the birth of my second brother; the redness of the red ants that attacked my third brother as he lay in bed next to my mother a day after he was born; the navy blue of the sailor suit my first brother wore when my father took him to a cricket match; the absence of red lipstick on my mother's mouth after they were all born" (p. 131). A cameo in black and white immediately follows: "The men from the prison in their black-and-white jail clothes came to cut down a plum tree that grew in our yard" (p. 131). Metonymically inscribing herself as a prisoner — a person living on the borders — in her own home and homeland, she was forced to kill life (a tree) back then (as Annie John?). Now with a powerfully emerging code of her own, she lives and affirms herself in violation of the dual codes. But right then, these realizations are too much for Lucy and her major mode of confrontation fails her: "But I couldn't speak, so I couldn't tell her that my mother was my mother and that society and history and culture and other women in general were something else altogether" (pp. 131–32). At this point, with the best Eurocentric will in the world, Mariah gives Lucy a copy of Simone de Beauvoir's philosophical treatise on sexual politics, *The Second Sex.*[21] Lucy understands this gift as another representation of cultural imperialism that signs Mariah unmistakably as part of the colonizing project. Lucy knows full well how Mariah has "completely misinterpreted my situation." Having loaded her problems with motherhood and colonial intervention on Mariah, Mariah then exchanges for this (unwelcome?) knowledge a famous bourgeois feminist text embedded in Eurocentric beliefs and principles.

Lucy's perceptions here go well beyond those of the narrator of *At the Bottom of the River* and *Annie John*. Lucy lines up in terms of political savvy with the narrator of *A Small Place* and (later) "Ovando."[22] Though she may not say so explicitly, Lucy notes connections between her private and political estrangement. She airs concepts and proffers examples of subjugation almost in the same breath, from daffodils and minions to plowed fields and cameras. This self-critical use of language, this hybrid form — the self-knowledge implied in growing up fragmented — yields a decolonizing of the mind. She claims the right to what Edward Said calls "the audacious metaphoric charting of spiritual territory usurped by colonial masters."[23]

In an epiphanic moment, Lucy comes face to face with the end of innocence, recognizing how her mother's social condition and Antiguan history doubly affected her. Lucy sentimentally relates a story about how she used to think life would have been preferable if the French and not the British had been colonizers. She reasons that French stamps she received from her pen pal bore a more progressive message: "The stamps on her letter were always canceled with the French words for liberty, equality, and fraternity; on mine there was no such words, only the image of a stony-face, sour-mouth woman" (p. 136). In her evolving maturity, however, Lucy shies away from that preference, but still with some reservations: "I understand that, in spite of those words, my pen pal and I were in the same boat; but still I think those words have a better ring to them" (p. 136).

But the motif of stamps strikes a more explicitly political chord also. In *A Small Place*, Annie John's mother reminds a government minister that he was involved in a scandal concerning postage stamps. Once again,

Kincaid's texts allusively connect. The speaker's biological mother is vindicated as a feisty activist who stands up to colonial guff. While insisting on her right to agitate, she exposes postcolonial corruption. Meanwhile, in *Lucy,* Lucy reveals her love of justice and her confusion about how to judge it. The parallel stories about stamps manifest the importance of the mother's example in teaching anticolonial insurgency and how Lucy has not yet internalized that lesson.

Just as much to the point, her conversation with one of the colonizer's daughters — Mariah — clarifies her own history and culture. She sees the cover-up of colonialism in Paul's bright and breezy chatter. She comes closer to her mother. The conclusion of *Lucy* recapitulates her reconciliation with these perceptions.

In that final section, the protagonist is "making a new beginning again" (p. 133). She then pointedly rehearses her origins and the arrival of Christopher Columbus, intertextualizing the previous text in this ongoing bildungsroman that features a many-faced protagonist: In her own ironic words, "[He committed a] foul deed, a task like that would have killed a thoughtful person, but he went on to live a very long life" (p. 135). Subsequently, Lucy tells the story of refusing to stand up and sing "Rule Britannia" at school, attributing her disobedience to the unattractiveness of Britons and the fact that "I was not a Briton and that until not too long ago I would have been a slave" (p. 135). In school at the time, her action was not deemed especially scandalous (because it was expected, presumably) and "instead, my choir mistress only wondered if all their efforts to civilize me over the years would come to nothing in the end" (p. 135).

She then categorizes her life up till then: "I had begun to see the past like this: there is a line, you can draw . . . yourself, or sometimes it gets drawn for you" (p. 137). She wants to be a woman shedding, not embracing, illusion. She sees through Paul: "I could have told him that I had sized him up" (p. 156), and her friend Peggy, too, in terms of colonial mimicking: "Her hair smelled of lemons — not real lemons, not lemons as I knew them to smell, not the sort of lemons that grew in my yard at home, but artificial lemons, made up in a laboratory. Peggy did not know what a real lemon smelled like. How am I going to get out of this?" (pp. 154–55). But solutions are not yet available: "I quickly placed a big rock on top of it [her feelings of being trapped]" (p. 155).

She prides herself on seeing through Lewis's snobbish veneer to his sheer ordinariness; his character is summed up in his perverse final present to the environmentally conscious Mariah of a coat made of animal fur. Lucy sees that the family members scarcely know her, although they consider it their First World right to know and therefore manipulate her. With no way of undoing their own infinite play of dissimulation and self-deception, they scarcely see beyond Lucy's phenomenal appearance of differently curled hair and a darker complection.

Nonetheless, Lucy will not forgive her mother and sends her a fake address. She still feels that to connect is to capitulate. She fears onto-logical erasure. Fiction and autobiography fuse. In a recent interview, Jamaica Kincaid stated: "Well, you know, in the battle of wills, I really couldn't stand up to her. In a way that's why I left and didn't see her for twenty years because I really had no defense."[24] By contrast, she is willing to rationalize Mariah's fury when Lucy says she will leave: "Her voice was full of anger, but I ignored it. It's always hard for the person who is left behind" (p. 141). She is even willing to forgive Mariah the mark of the colonizer; understandably the trauma of separation and insecurity is not totally fractured: "Mariah spoke to me harshly all the time now, and she began to make up rules which she insisted that I follow. . . . It was a last resort for her — insisting that I be the servant and she the master. . . . The master business did not become her at all, and it made me sad to see her that way" (p. 143). Interpreting Mariah's behavior positively, Lucy practices restraint — the kind she cannot extend toward her mother. She evinces compassion. This implied link between Lucy's compassion for a colonial mother in Mariah and the absence of compassion (because of displaced anger?) toward her biological mother is not quite within Lucy's grasp at this point. But she verges on an understanding of that link when she reapplies knowledge gleaned from her mother at home.

The complexity of Lucy's feelings is evident, too, in her desire to use her mother's knowledge to explain to Mariah the everydayness of her situation. Lucy recognizes, too, that her knowledge of Antiguan mores has empowered her to avoid Mariah's dangerous innocence: "I wanted to say this to her: 'Your situation is an everyday thing. Men behave in this way all the time.' . . . But I knew . . . she would have said, 'What a cliché.' But all the same, where I came from, every woman knew this cliché, and a man like Lewis would not have been a surprise" (p. 141). Additionally, in a neat parthian shot, she terms Mariah a stony-faced woman, echoing earlier descriptions of Queen Elizabeth II (p. 136). She slowly begins to discern finer distinctions among Mariah, Lewis, and her own mother, or rather she begins to judge them in terms of their attitudes toward colonialism, a self-preserving tactic for Lucy. Lucy has turned the tables against the family and their maid who sought to control her. As far as she is economically able, she takes charge of her environment, right down to sexual encounters. She fractures any attachment between sexuality and the damaging force of empire.

Toward the end, Lucy names who she is. Kincaid's protagonists are always specially named or deliberately unnamed. Annie John's name is also her mother's; at another anticolonial level, she must stop mimicking the master's name. She must refuse to mimic, or do so only as long as she chooses. In *At the Bottom of the River,* the speaker claims a name at an epiphanic moment, but does not disclose it. In *A Small Place,* although Jamaica Kincaid never names herself, she speaks (it seems) in her own voice. The speaker in "Ovando" resolutely refuses a name. Lucy, by contrast, recites her given name and the names she attempts to adopt: Lucy (Lucifer) Josephine Potter — names associated with plantocratic lineage, slave traders (the English Potter family), with imperial Napoleon (the Martinican Josephine), and with a Western-Christian symbol of evil — plus the possibilities of other names mentioned or referred to in the text — Emily, Charlotte, Jane, and Enid.[25] These names signify a white female hero like Jane Eyre who lives in a house with a locked-up white-Caribbean woman (and the creator of them both, Charlotte Brontë, and her sister Emily), and Enid Blyton, notorious in Britain for her racist characterizations in children's books.

In *Lucy* in particular, *Paradise Lost* resonates with the implications it harbors in *Annie John.* Lucy now knows that she has permanently lost the paradise of her innocence. She embraces the antithetical name wholeheartedly. Lucifer is configured, after all, as the perfect Western villain. Lucy finds part of her postcolonial identity in that name, a female version of the quest for identity that involves confrontation with the mother-God: "It was the moment I knew who I was. . . . Lucy, a name for Lucifer. That my mother would have found me devil-like did not surprise me, for I often thought of her as god-like, and are not the child of gods devils? I did not grow to like the name Lucy — I would have much preferred to be called Lucifer outright — but whenever I saw my name I always reached out to give it a strong embrace" (pp. 152–53).

Lucy has begun to dispense with surrogates, positively announcing to herself a personal capacity to abandon not just Mariah and Peggy but Jane and Enid too. Instead, she tunes into herself. This interior listening and observing is not unusual in Kincaid's protagonists. Both the narrator in *At the Bottom of the River* and Annie John listen inwardly. The difference is that Lucy is beginning to root herself more thoroughly in externality.[26]

But she is able to act pleasantly when Mariah effects a reconciliation and gives Lucy a notebook she had bought in Italy "a long time before" (p. 162). In a sense, Lucy is reversing the colonial project since, in its red, white, and blue composition, that notebook visually signs patriotism.[27] In its nationalist association, it refers back to the fall of Rome mentioned earlier, but this time Lucy is the Vandal who conquers the original invaders. She will use the mark of the colonizer on behalf of postcolonial agitation.

The blank pages of her life that now stretch before her, like the potential but unused frames of a camera spool, stand a better chance of being imprinted authentically. The conscious articulation of a desire — "I wish I could love someone so much that would I die from it" (p. 164) — problematizes her past, present, and future. Yet her allergy to the grand narratives of marriage, religion, and cultural conformity persists. She begins to confront herself.[28]

The angle of refraction passes through her mother's voice, passes through the sacred, hesitant, yet angry voices that close earlier texts. In a ritual of purification, her psychic life and the pain she has been suppressing for so many years spill out when she finally attempts a self-articulation.[29]

Lucy is now on her way, having come to recognize the tunnel vision of the homogeneous imperative.[30] Not only does she comprehend who has the blemishes, she further discerns that she has the ability to impose scars herself. Not only the colonizer imposes the disfiguring mark of the dominant culture. These recognitions recall Lucy's trickster story of the monkey who retaliated when Lucy's mother, irritated by the monkey's stares, threw stones at it. Just as Lewis's monkey metonymizes Lucy, so the monkey who permanently scars Lucy's mother is an insurgent who refuses extinction (pp. 154–55). At the level of minianecdote, Kincaid's texts are paradigmatic of a quest for independence and freedom, both personal and political. But it is a precarious state and she recognizes her unease: "I am alone in the world. It was not a small accomplishment. I thought I would die doing it. I was not happy, but that seemed too much to ask for" (p. 161).

Lucy can love Mariah on Lucy's terms, no longer so confused about Mariah as a substitute mother or her own ability to love without encumbrance. She can take it or leave it. The earlier persuasive words of her biological mother have "ceased to mean."[31] The girl in *At the Bottom of the River* and *Annie John* is becoming comfortable with all the parts of herself: "I had seen Mariah. She had asked me to come and have dinner with her. We were friends again; we said how much we missed each other's company. She looked even more thin than usual. She was alone, and she felt lonely. . . . When we said goodbye, I did not know if I would ever see her again" (pp. 162–63).

In addition, the camera has helped to trace Lucy's maturation: "a picture of my dresser top with my dirty panties and lipstick, an unused sanitary napkin, and an open pocketbook scattered about; a picture of a necklace made of strange seeds, which I had bought from a woman on the street; a picture of a vase I had bought at the museum, a reproduction of one found at the site of a lost civilization" (p. 121).[32] Lucy was a mixture of unpreparedness, historical lineage, and unpredictability. By the end she is more prepared for what will come. Just prior to the act of writing, she states: "I did all sorts of little things; I washed my underwear, scrubbed the stove, washed the bathroom floor, trimmed my nails, arranged my dresser, made sure I had enough sanitary napkins" (p. 163).

Most importantly, the second vignette of sanitary napkins, emblems of maturation, are no longer confined to or within the camera's eye. Lucy will prepare her affairs as she pleases. She is no longer the child of *At the Bottom of the River* or *Annie John*. Her menstrual blood links her not only to life and maturation but to the blood-red Italian notebook that Mariah gives her at the end, signifier of creativity and survival.[33]

Lucy writes down what could be read as an exaggerated sentiment about love and death, but her statement is also a way of coming to terms with blockage: "I wish I could love someone so much that I would die from it" (p. 164). Tears dissolve the power of her separate past, her closure in water (the beautiful blue ink resembling the color of the Caribbean) echoing comparable liquid closures in earlier texts.

Jamaica Kincaid's fiction invariably ends in water that cleanses, fertilizes dry ground, and opens up new radical possibilities. Symbolically, water is also a place of indeterminacy where anything can happen; it returns Lucy to amniotic fluid and new beginnings; as the beautiful Caribbean represents her as a black Antiguan and a colonial subject, so now does the ink in her pen; she is the community recorder who connects her life in Antigua with what lies ahead; she provides a link between personal and political lives; she displays the effect of colonialism and postcolonialism on an African-Caribbean woman. As the final sentence denotes, weeping is erasure: "As I looked at this sentence [about loving someone so much she would die] a great wave of shame came over me and I wept so much that the tears fell on the page and caused all the words to become one great big blur" (p. 164).

Talking about water, arriving at it, finding comfort in it, as Kincaid's protagonists do, returns them all to a time of harmony and safety. Kincaid returns us first to *At the Bottom,* where the protagonist enters the sea. After that she steps into a lighted room and sees a pen, ripe fruit, milk, a wooden flute, and clothes. With these tools of basic survival — physical, spiritual, and intellectual — she claims herself. In *Annie John,* Annie is embarking on a voyage, surrounded by water, that will transform the past. She ends the drought she so deplores in *A Small Place.*[34] Now, less is clear and more things are spotlighted. Lucy is left with uncertainty, "one great big blur," no longer with hard and fast answers. The blur means everything is out of focus; it returns us to the camera-eye view, to a sight metaphor involving confusion coupled with determination. With the blur, Lucy comes close to an adult admission that her voice is youthful and still one-sided. On the other hand, Annie John–Lucy plays out exactly what she was warned against. Her forbidden actions have positive consequences. They squash racist suppression and enhance her autonomy.

The oscillation of meanings signifies that nothing is privileged, resolved, or closed off. This ending, however, is not constitutive of mystification and metaphorical density; it is neither the dream world of *At the Bottom of the River* nor the outpouring of hatred in *Annie John* and *A Small Place.* Yet it is all of these too.

Through the metaphor of water, Lucy contextualizes her own inchoate, earlier metaphor when she observed Mariah acting in her usual manner, "which was that the world was round and we all agreed on that": Now Lucy knows the world is flat and she can fall off if she ventures to the edge. She knows the fraudulence of the overall "consensus" Mariah is sure of, its relation to a blonde, European world, the one that Peggy tries to simulate with her artificial lemon shampoo.[35] In questioning roundness and stepping closer to the edge, Lucy realizes she can see forwards and backwards. Having refused enclosures built by others, she begins to forge a site (sight) of her own.[36] She refuses assimilation and embraces cultural difference and an "alien status." Lucy chooses her own margins.[37]

In this enactment of cultural revenge, of the dissolution of authorities, of others both family and foreign who overshadowed her life and her decisions, Lucy claims her right to feel, to drown out cognition for the time being. Revealing the duplicity of the colonizing economy by mapping herself onto earlier texts, she creates a new postcolonial cartography. She is ready to write.

Last, at a transcendent level, Lucy is also Antigua of 1967, a territory freeing itself from the colonizer, already tentatively entering an early postcolonial phase. In the late nineteen sixties Antigua was struggling toward partial independence and the United States was becoming a contestational zone of antiwar protestors, just as Lucy struggles successfully toward a form of independence. Lucy has begun the process of self-decolonization. In that sense, Jamaica Kincaid, a postcolonial subject herself, has made an ex post facto intervention in describing a colonized subject about to be legally and personally freed. The deathlike green, black, and cold January of the opening transitional period on page one of *Lucy* has been transformed through Lucy's awakening and agency into a blood-red, milk-white, Caribbean-blue temporary closure, but one that is very much alive.

Fray Nicolás de Ovando, Apocryphal Texts, and the Quincentenary

Chapter 5

> As I sit here enjoying myself to a degree, I never give up thinking about the way I came into the world, how my ancestors came from Africa to the West Indies as slaves. I just could never forget it. Or forgive it. It's like a big wave that's still pulsing.—**Jamaica Kincaid, interview**

> What can Christopher Columbus mean to us? He was the advance guard of racism and imperialism.—**Molefi Kete Asante**

✶ PUBLISHED IN THE journal of experimental fiction *Conjunctions* in 1989, Jamaica Kincaid's short story "Ovando," is a myth of origins, a portrait of colonialism at work through the ages and dying as it enters the future, having sown the seeds of its own destruction.[1] Within the chronology of Jamaica Kincaid's texts, "Ovando" comes between *A Small Place,* an anticolonial polemic, and *Lucy,* a poetic, mainstream novel. "Ovando" begins with a primal encounter between a transhistorical, all-knowing narrator who is naive at first but compassionate and ultimately wise, and Ovando — a man made of plates of steel, stained with blood, in various stages of decay — who plops himself down in the narrator's living room thousands of years ago and schemes about how he can gain global ascendance. The narrator feels sorry for this metal man, hugs him, and kneels at his feet. Collapsing and expanding time at will challenges an orthodox Western mode of apprehending material reality.

"Ovando" extends *A Small Place,* where Kincaid stressed the "strange, unusual perception of time" harbored by Antiguan people (p. 9); the polemic reminds readers that colonizers imaginatively construct colonized people as "monkeys just out of trees," that "exploitation, oppres-

sion, domination" (p. 10) — a cumbersome but key phrase — and hegemonic power relations are the order of the day.[2] At one point she states
the facts boldly: "You murdered people. You imprisoned people. You
robbed people" (p. 35). "Ovando" returns us to the source of genocide
and corruption.

The narrator's last word on colonizers in *A Small Place* — "human
rubbish from Europe" — leads directly into the encounter of the narrator
with Ovando, a key player in the early history of the Americas. "Ovando"
explains why the pent-up, ostensibly polite narrator of *A Small Place*
warns the colonizer that "people like me cannot get over the past, cannot
forgive and cannot forget" (p. 26); the short story unravels what the
narrator of *A Small Place* meant when she firmly stated: "Sometimes we
hold your retribution" (p. 27).

In "Ovando" the stunned narrator is physically unprepared for Fray
Nicolás de Ovando's entrance, summed up in the fragment that opens
the story: "A knock at the door" (p. 75).[3] Thus Ovando arrives — out of
the blue, but with willful intent to impose a mode of arrival that matches
his political outlook. Although these matters are never clarified in Jamaica Kincaid's early texts, it becomes clear that Ovando resembles the
shorn, lamblike clouds in *Annie, Gwen, Lilly, Pam and Tulip* in which Pam
is lost. Their appearance is deceptive and they bode ill for the inhabitants of that small place. Ovando is a visitor cum would-be victor who offers nothing but authoritative discourse; he announces himself without
warning as if he were entitled to be there. With this intrusive disem-
bodied opening, Kincaid conflates Columbus's and Ovando's separate
entries into Hispaniola and foregrounds a protagonist unacquainted
with Europeans. Instantly sympathetic, shocked by the knight's physical
condition, the narrator assumes no danger. Her confession — as if in
retrospect — that she was immediately struck by the knight's innocence
resembles a strange textual mirror that reflects back her perilous unpreparedness.

Why, the text challenges, does the speaker welcome the colonizer so
readily, a complex question, given contemporary controversy. First, as
foreshadowed in *Annie, Gwen, Lilly, Pam and Tulip*, the Arawaks were
traditionally a peace-loving nation. Second, rumors spread about a possible divine association of this unusual-looking people. Last, by opening
the gap about why an Arawak narrator welcomed a duplicitous ma-

rauder, Kincaid challenges any acceptance by contemporary readers of a colonizer's reworked narrative of events. There is a further complication about the Amerindian narrator. In the character of the narrator, Kincaid may have conflated two different Amerindian populations to highlight the magnitude of Ovando's damage. The narrator is, for example, initially serene and unaggressive, characteristics customarily attributed to the Arawak civilization that peopled Hispaniola when Columbus arrived in 1492. On the other hand, the narrator also assumes more combative traits usually attributed to Carib people from whom Jamaica Kincaid herself descends. Kincaid's maternal grandmother was one of the few remaining Caribs in the world. This conflation in the narrator of Arawak and Carib dramatically crystallizes the imperial project and the power-ridden colonial gaze. By fleshing out the embedded histories she presents in *At the Bottom of the River* and *Annie John* and the overt contemporary history in *A Small Place,* Jamaica Kincaid refuses to present the Caribbean landscape in reductive terms that belie its cultural complexity. By rendering the narrator warmly open-armed and then resistant, Kincaid thereby dissolves binary thinking about Arawaks and Caribs.[4] The narrator accepts the finiteness of borders. She is neither greedy nor does she want to invade. "I am not tempted to transgress" (p. 78). Kincaid explodes the idea that Columbus met a peace-loving Arawak as opposed to hostile Caribs who made trouble later. To put the case bluntly, reductive categories of good Arawaks and bad Caribs are suspect because they come from Europeans. Her matter-of-fact tone affirming a trusting disposition, the narrator still ventures a veiled, anachronistic, somewhat anxious comment about manipulation and profit: "In banks, really, . . . he stored the contents of his diminishing brain" (p. 75). Besides, Kincaid mockingly predicts, if Ovando's brains were diminishing, why would he need a bank? How could he gain interest on capital dropping in value?

The almost immediate reference to Ovando as a "stinky" relic — the narrator rapidly conjoins the past to the present — suggests not only the speaker's youth in using such a childishly slang term, *stinky,* but an already dual view of the present, her before-and-after impressions: On the one hand, Ovando is an object that has survived from the past, whose age and associations yield historic interest; on the other, he consists of fragments or ruins, revered only by himself. Most of all, he and his kind are dead, another optimistic prediction about colonialism, doubly ominous given the fact that the Spaniards virtually exterminated the Arawak and Carib populations.

Kincaid's use of Ovando's name in particular morbidly plays on this initial scenario. The ovum—the reproductive cell that produces a new individual—that packs into the word *Ovando* derides his relation to indigenous people.[5] The ridiculed tourists in *A Small Place* are Ovando's cultural heirs in the Caribbean region who continue to negate the post-independence motto of Antigua: "A People to Mold. A Nation to Build." Later in the story the idea forcefully enters that Ovando and his relatives generate themselves through the rape of the narrator. As a near homonym for *ovan,* ovum is also Arabic for zero and cipher, hence a mere nothing. Ovando is a seed of genocide. He is the possibility of colonialism multiplied, its ubiquitous, prolific embodiment; he is both the egg fertilized and the eggs about to be fertilized, the past, present, and future in a single incarnation. Symbolically through the eggs, time becomes seamless.

FRAY NICOLÁS DE OVANDO

On September 3, 1501, Fray Nicolás de Ovando, a distinguished knight of a religious order, a Comendador of Lares of the military order of Alcantara was appointed governor of the Indies by King Ferdinand and Queen Isabella of Spain. Having been accorded full civil and criminal jurisdiction by the monarchs, he ruled Hispaniola (now Haiti and Santo Domingo) from 1502 to 1508, setting a standard of imperial excess for other conquistadors.[6] Although Ovando's barbarities are notorious, since even by colonists' standards he was an excessive autocrat, he is still featured in Eurocentric textbooks as the man who established a successful settlement in Hispaniola, credited with rendering the island a base for the Spanish empire in the "Americas."[7] On September 16, the king and queen gave him the following instructions, which he later freely interpreted:

> First of all, you are to work diligently in those things that pertain to the service of God and ensure that divine services are conducted with the proper respect, order, and reverence.

Also, because it is Our will that the Indians be converted to Our Holy Catholic Faith and their souls be saved, since this is the greatest benefit We can desire for them . . . you are to take care, without using any force against them, that the priests who are there teach and admonish them for this purpose with much love, so that they are converted as quickly as possible; and you are to provide all the support and help needed for this. . . . And you are to ensure that all live in peace and justice, treating all equally without exception; and you are to appoint for this purpose the subordinate officials that are necessary and to punish those crimes that justly should be punished.

Also you are to ensure that the Indians are well treated and can walk safely throughout the country without anyone assaulting or robbing them or doing them any other harm. . . .

Also, because it will be necessary to use Indian labor in mining gold and other tasks We have ordered done, you are to require the Indians to work in the things of Our service, paying to each the salary that seems just to you with regard to the quality of the land. . . .

Also, because it benefits Our service that those who are foreign to Our Kingdoms and Realms not live in the above said islands, you are not to allow such foreigners to settle in the said islands and mainland.[8]

On September 26, to demonstrate further their approval of this appointment, the monarchs drew up a Cédula that "gave him [Ovando] permission to wear silk, brocade, precious stones, etc., notwithstanding the regulations of his order."[9]

Bartolomé de Las Casas, son of one of Christopher Columbus's shipmates of his first voyage and the first priest ordained in the Indies, published in 1698 an eye-witness account of those times entitled *History of the Voyage and Discoveries the Spaniards have made in the East Indies.*[10] Las Casas's chronicle suggests why Jamaica Kincaid uses Ovando's name for the title of a story about the Spaniards' arrival. Not only did Ovando take the law into his own hands, he was responsible for massive genocide. In Las Casas's words: "In the eight years of his government, more than nine-tenths (of the Indians) perished."[11] If the original figure given for the population is accurate — 1,200,000 — then, 1,080,000 were massacred in an eight-year period.[12] From the moment of landing, the exclusively male Spanish force was bent on acquisition: "The Indians now conducted the Spaniards to their houses, and set before them cassava bread, fish, roots, and fruits of various kinds. They brought also great numbers of domesticated parrots, and indeed offered freely whatever they possessed. . . . All that [the Spaniards] complained of was that they saw no signs of riches among the natives."[13]

The administration of this conquistador can be summed up as follows: Ovando replaced Fray Francisco de Bobadilla who was sent by the king and queen to replace Columbus. Exceeding his orders, Bobadilla brought Columbus and his brothers back to Spain in chains.[14] Ovando was then sent to relieve Bobadilla of his command.[15] His government extended over the islands and over Terra Firma, of which Hispaniola was to be the metropolis.[16]

Ovando embarked for San Domingo on April 15, 1502.[17] Las Casas arrived in the same fleet. Before long, a thousand of the 2,500 people whom Ovando transported from Spain perished. Many among them were hidalgoes, agricultural workers, and laboring-class people as well as people set free from the jails. To comply with the monarchs' request that the Indians should work for wages, Ovando skillfully modified his sovereigns' ordinances, developing a system that redistributed Indians entirely for Spanish benefit. Effectively, he instituted serfdom. The loophole he used to get round the orders was the stipulation that Indians were to be compelled to work in the mines for royal service, a condition that opened the door to genocide.[18] Ovando gave an Indian village or a group of villages, often about 50 Indians, who collectively were called an *encomienda,* to each Castilian.[19]

> It was arranged in the form of an order on a cacique for a certain number of Indians, who were to be paid by their employer, and instructed in the Catholic faith. The pay was so small as to be little better than nominal; the instruction was little more than the mere ceremony of baptism; and the term of labour was at first six months, and then eight months in the year. Under cover of this hired labour, intended for the good both of their bodies and their souls, more intolerable toil was extracted from them, and more horrible cruelties were inflicted than in the worst days of Bobadilla. They were separated often the distance of several days journey from their wives and children and doomed to intolerable labour of all kinds, extorted by the cruel infliction of the lash. For food they had the cassava bread, an unsubstantial support for one obliged to labour; sometimes a scanty portion of pork was distributed among a great number of them, scarce a mouthful to each. When the Spaniards who superintended the mines were at their repast, says Las Casas, the famished Indians scrambled under the table, like dogs, for any bone

thrown to them. After they had gnawed and sucked it, they pounded it between stones and mixed it with their cassava bread, that nothing of so precious a morsel might be lost. As to those who laboured in the fields, they never tasted either flesh or fish; a little cassava bread and a few roots were their support. While the Spaniards thus withheld the nourishment necessary to sustain their health and forces, they exacted a degree of labour sufficient to break down the strength of the most vigorous man. If the Indians fled from this incessant toil and barbarous coercion, and took refuge in the mountains, they were hunted out like wild beasts, scourged in the most inhuman manner, and laden with chains to prevent a second escape.[20]

Multiple acts of base treachery lie at his doorstep, the most notorious suggesting how Kincaid obliquely embeds gender in the tale. Along with local chiefs called the Caciques, the Indian Queen, Anacaona of the principality of Xaragua, seventy leagues from San Domingo, was led into a trap by Ovando and his retinue. Her fate foregrounds Ovando's style of colonial administration: "At the signal of Ovando the horsemen rushed into the midst of the naked and defenceless throng, trampling them under the hoofs of their steeds, cutting them down with their swords, and transfixing them with their spears. No mercy was shewn to age or sex; it was a savage and indiscriminate butchery. . . . The mockery of a trial was given her, in which she was found guilty on the confessions wrung by torture from her subjects, and on the testimony of their butchers; and she was ignominiously hanged in the presence of the people who she had so long and so signally befriended."[21] The chiefs, furthermore, were burned alive: "Having at length hunted them out of their retreats, destroyed many, and reduced the survivors to the most deplorable misery and abject submission, the whole of that part of the island was considered as restored to good order."[22] After these murders, Ovando formed a town out of the settlement at Xaragua, renaming it La Villa de la Vera Paz, the city of the true peace. His coat of arms consisted of a dove with an olive branch, a rainbow, and a cross.[23]

Kincaid intertextualizes known facts of Ovando's atrocities underscored in Las Casas's account when he chronicles the tale of thirteen Indian boys hanged to pay reverence to Jesus Christ and the twelve apostles: "These men, hanging at such a height that their feet could just touch the ground, were used as dumb figures for the Spaniards to try their swords upon. . . . On another occasion he saw some Indians being burnt alive in a sort of wooden cradle. Their cries disturbed the Spanish Captain taking his siesta in his tent; and he bade the Alguazil, who had the charge of the execution, to dispatch the natives. This officer, however, only gagged the poor wretches, who thus fulfilled their martyrdom in the way he originally intended for them. 'All this I saw with my bodily mortal eyes,' emphatically exclaims the witness for the fact."[24]

One of the last acts of Ovando's government was to lure as workers to Hispaniola the inhabitants of the archipelago that included the Bahamas.[25] The Indian civilization in Hispaniola had been worked to death and died on such a mass scale that necessary daily chores were being neglected. To capture the Bahamian Lucayans, the Spaniards flatly lied to them and pretended they had come from the heaven of the Lucayans' ancestors and that they would return the people to that land. In five years, this fiction drew 40,000 Lucayans to Hispaniola. Many suffered the same fate as the original Indians; some escaped to the north. This dislocation of the Lucayan population was so well publicized that minor eighteenth-century poets wrote about it.

Despite overwhelming contemporary evidence to the contrary, ethnocentric historical views are still frequently represented. Samuel Hazard, comments for example, traditionally: "[The Indians] made several attempts to recover their liberty. . . . The Spaniards always treated these efforts as rebellion, and took arms against the natives with this idea. It is easy to imagine the result, in a contest between savages, entirely naked, on one side, and, on the other, one of the most warlike nations of Europe, where science, courage, and discipline were pitted against timidity and ignorance."[26] To drive the historical point home, Kincaid writes "Ovando" to precede by a year the quincentenary of Christopher Columbus's arrival in the Caribbean in 1492; she also takes usually unsuccessful Indian resistance for granted. Several historians and engravers, for example, have noted the numerous forms of Indian suicide, an unsurprising fact given how severely Spanish overlords exploited the people: they yoked Indian men and women together like oxen and forced them to work in this condition; they also drove Indians into the mines, or obliged them to work almost ceaselessly in burning sun.[27]

Kincaid indicts all aspects, buried and overt, of the imperial project, especially those conducted under a peace-conferring guise. In "Ovando," Kincaid recreates a myth of the original colonial intervention that chronologically precedes and infiltrates her collective texts. By elaborating on the conquistadorian encounter from the point of view of the colonized, she underscores its crucial cultural location.

Kincaid also highlights the abusive treatment of women in these invasions. Aside from the allusion to Queen Anacaona, Kincaid obliquely intertextualizes gender in the speaker herself. She transposes into Ovando's scenario the woman with the gold nose-ring who was brought to Columbus after being captured and alerted him to the island's natural riches.[28] Kincaid adds a female figuration to this transposed Arawak guide, referring early on to the tender familial love this woman harbors: "I love him then, not the way I would love my mother, or my child" (p. 75), she says as she welcomes Ovando into her own domestic arena. "Think of this," she goes on, "as your new home" (p. 75). Later when she speaks of Ovando's forcible replacement of Arawak people in various stages of degradation, she alludes to other force used by the Spaniards, namely the raping of Amerindian women.[29] In the following sentence — "In unison, like a clap of thunder, they all said, 'Mine!'" — Jamaica Kincaid imagistically suggests that sexually transmitted European diseases helped to wipe out a high percentage of Amerindians.[30] Simultaneously, she inscribes the constancy of rape, both of land, resources, and the female population. Customarily a sign of female space, home has fundamentally altered its meaning.

The opening of "Ovando" collapses past, present, and future. In the past, the knight knocked on the door of the narrator who exhibited an amazed response (as anyone would) to someone in his bloody condition. Yet in that same split-second of shock, she senses his duplicity. Ovando assumed that she would not recognize how artificial he was: "He thought I would not know the difference." Yet one of the first things metropolitan invaders typically do when they write about colonized people is comment negatively on their host's customs and appearance. Demeaning the culture of the about-to-be-colonized is a colonizing sine qua non. In this case, the indigenous person so pities the intruder's appearance that she wants to help him. Thus in a brilliant reversal Kincaid reconstitutes the Eurocentric gaze.

Whether Ovando replies or the narrator imagines that he replies is unclear, but Ovando makes his spiritual claim to the land. He subscribes, he boasts, to the divine right of kings, a tenet of imperial belief that validates any interventionist action, since all acts are theoretically under-taken in God's name. Ovando's divine association renders all his doings (Ovan-do), moral and ungainsayable.

Through different expressions of the same events, the narrator again stresses the importance and relativity of cultural position: "What was in-vasion to me" — she firmly pronounces — "[was] a discovery to him." Her subsequent claim that her powers could have terminated his inva-sion but "he was horrible on a scale I did not even know existed before" (p. 76) raises more questions about cultural difference. Why does she think she could have stopped him in his tracks? With what? Presumably she and her people could have chased him away. But their sense of com-munity, their lack of knowledge and an arsenal prevented such a re-sponse. "I could have stopped him" also voices a wistful retrospective insight that her society was no match for armed metropolitan agents bent on conquest. In a colonizer's vision, this utopian moment is what might have been. The narrator's mysterious invocation of potential retaliation could also be a postcolonial vision of unspecified guerrilla warfare.[31]

Another reading foregrounds Indian cultural practices. The narrator's assertion that she could dispense with Ovando if she wanted to hinges on a belief in obeah. Since Ovando governed Hispaniola, he would be ruling a people with plural subjectivities who subscribed to indigenous beliefs, also known as residuals, that are coordinated with obeah or voodoo. The term *voodoo* (or *vodu* or *vondoun*) "is a generic one which encompasses at least two denominations of an African-Haitian-Indian culture. . . . The Petro [cult is] generally traced to Carib Indian origins. To a large extent, much of the atavistic energies as popularly associated with Voodoo appear to have their origin in the Petro."[32] Such a religion, "where to impart to the individual of the community a system of mental and emotional convictions upon which the very survival of the commu-nity is dependent, does not, and could not require of them that they perceive and understand its principles on an abstract, metaphysical level in order that they be inspired to participate in it."[33] Hence the narrator feels potentially triumphant. If supernatural power had become an issue, the people, she suggests, might have won. Moreover, the narrator's deci-sion not to intervene underwrites a belief that no matter what Ovando does, he cannot obliterate a people because "a corpse, mummified under white domination, can be resurrected by the ancestral spirits and refined into a force that will liberate the whites also."[34] In Haitian as much as in African cultures, only "moral blindness, esthetic treachery and intellectual and emotional counterfeiting, the results of assimilationism . . . constitute death or mummification."[35] Hence the unassimilable narrator and like-minded people never die.

The narrator verbalizes views of a traditional society exploited by a self-involved colonialism. Ovando strikes her as helpless and pitiable, his flesh weak and broken, his mind shrinking, unable to communicate or to hear. The eyes of Ovando's Spanish-imperial society are shut so tight that it registers tunnel vision, seeing only what it wants to see. To add to the complex of a culpably ignorant society, Ovando himself has no ears.

In a form of postcolonial self-criticism, the narrator apprehends how her kindness tripped her up, made her an easy mark as she projected onto Ovando how *she* would feel in that situation. Ashamed of how he looked, he would deny his condition. Nonetheless, she is still uneasy about his presence, a disquiet soon confirmed by a third-person commentary, helpfully tendered toward her: "Many people have said that this was my first big mistake, and I always say, How could it be a mistake to show sympathy, to show trust, to show affection to another human being, on first meeting" (p. 75). Extolling cultural values, she reassuringly replies: "I loved him then . . . with that more general and spontaneous kind of love that I feel when I see any human being" (p. 75). The narrator's retrospective indictment of her initial naiveté is palpable. This recognition erupts again in an almost disguised form. As the white knight imperiously enters the living room, the narrator talks (sarcastically?) of her "great exaggeration" in ushering him in. But he needs no invitation. Not until he openly comments on his impending predations does the narrator permit herself a troubled thought: "So many things at once seemed wrong to me that it was hard to know where to begin" (p. 76). Even at that, the unnamed narrator tries to proffer acceptable explanations. She feels sorry for Ovando's global relatives because she assumes they will resemble him in appearance. Her severe discomfiture with his unilateral decision to invite Europe into her home fosters such confusion that she persists in explanations that will justify his egregious conduct: He is, she rationalizes, blind.

Similarly with respect to language, the narrator turns the tables on orthodox Eurocentric constructions of the colonial encounter. These odd-looking people, she realizes, cannot even speak conversationally; they can only "make pronouncements." Countries of people who have invited themselves to sit down in her house "without asking my permission" function in near silence, like animals in the dark.

Ovando invokes some arbitrary right to stake territorial claim: His relatives will enjoy life in her land, he asserts, because "we have met the same fate in the world" (p. 76). Articulating an imperial doctrine which he coyly calls fate, Ovando embodies an early form of what was to be later termed manifest destiny. In his eyes and in the eyes of those who subscribe to supremacist beliefs, European hegemony is inevitable. Still in the present, the narrator realizes that Ovando is beyond negotiating on an equal basis.

Given her background, the narrator has trouble confronting Ovando's excessive self-interest, a phenomenon that fights her ideological construction, premised on collective harmony. Up till then, she has responded sympathetically, excused him, defended him to concerned people, and remained confused. Now she states her opinion—albeit silently—while pointedly naming him and politely acknowledging his presence. Her conflicts are growing insupportable, her patience tried to its utmost. Yet she still rather artlessly locates herself in the role of quasi host and (even) mentor: "Ovando, look, let us be reasonable. All of your words and deeds towards me so far have been incredibly unjust. Already, just in the first few moments of our meeting, you have done me irreparable harm. Stop now, let me show to you the grave errors you have made" (p. 76). His response alerts the narrator to their sharply diverse vantage points, the implications of his invocation of divine right. She begins to discern that she constitutes his other: "Really, there is nothing I can do about this, [he replies]. A power outside and beyond me has predetermined these unalterable events. All of my actions have been made for me in eternity. All of my actions are divine" (p. 76).

The narrator's response to his "knock" or his invasion—"Though I was not expecting him, he was bound to come"—then becomes a projection of Ovando's confident sense of his fate, his historical role, and the direct and indirect bondage that defines that situation. In harsh "real world" terms, Ovando is scheming to establish metropolitan centers of domination abroad, a heterodox network of West European hegemonic control. In a broader context, the malignant colonizer who is carrying "bibles, cathedrals, museums (for he was already an established collector), libraries . . . the contents of a drawing room" (p. 75) is now appropriating civilizations — religious, state, and financial institutions.

The speaker mimics Ovando's linear thought processes to cope with him; contemplation confronts "might is right." Then she moves into time future and sketches Ovando's actions in a world of his own making — a round world that is "small and bare and chalkwhite, like a full moon in an early evening sky." Ovando renders the universe according to his own perceptions. Only the narrator can see how it will have to give way, like an early evening moon, to darkness and the morning sun. The narrator later basks in this sunshine.

Ovando sees the world as round because imperial ideology ignores frontiers; it dictates that frontiers do not exist for (stand in the way of) history's chosen pioneers. Round is a metaphor for marauding. It signifies aspirations of permanent travel and conquest, narcissism reencoded. In proving that the world was round in one sense, Columbus proved it in another.

The narrator's viewpoint dramatically challenges his own. The world is flat to her, flat signifying stability, a sense of community, of relating, and belonging. Ironically, to be flat is to lay yourself open to conquest. But flat also contains within itself its converse. It halts perpetuity and circularity or roundness. It can sign resistance. To be flat is to oppose Columbus and an imperial mentality. The horizon is endless. Everything and everyone — the aged and poor alike — have a place. The speaker learns some of the colonizer's corrupt ways, for she begins to perceive that to see things as flat, to be open and welcoming, is perilous. His actions teach her to simulate his duplicity in order to survive. In retrospect, we know that the narrator's flat culture assumes an open-door policy.[36] People imbued with compassion and generosity welcome strangers since sharing warmth signals humanity and earns people a worthy place in the global community; only people made of steel — scarcely human — are devoid of those feelings. At that time the speaker does not know that these metal people are also (homonymically) thieves, another kind of steel (steal) people.

This discussion reminds readers that the narrator has lived through hundreds of years in the world, say, of *At the Bottom of the River, Annie*

John, and *A Small Place.* Kincaid's narrator was the one who reacted to Ovando's depredations in time past, present, and future. At this point, Kincaid's bildungsroman—her ongoing saga about growing up (trans-historically) colonized has taken a turn backwards, *and* into the future. "Ovando" becomes a synthesizing text of sorts, one that "explains." By implication, that is, "Ovando" elaborates on and culls from Kincaid's resonating earlier texts; in denoting the origins of Hispaniola, she suggests a political unity among Caribbean peoples and a foreswearing of colonial and postcolonial influence. Even Kincaid's most recent protagonist, Lucy, goes to New York with baggage that Ovando historically dumped on her. These intertextual motifs and allusions argue for global interconnection. They insist that everything is part of everything else, that the world is flat, in opposition to the colonizer's view. It is a continuity over time and only corrupt mentalities and rationales for European intervention would suggest otherwise.

Hence the narrator's earlier statement that "he had made himself a body from plates of steel, and it was stained with shades of red, blood in various stages of decay" turns out to be literal as well as metaphorical. Ovando's expedition that embarked on Xaragua consisted of 300 well-armed foot soldiers and 70 horsemen who were wearing cuirasses, as well as holding small round shields or bucklers, and lances.[37] These cuirasses are the very plates of steel the narrator identifies; pieces of close-fitting armor for protecting the breast and back. The supposedly more sophisticated soldiers—Ovando included—wear breast plates which to the narrator's eyes—another sign of political youth and her distance from European warfare—look like "plates of steel." The narrator assumes that the reader belongs to the round world and hence does not understand.

The colonizer considers his self-proclaimed power eternal, with new worlds constantly available for conquest. As the architect of this new dispensation, Ovando fashions it serenely, dividing it up into lots until he realizes gold and jewels are also on hand and can be extracted from the mines. The discovery of precious natural resources, particularly gold, intensified conquistadorian greed; it stopped a certain kind of colonial gentlemen's mutual redistribution of others' territory. Discovery of gold caused Ovando to reshape the world through a language bound up in false beliefs.

Only the narrator and people like her can see how bogus Ovando's created world is. He is seriously sight-impaired. His preoccupation with bloodletting signifies his fundamental bankruptcy. In all senses but the technical, he is a dead man. The volumes he writes abut phlebotomy, liberation, and divinity are already contaminated. Given the situation, the narrator's quiet sarcasm, which resembles her opening queries, assumes more ominous overtones. Now she employs a similar kind of bathos to underscore Ovando's worldwide fracture of peace: "To say that his meditations were nothing more than explanations and justifications for his future actions might seem unfair, for after all is it not so that all human beings are, from moment to moment, vulnerable to overwhelming self-love?" (p. 77). Ovando is too narcissistic to know that self-love is all he possesses with any certainty. Only the narrator and her allies understand his overall position of power. Yet they cannot defeat him because he has erected an interlocking global arsenal of apocryphal texts — weapons to vindicate his narrow vision and crush those who would expose him.

Ovando, then, draws a map to stake out his potential claims. Defying an authentic past, his map insists that nothing existed on the earth before Europeans landed on it; he redistributes the globe as he pleases. But no sooner is the refashioned map of the world complete than it collapses. Put another way, after he arbitrarily expropriates territory on the map, resistance instantly sets in, expressed in the terse phrase "the world broke." The map of the world which is "sadness itself" is so much his construction that he can trace a path from where he is across what he owns that arrives back in the same place. Give or take, he is the universal conqueror on (of) this map. A tension informs his description. This path across the globe is described as a line, but it is also configured as a full circle that metonymically echoes the small, bare, chalk-white world. Only then, when the circle is complete, when the waning moon complements Ovando's global construction does the edifice break. The very line that he traces — that in his terms is a circle — is indeed a (flat) line to the narrator who will eventually become a counterintuitive cartographer.

Graced with a flat vision, the narrator has power to envisage doing what Ovando did. She imagines him surrounded by signs of conquest: "What can I do with all that I am surrounded by? I can fashion for myself bracelets, necklaces, crowns. I can make kingdoms, I can make civilizations, I can lay waste" (p. 78). Ovando fails to see that natural resources — what he views as his treasures and wealth — will outlive and outwit him. Despite his pillage, he cannot control nature and time. The point is that the narrator — more far-sighted and rights-oriented than Ovando — espies where all this will lead. In caring about these matters, she states pithily and elementally: "I can see the destruction of my body, and I can see the destruction of my soul" (p. 78).

The narrator forthrightly condemns and rejects authoritative discourse and arbitrary usurpation of land. In their place, she urges a richer view of the world based on the concept of live and let live. "I can prevent myself from entering the dungheap that is history," she says, meaning those wearing blinders create such a phenomenon. History, then, is a product of colonizers — it is their tale of events, their attempt to control communication, the very kind of history the narrator scorned in *A Small Place*.[38] This association of the narrator with all-inclusiveness is an association frequently linked to females. Moreover, in the sense of a transhistorical, transoceanic contestation, Jamaica Kincaid hints at gender difference as well as colonial difference. Though the sex of the narrator is left indeterminate, her sensibility radiates a nurturance traditionally linked to females. Ovando's attempt to obliterate her echoes standard institutional practice in erasing women. The narrator is the repressed term of Ovando's discourse.

The narrator elaborates on Ovando's territorial expansion and his egotistic engagement with a mirror. Ovando's history of acquisition is a tale of gaining power. Yet that power is disguised as treasure. Greed metonymizes into political hegemony, bracelets are manacles, necklaces are neck irons, crowns are tyranny. Ovando's forte is laying waste and forcing "civilization" upon people, a much-mocked word that rings hollow. Ovando's actions are self-defeating and potentially fatal. He might have conquered the ages but his conquests are millstones (or medallions) around his neck, his waist, his wrists, and his ankles (p. 81).

For the narrator, history is a continuum. Those who belong to her land recognize the ebb and flow of the tide: They see that things and people — like colonialists — come and go. Round-world people, by contrast, see no end to things. The horizon, they believe, stretches endlessly before them, ripe for conquest. Round people do not understand, follow, and accommodate the tide. They neither keep pace nor stay ahead of it. Round people consider themselves the tide of history, making peri-odical pronouncements along these lines.

But Ovando's round view of history is dangerous even to those who see a flat world before them. It causes the narrator to "stumble over the glittering stones that are scattered in my path" (p. 78). In one sense, these stones represent a certain kind of false consciousness — desirable gold — the glitter of which hinders her and holds her back. The narrator realizes that everything passes and only life can be appreciated. Gold and jewels possess the owner rather than the reverse. They corrupt and ruin a society if a society only exists to administer its wealth.[39] Their beauty is so deceptive that they might be better left alone. Were Ovando to wear gold and jewels to underscore the trappings of his power and enhance his image as a man of steel, a metal man, the narrator would reconsider the possibilities of her own natural resources. That is, the narrator by exten-sion would have to reconsider the person she had come to be and decide whether her "self-constitution" was still appropriate to the changing environment.

Between the lines, the fight between Arawaks and Caribs in early Antigua quietly inserts itself.[40] Do the British alone seek gold or is it a different situation when indigenous people fight among themselves? When the narrator rubs her toe, she spots gold and leaves it; she marks that the value ultimately put on this metal is a created value. How ironic, the narrator stresses, that Ovando "had spent many years in preparation for this moment, the moment in which these words 'My Sheer Might,' could be said. The moment in which the words 'My Sheer Might' could be said was the moment in which the words would be true. And so for a long time Ovando stood in front of a mirror" (p. 79).

Ovando changes the "usually serene and pleasing contours" of the narrator's world. He shifts her position with his "sheer might." When he finally discovers his imperial subjectivity through these words, the narra-tor pokes fun at his histrionic parading: My Sheer Might is his battle cry, the colonial imperative. Ironically, this might that belongs to him can presumably be taken away; moreover, it is *sheer* might, in the sense of bright and absolute — but sheer also in being diaphanous and even frail. Once again the question arises: Who is taken in and who believes? Only the person in the mirror, a distorted solipsist, she grimly suggests.

In addition, the sun that the narrator sits in emblematizes a relation to the world. While Ovando and his relatives sit in other people's houses uninvited, the narrator and her allies sit in the sun's rays. It is the natural center of their lives; they live by it, but their (literal) solipsism is undistorted. The narrator describes the apocalyptic nightmare of those on Ovando's receiving line where words demolish civilizations.

Mirrors and glass shine everywhere, reflecting back gullibility as well as greed.[41] The mirror Ovando looks in that signifies woe connects with the splintering world (pp. 77, 79, 80). His world and his words are reflectors and engorgers. The mirror is fracture; fracture is pain and ugliness; centuries-old harmonies are broken by cupidity, so human beings repopulate the world in new ways. In multiple relations, masters with servants or slaves constitute a changing social formation. The allegory of Ovando explicates the beginning of international struggles against colonial ruling-class hegemony.

The jagged edges of Ovando's shards witness his unpredictability, his instability, his ultimate fragility and fragmentation. He has perpetuated certain conditions, but the mirror that returns his image and his dreams is shattered into pieces of evil. Around Ovando, Kincaid weaves the numbers associated with the devil: 13 and 600 and 66. They stress Ovando's negativity and intensify the racist iconography.[42]

Furthermore, those surrounding mirrors and glass echo one myth variant about Narcissus who lives indifferently to the people around him. In vengeance for his lack of giving, he falls in love with his reflection in a stream and continues his indifference, concentrating only on his mirror image. When he tries to see himself in the river Styx that runs through hell, he causes his own death.[43]

Ovando, then, becomes a self-parody that he maliciously forces colonized people to construct on his behalf: the beast, a tail, horns, and a forked tongue that he himself cut. The narrator presents this matter-of-factly, as if to say look behind the facade and there he is. He uses precious natural sources — a millennia of trees — to produce his obscene documents. His machinations now follow thickly upon one another. Having reduced the forest to a 6″ by 6″ piece of paper, Ovando tries to reduce the narrator comparably. He sees no irony in his rejection of the narrator whose land and people he has stolen. Through the sign of the trees, Ovando seeks to colonize, but the narrator's sarcasm about the millennia of rain forest he has destroyed overnight voices a decolonized perspective. Defoliation enables the narrator to shift location. Chronicling the loss of the rain forest constitutes a countermemory. The people may be physically defeated but they do not forget.

There is more. In the discussion of trees, Kincaid conflates people and trees in a long discussion about degradation. Ovando orders them to be "cut down so that only stumps remained, and boiled and pounded and dried." Here Kincaid describes unspeakable tortures perpetrated against Indians that range from being nailed to the ground and burned alive to being chained up like dogs (p. 80).

Additionally, just as Ovando thinks he can reduce valuable trees "to something held between the tips of two fingers," he also thinks he can hold time past in his hand. That is, he assumes he can capture history and fashion it to his own liking. The trees of the past and the present are his possessions, just like the people. He claims he can possess "their origins, their ancestry, and everything they had ever, ever been, and so too," the narrator states, "he held me" (p. 80). Beyond that, Kincaid highlights the arbitrariness and persistence of female rape: "On this paper, which constitutes millions of trees, Ovando wrote that he dishonored me." Everything Ovando says and does confirms the narrator's nothingness. The point is that the narrator's refusal of Ovando's position and status cancel out that attempted observation.

Ovando is happy to circulate false pronouncements that the narrator is dead, his confirmation of the narrator's "nothingness" just one more dimension to his subsumption of the other. But Ovando has become so close to sightlessness that he can recognize almost nothing but vestiges of a supposed power. He must reject the other outright to try to live. He cannot see the other in himself.

The narrator counters with a use of language that echoes her refusal of assimilation. In another brilliant transformation of the subject-other relationship, Ovando expatiates on his oppressed condition despite the narrator's colonized position; she is the one with feelings and political insight as well as a sense of resistance: "Should I not be touched by my own pain, should I not be moved on seeing a picture of myself humbled by a power over which I had no desire to triumph, a power I wished would stay out of my way" (p. 81).

This insistence on explaining why her speech is heartfelt invites readers to consider the continuing global complicity of hegemonic apologists — conscious or unconscious — readers with sympathy for Ovando, those who write Eurocentric histories, the colonists themselves and their allies.

Adopting an epistemology that relativizes modes of knowing, Kincaid categorically debunks the Cartesian mode. The colonizer's mania for accumulation of any sort — of things and data and buildings — is his corruption and ultimately his undoing. The narrator, on the other hand, represents well-known political landscapes with optional points of entry, through connection or through banditry.

As the narrator concludes her exposure of Ovando, she paints a gruesome, albeit ridiculous picture, deftly combining Ovando's intentionality with external perceptions of his parading in a diabolical outfit. Ovando himself becomes theatrical as if he were beginning to accept role-playing as a transcendent subject position: "I shall raise the curtain, and my relatives shall now make their appearance" (p. 81). Ovando's relatives who magically appear in a covered floating vessel (is the *Santa Maria* the flagship?) kiss the earth as a sign of possession. In this reminder of European intervention abroad, we return to the historical roots of the text, for the first thing Columbus did when he set foot in Guahania was to kiss the earth and instantaneously rename it San Salvador.[44] The author pointedly reminds us that his act was no fantasy:

> It was on Friday morning, the 12th of October [1492], that Columbus first beheld the new world. . . . [The inhabitants] were perfectly naked, and, as they stood gazing at the ships, appeared by their attitudes and gestures to be lost in astonishment. . . . On landing Columbus threw himself on his knees, kissed the earth, and returned thanks to God with tears of joy. . . . Columbus then rising drew his sword, displayed the royal standard, and assembling round him the two captains, with Rodrigo de Escobedo, notary of the armament, Rodrigo Sanchez, and the rest who had landed, he took solemn possession in the name of the Castilian sovereigns, giving the island the name of San Salvador.[45]

Since conquistadores are infatuated with extensions of themselves through conquest, they fittingly kiss the dirt, dismember the narrator, and ultimately one another. They have lost, or perhaps they never had, any sense of peaceful coexistence. With warfare not love they propagate themselves, as if collective rape were their only hope for self-replication:

"Wherever their blood was spilt new versions of themselves grew up. It was in this way that they multiplied, by spilling blood over the earth itself" (pp. 81–82). Even before colonizers' in-fighting, Ovando's reputation among fellow Europeans was harsh. In Washington Irving's words: "He appears to have been plausible and subtle, as well as fluent and courteous, his humility to have covered a great love of command and in his transactions with Columbus, he was certainly both ungenerous and unjust."[46]

Thus Jamaica Kincaid explodes an important colonial myth that early invaders enjoy their spoils in an undiluted way. She pictures colonizers living in "that part of the night where all suffering dwells, even death." Their bodies are covered with sores bred of injustice, imaging isolation and presumably a kind of suppurating inhumanity, a particular disease contracted by colonizers. Ovando is left with no one to make love to but himself. He is a beast of prey that repels and puts people on their guard.

Ovando is not permitted to lie on an object as sacred (to many) as nails: "He lay in a bed of broken glass bottles (not nails)." For some, a purifying mystical element signifying power, resistance, patience, and endurance inheres in a bed of nails. Nails that Eastern Yogis lie on cannot be crushed. Instead, Ovando lies on glass and mirrors. His barbarity comes full circle on the bed of broken glass bottles he lies on, for he is effectively lying on himself, on a form of advanced technology. Kincaid might also be wryly hinting at the old communication of shipwrecked people with messages in glass bottles since Ovando has broken even desperate and odd forms of communication. Through his own force, he crushes down on these shards, on pain of his own making, finally obliterating himself. He has occluded his own humanity.

The narrator's last position is embedded in conflict. On the one hand, despite the squalor negatively exercised on a people by the invader's actions, the narrator's tender response signifies that vice cannot last. Her sense of community and her human love may be unusable tools for the time being, but the world cannot endlessly self-destruct. Thus the respective visions of the colonizer and the colonized implicitly contain the tools of retaliation. On the other hand, although the narrator's response to usurpation wins out, as a representative of all colonized people she pays a heavy historical price for tolerance and contemplation. An inner resourcefulness unknown to the colonizer may buoy her up, but such personal harmony does not last. Over centuries, it may surface only rarely. "Ovando" points out the complexity of regaining independence. How can the leap to self-rule be effected, be executed by and on behalf of the (representative) narrator? The people who try to implement self-rule are those who have adopted the mimicking strategies of colonizers and have endured. They have lived their lives in the knowledge that a death-dealing force assaulted their world. This force has to be removed, the instruments of domination dismantled, and the people who remain behind have to negotiate through a corrupt colonial legacy to a postcolonial process that inevitably attracts and begets corruption.[47]

Once again, *A Small Place* comes into focus. In that polemic, the narrator complains that formerly colonized people live from day to day and rarely try to change their situation. They are happy to read the contents of the principal colonial library even if half of the books are in quasi-permanent storage and the other half falsify events. At some level, intertextualizes Kincaid, Antiguan people in *A Small Place* are intertextualized as Ovando's political legatees.

The damage of imperialism, both narratives argue, may be somewhat reversible but it is never fully so. Over centuries most wounds heal slowly, but some never do. In the last instance, historical memory and a sense of cultural location remain.

In the ultimate confrontation, Ovando's narcissism confronts the narrator's discernment and exhaustion. His self-love is compared to a worm, an image that surfaced two pages earlier when Ovando is described as a ground worm without ears. Worst of all, this worm is described as asleep in every living person. Everyone is affected by Ovando's presence that resembles an infectious, incurable disease. Ovando is a parasite living off a host, his overweening self-love an uninvited intruder who distresses the global body politic. Wormlike, he is the slimy, supine invertebrate who has insinuated himself into a people's land to wreak devastation.[48] He is the inversion of the narrator who, in her response to his depredations, claims agency. For a while, this body yoked together in segments can maintain itself, can even split apart and live. And like worms, his "relatives" do endlessly regrow and regenerate. But eventually that sick body dies if the host refuses it.

This plural image of a wormlike Ovando becomes a privileged signifier for colonialism's consequences. Metaphorically, certain well-known facts about worms attach to Ovando and his kind. In terms of feeding habits, worms are scavengers in dirt and mud. And while they feed parasitically, expropriating others' natural resources, they also attack themselves internally or feed on their hosts. Since they have unprotected bodies, moreover, they live in dark concealed places, afraid of life and light. However, their physiognomy in the form of musculature (the colonialist's highly developed technology) allows them to slither in and out whenever they want, with "alternate push and pull movements of creeping, looping, and crawling."[49] Notably, too, they harbor an exhaustive range of physiognomical tolerance.[50] Their reproduction is both asexual (vegetative) as well as sexual, and their life span varies from twenty-seven years (the medicinal leech) to the six years of the common earthworm.[51]

Another feature of worms — their bilateral symmetry — applies to Ovando's so-called relatives; they may be from all over Europe but they are virtually identical. Worms, moreover, are found everywhere — hence there is a worm in every heart — "from the highest mountains to the greatest ocean depths."[52]

In her final adversarial speech, the narrator is ill and incoherent because these worms have partly eaten her away. Her land has been infested and is worn out. Nonetheless worms can be caught, and, more to the point, they can die of their own nature. Ovando multiplies through cutting himself when he is alive and ends up, as a perverse consequence, bleeding to death; he has become so greedy that he has cut himself into too many pieces. Despite being torn apart by Ovando and his relatives — the different segments — the narrator refuses such a groveling subject position. Instead, against severe odds, the narrator retains her humanity just as Ovando's inhumanity poisons him. At the end, in a complex act of self-preservation and validation that recognizes her debt to the colonized as well as herself, the narrator refuses to coddle Ovando's self-pity. She ceases to warn him of (the consequences of) his crimes. She stands apart and mimics him no longer. If anything, she uses him. Ovando has helped to locate a new cultural identity, namely, the speaker's status as an oppositional agent who resists. Thus she stands in two places at once. "Ovando" marks the narrator's "becoming" because, try as he might, he can neither expropriate her identity nor silence her voice.[53]

A subaltern text, "Ovando" is a combination of hardcore political history, a polemic against colonialism and the displacement of Amerindian people, a supernatural tale, and an oblique commentary on mother-daughter bonding. "Ovando" looks backward to *At the Bottom of the River* in its subtly inflected anticolonialism, to *Annie John* and *Lucy* with their multiple allusions to the ravages of invasion, and most of all to *A Small Place* in which anticolonial excoriation is unequivocal. Like *A Small Place*, "Ovando" adds a crucial political dimension to the loosely constructed bildungsroman, only this time, Kincaid returns the reader to historical rather than biological origins.

"Ovando" also introduces a more personal dimension. First, Jamaica Kincaid states several times that the feelings in texts she writes — though not necessarily their specific chronology — are autobiographical.[54] When she began "Ovando," she wanted to explore that precarious and tyrannical relationship between the colonizer and the colonized as well as intersect that history with her personal heritage. She intended, she says, to write a "grand work about the question of dominion."[55]

Second, Kincaid talks of the effect of sun, light, and obeah in her life. In terms of the narrator's statement in "Ovando" that the Indians could have overcome the Europeans, she indirectly responds: "[we need] to postulate that there is another reality over which we, in our modernity, have no control — and certainly of which we know very little, because we're too scientific."[56] She stresses the importance "of not believing what I saw, of really not being deceived by appearances."[57]

Obeah — she states as a case in point — "seemed to happen in the dark and be part of darkness." Thus light became important in clarifying how things looked: "This was false and this was right. I think it was my obsession."[58] On the other hand, the sun does not always signal positively: "But the sun is almost hellish, really. Sometimes it would turn from something wonderful, the light of the sun, into a kind of hell."[59] Kincaid's comments on light and dark affirm her pervasive though nuanced assertions that material reality can change, given variant historical circumstances. Nothing is fixed.

Third, in "Ovando" Kincaid draws on the fact that her Dominican grandmother is a Carib, Caribs constituting a historical pivot in the text. Her mother's parents, her crucial Amerindian ancestral influence, were land peasants in Dominica. In an early essay, "Antigua Crossings: A Deep and Blue Passage on the Caribbean Sea," Kincaid explores the connection between her indictment of Spanish colonialism in "Ovando" and her grandmother: "I know this because my grandmother is a Carib Indian. She is very tall and very dark and very fierce looking. . . . I have seen the way she hunts agouti and I know that she has not forgotten the history of her ancestors and it makes me glad."[60] Kincaid knows these facts — she states — because they have been orally handed down. On another occasion, she asserts of her grandmother: She "was an *obeah* woman, perhaps not on the Haitian scale — they are very different — but she did believe in spirits." . . . If I were a person who did compare [Christianity and native religion], I would obviously choose my grand-mother's original religion because, to be quite frank, my grandmother's religion committed no crime against humanity. . . . She felt her beliefs would have saved [Jamaica Kincaid's uncle], and he [her husband] felt that his beliefs — his beliefs being faith in God and Western medicine — would have saved him. Well, it turns out that his illness was of a type that my grandmother's beliefs would have cured."[61] When Kincaid wrote this section on Caribs in "Antigua Crossings," she was incensed, she told one critic, about the conquista and what had transpired. She read ethno-centric histories. She volunteered to fathom this colonizing mentality and follow their fictional version of events.[62] In the following passage, Kincaid figuratively explains her reaction to genocide:

> The other insight I have into history is that it's a bit like musical chairs. When the music stops some people are standing up and some people are sitting down, but at any moment you don't know if you will be among the stand-ups or the sit-downs. I feel as though if I am among people sitting down I always will identify with the people who are standing up — that my knowledge of my history tells me that I have to always make room on the chair for the people standing up. In writing "Ovando," I was trying to understand how for some people who found themselves sitting down it would become important to try to remove the apparatus for the game to continue — so that they would never again be standing up.[63]

In an interview on National Public Radio, Kincaid further explained her desire to recapitulate the etiology of oppression, her vision of events through a variant lens. To be a recorder of people's history is a matter of survival for her, a way of preserving wholeness: "No matter what you have it's just very difficult to live. But in my case, I was born into certain realities that if I weren't angry I should have been placed in an insane asylum just because I wasn't angry."[64] Her art also empowers her: "By the transforming powers of the imagination, what appears to have been irretrievably lost may be recuperated—indeed in the very energy involved in violent and destructive acts reside the seeds of creativity."[65]

Jamaica Kincaid's earlier texts are informed by concerns that "Ovando" most overtly expresses. In that sense, "Ovando" is an anchor text. In response to a question that her work "strike[s] at the physical core of the entire Americas," Kincaid replies that at one point in her life "I never knew whether the ground would hold, whether the thing next to me was real or not."[66]

However, she admits that she could not finish "Ovando" until she learned more about the explorers-invaders. "I need to be older."[67] Thus the end of "Ovando" remains untold for the time being. She had more ideas about colonialism—she hints—than her short story could contain. Perhaps that explains why she said in a recent interview that she had begun to write on British colonialism, a future project that might well take up where "Ovando" left off: "I'm just about to get to this in my own fiction, this commodification of relationships. The commodifying of things is what I wanted to discuss in 'Ovando.'"[68] Nonetheless, while Kincaid can enjoy the spirit of adventure that these explorers display—"it had an individual element that was admirable and surprising"—their end and means wildly collided to the detriment of native peoples. This, understandably, she can neither forgive nor forget. Kincaid's historical pronouncement on the eve of Christopher Columbus's quincentenary directly confronts the celebrations that highlight his rediscovery of the Americas. "Ovando" foregrounds a crucial and highly problematized dimension in all her texts: "By the time they made their discoveries, everything admirable about them becomes lost."[69] Quod erat demonstrandum.

This intensity of textual-political oppositions has undergone drastic change. At the end of *At the Bottom of the River,* the man who measured—possibly the narrator's father—metonymically signed colonial expropriation. By "Ovando," written seven years later, the one who thinks in a unitary way, who measures how much of the globe he possesses, is the

heinous protagonist, Ovando. Measurement has become a primary signifier of intervention and theft. And the debate no longer exercises a
fluid, visionary dimension; it has become much more concrete, albeit
couched in magic terms. Where before variant voices embodying different roles and subjectivities internally debated diverse ways of thinking, now a female narrator represents colonized peoples unambiguously.
The narrator's inner turmoil remains, but opposition is now external-
ized. Nonetheless, she still thinks of the world as continuous; past, present, and future life is a whole in which she and all those whom she
represents participate. She still dwells in (on) the possibility of harmony.

Unlike *At the Bottom of the River*, the narrator no longer has to imagine
what the world is like since Ovando relentlessly unveils imperial reality.
This evidence forces her to face the powerlessness of living life without
choice; but shutting off choice paradoxically engenders choice, if only in
the realization that emotional and political possibilities exist. Ovando,
then, revisions origins. In *At the Bottom,* the narrator imagines herself
in a pre-bang world where she lives in a primordial state, before "the
green . . . was . . . the green from which all other greens might come."[70]
The woman [the narrator] discerns is one whose instep was high "as if
she had been used to climbing high mountains . . . like a statue . . . just
before it is to be put in a kiln."[71] That vision slowly dissolves throughout
the intervening texts. By "Ovando," via the plural experiences of protagonists in *Annie John, A Small Place,* and *Lucy,* the composite narrator
knows — without having to state it explicitly — that this vision is little
more than idyllic illusion.

However, connecting Kincaid's texts is not to imply that a unitary
meaning can be elicited or that one exists. To do so would be to fall into
the trap of the carpenter. The fact that the surreal, epiphanic vision of *At
the Bottom of the River* dissolves into Lucy's more pragmatic appraisal of
her world in North America is a function of respective environments and
relative perceptions. The vision may be illusory, but it still exists as a
possibility.

Ovando and his relatives do their best to obliterate indigenous culture. In the process, the vision is temporarily transformed into a nightmare that closes off many of life's options and chops the green away; it
kills the vital woman with the high bouncing instep. But hope is always
there to inflect potential despair.

Furthermore, by combining magic and realism, myth and supernaturalism with material existence, Kincaid asserts that multiple worlds exist. At least two logical codes function in an egalitarian way, without hierarchization: One fits the colonizer's distorted mentality and the other derives from countries and peoples who live by obeah. With these connections, the narrator reaffirms the importance of female ways since obeah tends to be associated with women.

By working magic, by shifting and reshifting readers' customary perspectives, Jamaica Kincaid accentuates the continuity of colonialism. The narrator's magical vision contrasts with Ovando's politics of linearity and ends-and-means thinking; she underlines the certainty that the institution is a ubiquitous, transhistorical phenomenon, its testimony human ravishment itself. The practice of obeah enables people to acquire a finer understanding of Ovando's reality for it penetrates his mystifying, supposedly practical outlook.

Invoking cultural roles and modes of perception that confront the conventional order also emphasizes ideological tensions between the narrator and Ovando. Magic offers a world that does not depend only on materiality. So does "temporal telescoping."[72] Power manifests itself in different ways, with magic encoded as a form of indigenous people's power.

In the end, the disjunction between Ovando's boasts and his pathetic physical nature closes. His force is subverted — it could not staunch people's time-honored culture: "In the face of what the conquistadores, the Creole oligarchs, and the imperialists and their flunkies have attempted, our culture — taking this term in its broad historical and anthropological sense — has been in a constant process of formulation: our authentic culture, the culture created by the mestizo populace, those descendants of Indians and blacks and Europeans."[73] Put slightly differently, "Ovando" draws attention to the creative continuum of African-Caribbean culture in the face of historical violence and discontinuities.[74]

Jamaica Kincaid makes Ovando (colonialism) accountable to all agendas: to private and public matters, to race, class, and gender issues. The greedy colonizer lying on his broken (glass) dreams, epitomizing disenablement and finiteness fits well into a conventional white iconography of acquisition. Thus Jamaica Kincaid mythically subverts imperial incursion and dissolves (or grinds into the dirt along with the glass fragments) the privileged signifier of whiteness. Countermemory is one of her weapons. So is acceptance of the fact that realpolitik is saturating her environment and must be transformed. The continuum of Kincaid's texts constitutes one dimension of this crucial countermemory fused with a personal saga. These interventions, her collective texts argue, articulate an indispensable element of struggle.

Conclusion

Like other Black women for whom writing is both an act of liberation and salvation, Kincaid says she writes to save her life — that if she couldn't write, she would be one of those people who throw bombs, who spout revolution, who would surely be in jail or perhaps even dead. Or maybe just insane.
—*Essence*, 1991

The people of the West Indies have never felt that country belonged to them. They do not feel responsible for it. Something happens, and they get something, and something doesn't happen and they don't get what they expect: so somebody else promises that he will get it for them — that is how they live and that is how they have been living for a hundred years.—C. L. R. James

✪ To CONVEY A world unhinged by conquistadorian greed and its aftermath, Jamaica Kincaid writes about growing up on an island in the Caribbean and leaving it, all the while exploring the formation of personal and political identity.

A narrator in multiple guises and in generically diverse texts travels back through historical epochs to the beginning of known communities in Antigua and Hispaniola, and then lands in contemporary New York and indeterminate regions. A composite character, she is first a black Antiguan nine-year-old, then an adolescent, and later an adult. She is also an Amerindian. Semiautobiographical, sometimes inchoate accounts of life, death, and contestation in *At the Bottom of the River, Annie John,* and *Lucy* play off in *Annie, Gwen, Lilly, Pam and Tulip,* "Ovando," and *A Small Place* against a wider context of past, present, and future struggles in precolonial and Amerindian communities and black and white Antiguan communities.

Jamaica Kincaid's texts constitute a continuous and evolving narrative—what I have loosely called a bildungsroman—of a plural, multivocal, precolonial, colonial, and postcolonial female subjectivity by a postcolonial writer. These texts, that is, constitute an ongoing, checkered saga about colonial origins, the construction and interrogation of personal-political identity, and the conditions of possibility in psychic and material life. Together, the fictional and nonfictional narratives represent the formation of colonial and postcolonial subjectivities. In Trinh T. Minh-Ha's words, "Autobiographical strategies offer another example of ways of breaking with the chain of invisibility."¹ Narrative itself, furthermore, tells the history as well as marking the connections among narrative, history, and the writer's distant though resistant stance throughout.² Diverse protagonists eventually claim marginality as a badge of honor. More specifically, in *At the Bottom of the River* the narrator probes her relation to externality, trying to fathom her ontological status. In *Annie, Gwen, Lilly, Pam and Tulip,* she tries to recuperate a sense of life before and on the brink of intervention. Moreover, if *At the Bottom* introduces the first section of a personal-political bildungsroman, then *Annie John* constitutes its adolescent dimension. Annie John tries to work through her adolescent feelings, how relationships coexist, how they falter, disappear, and reappear in a refashioned form. She learns and teaches herself to cope.

Coterminous with her investigation of how gender is implicated in the formation of the female subject are Kincaid's formulations of motherhood and colonialism—a doubled negotiation. In *Annie John,* Jamaica Kincaid parallels the fictional daughter's ire at her mother with her anger at Christopher Columbus; she inflects daughterly domestic rage with fury at metropolitan expropriation. Biological motherhood is a mise en abyme that conveys the diatribe against colonialism. Muted yet subtly present in *At the Bottom*—more so in *Annie, Gwen, Lilly, Pam and Tulip*—anticolonial resistance provides Annie John with inner security and a public identity, not dissimilar to her mother's identity (we later learn in *A Small Place*) as a historical troublemaker.

For Jamaica Kincaid this choice of a semiautobiographical mode, at both personal and political levels, amounts to an act of self-exorcism, an avowal of what signs her cultural integrity. Jamaica Kincaid puts it this way: "I'm clearly the kind of writer interested in the autobiographical for [use in] fiction and nonfiction,"[3] and she further adds: "I would say that everything in *Annie John* happened — every feeling in it happened — but not necessarily in the order they appear. But it very much expresses the life I had. There isn't anything in it that is a lie, I would say. [I choose to write fiction over autobiography] because autobiography is the truth and fiction is, well, fiction."[4] Put another way, Jamaica Kincaid is, in her own words, "really interested in breaking the form."[5] In several texts, she presents discursive alternatives to a Western linear modality, a decolonizing style that is attuned to realpolitik.

In *A Small Place,* which doubles as an anticolonial, postcolonial polemic, Kincaid temporarily abandons the facade of fiction while at the same time recognizing that polemic can rarely be unmediated chronicle. In that polemic, the concentration on mother-daughter relationships that characterized sections of *At the Bottom* and *Annie John* has shifted to explicit assault on a colonial mother or motherhood. *A Small Place* attacks a dual foe–false friend of the majority — British colonialism and the present Antiguan government that ushered the island into a partially independent existence in 1967 and then full independence in 1981. An incensed daughter-speaker draws these two "motherhoods" together to explicate the consequences of colonialism on people's past and present lives. One of Kincaid's own statements underscores this nuanced use of maternal linkages: "I identified [maternal] restrictiveness with the restrictiveness of my surroundings."[6] *A Small Place* is part three of this ongoing story that now plays itself out against a broader historical and more explicitly political canvas.

The movement from *A Small Place* to *Lucy* is circumlocuitous. In a poetic, though seemingly conventional novel, Kincaid traces the next segment in the life of a young African-Caribbean woman. *Lucy* narrates the tale of self-imposed exile mediated through Lucy's growing awareness of her configuration as the other in the professional and artistic postcolonial milieus she frequents. The voice and sensibility of earlier narrators resonate in Lucy herself while the dialectic of conquest and contestation of *A Small Place* manifests itself. Additionally, the slippage of mother from one potent referent to another is particularly striking in *Lucy,* where the effects of postcolonial attitudes and Lucy's sense of retribution are at their most diaphanous. Hence Lucy's use of the camera, her stalwart decision to reverse the colonial (coded as maternal) gaze. She wants her turn at framing life.

Even in *Lucy*, too, the text that most closely resembles a mainstream novel, blanks in the chronicle resonate. The author, Kincaid intimates, is a questionable author-ity. Abandoning orthodox mimetic claims, Kincaid fictionally speculates on how events might have gone, how lives might have been diversely experienced, why people ambiguously reacted, how temporary solutions were reached.

This reading of multiple mothers clarifies what has never quite added up in Kincaid's texts as a whole: her love for her mother and brothers (*At the Bottom of the River* and *A Small Place* are dedicated to them) compared to the fury she collectively vents over these family members — indirectly as well as frontally. The love-hate ambiguity permeates the texts because Kincaid uses mother and brother as crucial discursive markers in a sometimes veiled, often overt anticolonial discourse.

By mapping *At the Bottom of the River, Annie John,* and *A Small Place* onto the terrain of *Lucy*, thereby concretizing cultural differences between Antigua and the United States, *Lucy*, furthermore, functions as a limit text. It establishes certain boundaries yet allows earlier texts to expand within them.

Hence Lucy's confession to Mariah about hating the advent of her brothers links not only to *At the Bottom, Annie John,* and *A Small Place,* but also to fears of unknown predators expressed symbolically by Annie, Gwen, Lilly, Pam, and Tulip and the Amerindian speaker's contestation with the arrogant conquistador Ovando, who arrives without invitation. Ovando slides into the role of Annie John's brothers, as well as the present Antiguan government; he comes equipped with many lethal disguises. Collectively, these and other males are precolonial, colonial, and postcolonial aggressors — first of Amerindian people and then of kidnapped peoples from the African continent. Lucy's maturation as a female and her evolution as a resistant postcolonial subject start coalescing.

"Ovando" ponders the cultural link in Kincaid's loosely connected diasporic bildungsroman. Resembling Annie, Gwen, Lilly, Pam, and Tulip, the speaker is an Amerindian, in tribute not only to aboriginal peoples but to Kincaid's family ancestors. Taken as a whole, then, Kincaid's texts are part of the process of historical reclamation. She perpetuates what Wilson Harris has called "the great chain of memory or being."[7] By highlighting the continuity of obeah and the ubiquity of Christopher Columbus as iconic signifier, she affirms a constant transhistorical opposition to the entrepreneurs of cultural imperialism. She marks the importance of relocating or, better still, displacing an Anglosupremacist historical vision in favor of one that is Carib-centric. In that sense, she embraces the border: "that space of refusal where one [who] can say no to the colonizer, no to the downpressor, is located in the margins."[8] Even Kincaid's chosen name — Jamaica — stresses that embrace of the Caribbean region, a sense of her voice as representative.

Time is important too. In "Ovando," the future is present because events in Hispaniola have already taken place in the 1790s whereas in *A Small Place,* the present merges with the past; historical corruption fuses with its latter-day counterpart. The conquistadorian mission provoked an unprecedented and triumphant revolution of slaves.[9] Hence the present is also the past and no one can escape antecedents. "Ovando" also commemorates the authenticity of a precolonial Indian cultural legacy. The future continues always in reference to the past. She problematizes the colonial category of law, right, anachronistic claims, and sovereignty, offering new vantage points, new critical paradigms that censure passivity. She holds marking time in contempt. A recorder of the people's history, Jamaica Kincaid affirms creativity as a combative weapon and a survival tool. Textual conclusions, that is, posit suggestive interventions for the postcolonial project. During a surreal transformation, the narrator of *At the Bottom* finds a pen at the end. The collective narrators of *Annie, Gwen, Lilly, Pam and Tulip* slowly and deliberately name themselves. In the ship, as the water releases, Annie John metaphorically births herself, by herself, into a new world. Motherhood and birthing are always bifurcated concepts. Quests enhance personal healing.

At a different level, *A Small Place* applauds agency and the voicing of resistance whereas Lucy comes to cherish solitude and self-sufficiency, capitalizing on experiences she formerly scorned. Lucy also reaches for writing materials, but now the water of the Caribbean, one of the key metonyms for life and growing up in *At the Bottom* and *Annie John* is integrated and coincides with other vital elements, blood and milk. At the end Lucy names herself, but the words blur, unlike the careful, precolonial enunciation of names by Annie, Gwen, Lilly, Pam, and Tulip, who claim themselves clearly and openly before intervention. The imperial mission makes the difference. Accompanied symbolically by the other protagonists, Lucy is still confronting Ovando's devastation.

Memories enter largely into Kincaid's elaborations of a worldwide, centuries-long scenario. By relying on memory that can always be rewritten and hence can also be faulty, she underscores the existence of a host of perspectives, questioning notions of absolute meaning or epistemological certainty; collectively the texts refuse a Cartesian, hegemonic modality, relying on nuance, inner resonance, reverie, self-reflection, and heterogeneous utterance to convey meaning. There is no normative archimedean point for political critique.[10] Unitary thinking is stillborn in these texts that acknowledge, too, some personal harmony, a healthy embrace of life. Thus Kincaid draws back from definitive closures, preferring not to conclude. Since all events have already happened — she argues — they are always in the process of being rescripted. Ends and beginnings continually merge and overlap but always with a sense that the imperial project constantly induces discontinuity and change.

Jamaica Kincaid's texts — as central trajectory — represent the articulation by a postcolonial artist of popular struggle, with Kincaid's voice as an Antiguan "organic" intellectual sounding the cultural void.[11] Collectively, her texts are part of the discourse — in Ranajit Guha's phrase — of opposition and counterknowledge; they project a transformed vision that privileges the former outsider.[12] Only through time and by dint of collective political acts — Kincaid's texts suggest — will popular victories erupt. The days of marauding tourists — metonymic for hostile external-internal forces — are numbered. Through multiple interventions in fiction and semiautobiography that document public lives and events in Antigua, Kincaid chronicles a minisaga of that island in all its unfolding complexity. She puts a new fast spin on social critique, reminding us that received patterns of events do not tell the whole story.

Given that Jamaica Kincaid is currently working on a project that discusses gardens as bountiful symbols of a ruthless colonial expropriation — Dutch tulips is one splendid example — this powerful counter-hegemonic discourse promises to continue.[13]

Notes

Bibliography

Index

Notes

INTRODUCTION

1. Morris and Dunn, " 'The Bloodstream of Our Inheritance,' " p. 219.

2. For a series of discussions on this issue, see Karen R. Lawrence, *Decolonizing Tradition.*

3. Hooks, *Yearning.*

4. Wilentz, "English Is a Foreign Anguish," p. 266.

5. Hall discusses the issue of cultural location and difference in "Cultural Identity and Cinematic Representation," pp. 68–81.

6. For the importance of seizing the means of communication and naming, see particularly Ashcroft, Griffiths, and Tiffin, *The Empire Writes Back,* pp. 79 ff.

7. Nasta, *Motherlands,* p. 219.

8. Fanon, *The Wretched of the Earth,* p. 247. In terms of the historical framework out of which contemporary Antiguans write, see, for a brief summary that encompasses political resistance, Murdoch, "Severing the (M)other Connection," pp. 326–27.

9. Minh-Ha, *When the Moon Waxes Red,* pp. 232–33.

10. Ibid., p. 233.

11. See Elliott, *Imperial Spain,* p. 51.

12. Minh-ha, *When the Moon Waxes Red,* p. 36.

13. Katrak, "Decolonizing Culture," pp. 161–62.

14. Minh-ha, *When the Moon Waxes Red,* p. 14.

CHAPTER 1

1. Perry, "Interview" with Jamaica Kincaid," pp. 698–99. The setting of *At the Bottom of the River* is the island of Antigua, where Jamaica Kincaid was born, a geographical and physical reality that constantly serves as contextual backdrop.

2. Kingsley, *The Water-Babies,* especially pp. 3–31.

3. Bachelard, *Water and Dreams,* pp. 11, 194.

4. Kingsley, *The Water-Babies,* p. 10.

5. Jamaica Kincaid, *A Small Place,* p. 29. See the Garis interview, "Through West Indian Eyes." For West Indian commentary, see, for example, Morris and Dunn, "'The Bloodstream of Our Inheritance.'"

6. Said, "Figures, Configurations, Transfigurations," p. 6. See also Ashcroft, Griffiths, and Tiffin, *The Empire Strikes Back,* pp. 152–54.

7. I thank Robert Haller for a valuable discussion of this and other hymns and scriptural points. Jamaica Kincaid notes also that each morning, as a schoolgirl, she began classes with "All Things Bright and Beautiful" (*New Yorker,* October 14, 1977, p. 27). She has also recently stated that it was the first hymn in her Methodist children's hymnal (ibid., March 29, 1993, p. 51). For information about the author of "All Things," Cecil Frances Humphreys Alexander, see Moffatt and Patrick, *Handbook to the Church Hymnary with Supplement,* especially pp. 9, 249–50. For allied information, see Routley, *An English-Speaking Hymnal Guide.* See also North, *The Psalms and Hymns of Protestantism,* pp. 3–12, and Reuel K. Wilson, "The Letters of Bruno Schulz, Jerzy Stempowski, and Especially Julian Tuwim," p. 246.

8. Robert Evans Snodgrass, *The Thorax of Insects and the Articulation of the Wings,* pp. 511–83; see also Snodgrass, *A Contribution toward an Encyclopedia of Insect Anatomy,* in *Smithsonian Miscellaneous Collections* 146, no. 2 (Washington, D.C.: Smithsonian Institution, July 12, 1963): 29–31; and *Insect Ultrastructure,* ed. Robert C. King and Hiromu Akai (New York and London: Plenum Press, 1984), pp. 35, 117, 492.

9. Dutton, "Merge and Separate," p. 409. See also "An Interview with Bruno Schulz," pp. 145–47.

10. Dutton, "Merge and Separate," p. 409.

11. Bachelard, *Water and Dreams,* pp. 109, 110.

12. The history of British rule in Antigua is a history of corruption. The neglect of the island can be seen to this day in the irregular and dangerous pavements and lack of lighting in the streets at night. There is still no adequate sewage system, another legacy from British colonial times, when there was none at all. See *The Revitalization of Downtown Saint John's, Antigua and Barbuda.* For John Bull and its association with English values, see Arbuthnot, *The History of John Bull.*

13. Castle, *Masquerade and Civilization.*

14. Cudjoe, "Interview with Jamaica Kincaid," pp. 396–411.

15. Hints of obeah emerge here. The author speaks of it in her "Antigua Crossings," p. 48. See also Ismond, "Jamaica Kincaid," pp. 336–41. See also Dutton, "Merge and Separate." Ramchand's view of the orality of this passage is riveting in his *The West Indian Novel and Its Background,* p. 110.

16. Bachelard, *Water and Dreams,* p. 109.

17. Joseph, "Black Mothers and Daughters: Traditional and New Perspectives," p. 99. There are several important analyses and commentaries on mother-

daughter relationships that have a bearing here. Among them are Murdoch, "Severing the (M)other Connection," pp. 328–29; *Daughters of the Nightmare,* a report "compiled from a number of recent sources," pp. 7–9; Davies, "Mothering and Healing in Recent Black Women's Fiction," p. 43; and Giddings, *When and Where I Enter,* pp. 47–55. For the view that females are more bonded to their mothers and hence would resent separation more than males, see Chodorow, *The Reproduction of Mothering.*

18. Anna Freud, *The Ego and the Mechanisms of Defense,* pp. 43–53, 101–5. See also Joseph, "Black Mothers and Daughters: Their Roles and Functions in American Society," pp. 75–126.

19. See Davies and Fido, *Out of the Kumbla,* p. 4. Additionally, for a rich probing of *At the Bottom of the River* in general, see Davies, "Writing Home," especially pp. 64–68.

20. Ferguson, "Interview with Jamaica Kincaid."

21. Note, too, how Bachelard associates blackbirds with water (*Water and Dreams,* p. 193).

22. In *Lucy,* the veiled suggestion of attempted abortion(s) is explicitly made: "She was pregnant with the last of her children. She did not want to be pregnant and three times had tried to throw away the child, but all her methods had failed and she remained pregnant" (p. 151).

23. Bachelard, *Water and Dreams,* p. 116.

24. The role that the monkey plays in Caribbean culture as a trickster is important here. I thank Robert Antoni for a conversation on this point. For the monkey as trickster and related issues, see Abrahams, *The Man-of-Words in the West Indies,* pp. 153 ff. and 178 ff. See also Dance, *Folklore from Contemporary Jamaicans,* pp. xix–xxv, 11–12, 16–17, and 23–26. As racist tropes for Africans, monkeys always have an identity in flux. In eighteenth-century England, monkeys appear in texts emblematic of foreigners. In 1713, moreover, among countless examples, Sir Richard Blackmore spoke of the great chain of being as follows: "So the Ape or Monkey, that bears the greatest Similitude to Man, is the next Order of Animals below him. Nor is the Disagreement between the basest Individuals of our Species and the Ape or Monkey so great, but that were the latter endowed with the Faculty of Speech, they might perhaps as justly claim the Rank and Dignity of the human Race, as the Savage *Hottentot,* or stupid Native of *Nova Zembla.*"

Jordan goes on to argue: "It is apparent, however unpalatable the apparency may be, that certain superficial physical characteristics in the West African Negro helped sustain (and perhaps helped initiate) the popular connection with the ape. By the latter part of the century, Bryan Edwards, a thoroughly good-hearted man, thought it necessary to discuss the apparent resemblance in the Ibo tribe" (*White over Black,* p. 237).

25. Hutcheon, *Narcissistic Narrative,* p. 7.

26. For a discussion of lizards and imagery, see Pope, *The Reptile World,* pp. 235–321. This fantasy finds resonances in Caribbean mythology. It inter-

sects with the dream of couvade, the subject of a story by Wilson Harris in which the purpose of the dream and its invocation of lizards is to pass on history and legacy to newborn children. See Harris, *The Sleepers of Roraima*. For further information about reptilian qualities in mothers, see Cartey *Whispers from the Caribbean*, p. 16.

27. LaPlanche and Pontalis, *The Language of Psycho-Analysis*, pp. 349–57.

28. See Ismond, "Jamaica Kincaid," p. 341.

29. In this episode, different pieces of Hindu mythology and other unique imaginings play themselves out. How the mother acts is very different from traditional practices of maternal suicide. See Sahi, *The Child and the Serpent*, pp. 153–56. See also Bailey, *The Mythology of Brahma*, p. 115. For the shedding of the epidermis, see "An Interview with Bruno Schulz," p. 146; see also Holland, *Popular Hinduism and Hindu Mythology* and Kinsley, *Hinduism*, especially pp. 82–91.

30. For this issue of merge and separate in Caribbean texts, see Ramchand, *The West Indian Novel and Its Background*, p. 109.

31. See Minh-Ha, *When the Moon Waxes Red*, p. 14; Jacobus, "The Difference of View," p. 51. See also Kristeva, *Revolution in Poetic Language*, pp. 102–3.

32. A haunting echo exists here of Nadine Gordimer, "A Lion on the Freeway," a story that Kincaid found influential. See Cudjoe, "An Interview with Jamaica Kincaid," p. 403. By implication, Jamaica Kincaid intertextualizes an attack on racism here through oblique reference to the antiapartheid stand in that story. See her *A Soldier's Embrace*, pp. 24–27. For a riveting postmodern interpretation of "Blackness" and "Wingless," see Covi, "Jamaica Kincaid and the Resistance to the Canons," p. 348.

33. Ehrenzweig, *The Order of Art*, p. 121.

34. Said, "Figures, Configurations, Transformations," p. 13. For a view of the last chapter as a "vision of androgynous existence," see Gilkes, "The Madonna Pool," p. 13.

35. An allusion reverberates here to Jesus' stepfather, Joseph, who was apparently a just but passive man. At the same time, Kincaid may be subtly indicting the fixity of Christianity. For measuring, see the *New Yorker*, January 3, 1983, pp. 23–24. For an expansion of the stepfather's opinions, see the *New Yorker*, July 19, 1976, p. 23. Given Jamaica Kincaid's statements about autobiography, we know that during the experiences of the speaker in *At the Bottom of the River*, Jamaica Kincaid's mother, Annie Richardson Potter, parted from her father, Roderick Potter, and she and David Drew began their relationship. In *At the Bottom*, however, she speaks of the father as if he were her own father. Even so, she probably knew how her own father, Roderick Potter, was incurring her mother's anger by refusing to help with child support.

36. Kloepfer, *The Unspeakable Mother*, p. 21. See also Covi's view, "Jamaica Kincaid and the Resistance to Canons," p. 349.

37. I take this metaphor from a recent movie of that title. So far I have been unable to trace its origin, although running is a traditionally important act in

many tribes, such as the Navajo and the Pawnee. I thank Dan Ladely for a conversation on this point. Cudjoe remarks that "Aimé Césaire utilized the technique of surrealism to plumb the soul of his being to arrive at his original self" (*Resistance and Caribbean Literature*, p. 184).

38. Jamaica Kincaid's short narrative entitled "Annie, Gwen, Lily, Pam and Tulip," published in 1986, makes a slant response — as a complement as well as a contestation — to the narrator's idyllic vision.

39. Note also that Davies brilliantly discusses the house at the bottom of the river as "a trope for her own writer-self [its A-shape] synonymous with the rudiments of writing: the alphabet" ("Writing Home," p. 68).

40. Gardner and Mackenzie, *The Poems of Gerard Manley Hopkins* (London: Oxford Univ. Press, 1967), p. 66.

41. Cixous, "The Laugh of the Medusa," pp. 260, 251; Minh-Ha, *When the Moon Waxes Red*, p. 124.

42. See, for example, Cixous, "The Laugh of the Medusa," pp. 245–64, and Irigaray, "This Sex Which Is Not One," pp. 99–106. See also Kristeva, "My Memory's Hyperbole," p. 221, and Kloepfer, *The Unspeakable Mother*, p. 148.

43. See note 41 and Minh-Ha, *When the Moon Waxes Red*, p. 144.

44. Kloepfer, *The Unspeakable Mother*, p. 21.

45. For the importance of obeah, see Johnson, *The Devil, the Gargoyle, and the Buffoon* and Kincaid, "Antigua Crossings," especially p. 50.

46. Ashcroft, Griffiths, and Tiffin, *The Empire Writes Back*, p. 150.

47. For Bruno Schulz, see, for example, Russel E. Brown, "Bruno Schulz's Sanatorium Story," pp. 35–46. See also Schulz, *The Street of Crocodiles*, and note 29.

48. Jamaica Kincaid repeats the same tropes (the lamb, water in many guises, measuring versus intuiting) as well as wholesale repetitions of sections to throw off the idea that events belong in one specific context. She uses transformations the same way — her mother and herself as lizards, her enactment of a dream in Michigan, her projection of herself as Tom, the nineteenth-century chimney-sweep cum water-baby in a modern incarnation. Note, too, that Bachelard characterizes water as the most maternal and feminine of the alchemical elements (*Water and Dreams*, p. 110). Given a slightly pessimistic view early on in her interviews, Kincaid may be projecting the potential of abyss in the midst of ecstasy.

49. Biographical details from Jamaica Kincaid's life suggest that the experiences in *At the Bottom of the River* take place when the speaker is around nine years old.

50. Hart, *Narrative Magic in the Fiction of Isabel Allende*, p. 21. Note, too, that in the sense that Jamaica Kincaid's texts are open, not closed, they are "parabolic" in Barbara Herrnstein Smith's coinage (*On the Margins of Discourse*, p. 44).

51. Jamaica Kincaid, in a phone conversation with Moira Ferguson, April 17, 1993.

52. Jamaica Kincaid and Eric Fischl, *Annie, Gwen, Lilly, Pam and Tulip*. All references will be to this edition.

53. Lyotard, *The Postmodern Condition*, p. 15.
54. See Tyler, *Two Worlds*, pp. 54–57.
55. Lyotard, *The Postmodern Condition*, p. 21.

C H A P T E R   2

1. Jamaica Kincaid, *Annie John*, p. 29.
2. Chronologically, *Annie John* seems roughly to follow *At the Bottom of the River*. The oldest the narrator appears to be in the first text is nine years old, although exact clues to her specific age are unforthcoming.
3. Jamaica Kincaid talks of resenting her brothers' arrival and presence in several interviews. See, for example, National Public Radio, p. 20, and Edwards, "Jamaica Kincaid Writes of Passage," p. 88.
4. Obeah features widely in Jamaica Kincaid's fictional texts and in her autobiographical interviews. As in many texts of Latin American magic realists, Kincaid features obeah as a way of life, democratically coexistent with otherwise material reality. In an interview with Selwyn Cudjoe, Kincaid explains her feelings toward obeah: "[My grandmother] was an *obeah* woman, perhaps not on the Haitian scale — they are very different — but she did believe in spirits" (p. 406). She also talks of people who gave consultations regarding obeah as "a sort of psychiatrist, someone keeping the unconscious all oiled up" (ibid., p. 409). Obeah is also an alternate mode of knowledge, part and parcel of everyday life, and enables her to ignore "the overbearingness of God from every direction, top and bottom" (ibid., p. 406).

For a discussion of obeah's influence, see also Roberts, *From Trickster to Badman;* Dutton, "Merge and Separate," in which *Annie John* is identified with conjure (or obeah or voodoo); it gives her private power (p. 409). Dutton further makes the point that creative women were accused of obeah. Jamaica Kincaid may be talking about her ancestry. Just as Annie John receives her "freedom" (to be a writer?) from Ma Chess, so Jamaica Kincaid is linked in her creativity from the original Caribbean encounter with colonialists over the centuries to her Caribbean grandmother. She wants to underscore the "survival of African cultures in West Indian secular life" (Ramchand, *The West Indian Novel and Its Background*, p. 123). See Dutton, "Merge and Separate," pp. 405–10; Jamaica Kincaid, "Antigua Crossings," pp. 48–50; Tyler, *Two Worlds*, pp. 53–54. See also Kloepfer, *The Unspeakable Mother*, p. 21; and Grieve, *The Last Years of the English Slave Trade*, p. 156.
5. Cudjoe, "An Interview with Jamaica Kincaid," pp. 397–98.
6. The use of an Anglican hymn that loves and embraces the world and sees it all as God's handiwork adds to the irony of the British-Anglican-colonial intervention in Antigua.
7. Throughout Kincaid's works, water is repeated as a symbol constantly shifting. In this case water associates with distance, travel, and authority. The

recurrence and shifting of the image suggests its power as well as its geographical and physical ubiquity.

8. Kincaid discusses her "real" father (as opposed to the stepfather who appears in most of her texts) in Cudjoe "An Interview with Jamaica Kincaid," p. 399. Drew is the surname of Jamaica Kincaid's stepfather; her mother's birth name is Richardson. See also Murdoch, "Severing the (M)other Connection," p. 328.

9. Bachelard, *Water and Dreams*, p. 120. See DeKoven, *Rich and Strange*, especially pp. 57–63. In regard to the image of the Kumbla and Jamaica Kincaid's eschewal of involvement in a Caribbean tradition, note also that Jamaica Kincaid's anecdotes about the mother's care for her daughter also include stories about what Cobham calls "protective devices used over the years by West Indian women to assure the survival of their children or the progress of the race" (Review, "Getting Out of the Kumbla," p. 34). See also Murdoch, "Severing the (M)other Connection," p. 328.

10. On the other hand, Insanally argues a convincing case a little differently. She contends that the protagonist was reared in a matriarchal society where the father cannot wear unmanly pink shirts. Ultimately, however, the child chooses not to resist established norms ("Sexual Politics in Contemporary Female Writing on the Caribbean," p. 87). The fact that males have more freedom also finds a resonance here. See Murdoch, "Severing the (M)other Connection," p. 328.

11. As a stepfather whom Annie John/Jamaica Kincaid has informally adopted, Annie John's father is not what he seems. He "takes care" of his charges" like British paternalists who are similarly doubleforked. However, there is no indictment of Mr. John, who is presented as a responsible father. He is simply linked at the metonymic level—bogus biological fatherhood and paternalist colonial fathers.

12. Bachelard, *Water and Dreams*, p. 146

13. For another compelling interpretation, see Perry's suggestive use of the trunk as a "suitcase of memories" ("Initiation in Jamaica Kincaid's *Annie John*," p. 248). For a psychoanalytic perspective on the trunk, see also Murdoch, "Severing the (M)other Connection," p. 330.

14. Barbara Christian also explains some of the diverse configurations of mother-daughter relations and the influence of place and time. Insisting on a less dependent maturation for her daughter, the mother refuses to share in any further "ritual of shared womanhood." She feels she should not nurture any longer if her daughter is to survive. Or rather, separation is the desirable form of nurturing at this juncture ("Gloria Naylor's Geography," pp. 357–58). For mimicking, see Bhabha, "Signs Taken for Wonders," pp. 163–84. See also Fanon, *The Wretched of the Earth*, pp. 53–54, and Ramchand, *The West Indian Novel and Its Background*, p. 54. Joseph talks pointedly about this necessity in another context. See "Black Mothers and Daughters: Their Roles and Functions in American Society," p. 106. Annie John's separation from her mother is deftly analyzed in Louis James, "Reflections, and *The Bottom of the River*," p. 68.

15. Cudjoe, "An Interview with Jamaica Kincaid," p. 399.

16. Gilbert and Gubar, *The Madwoman in the Attic,* p. 269. As they argue in a different context, parental sexuality bothers the adolescent child. Her entry into adolescence and the unfamiliar feelings it generates transform the stirrers of these feelings into "alien parents" (ibid.).

17. Through allusive references, Jamaica Kincaid links all her texts, not just the first two, as if the texts constituted a long but discontinuous saga that sometimes had to be retold a different way to be understood. The references to death, absorption, and skeletons in *At the Bottom of the River* and *Annie John* exemplify how richly Kincaid makes her recurring images reverberate.

18. Jamaica Kincaid, *Annie John,* p. 40. See also Warren, "'Mothers for the Empire'" pp. 96–109.

19. Jamaica Kincaid has frequently spoken about the autobiographical component of *Annie John.* In the anecdote about Rat Island, she tenders oblique commentary on her view of autobiography. See Covi, "Jamaica Kincaid and the Resistance to Canons," p. 350.

20. For possible psychological implications of Annie John's intimate relationship with her mother, see Kloepfer, *The Unspeakable Mother,* pp. 19–20.

21. Bachelard, *Water and Dreams,* p. 170. Bachelard argues that terrestrial water is superior to marine water.

22. Jamaica Kincaid locates herself in a Caribbean literary tradition of focusing on the mother-daughter relationship. The examples are numerous, from Merle Hodge, *Crick Crack, Monkey,* to Lorna Goodison, *I am Becoming My Mother,* and, recently, Paule Marshall, *Daughters.* I would further argue that these relationships (*Daughters* is the clearest example) are deeply inflected with and inextricable from an anticolonial dimension. Note also that one critical dimension in the mother-daughter relationship is the fact that Annie John is "a mass of repressed feelings," not only because she wants more love from her mother but because she subtly resents British cultural norms and political misrule (de Abruna, "Family Connections," p. 276). In the sense of Annie John's dual antipathy to her mother and her motherland, the daughter's anger is logical.

23. Blyton, *Here Comes Noddy.*

24. Dixon, *Catching Them Young,* pp. 56–73. For *Here Comes Noddy,* see particularly Ray, *The Blyton Phenomenon,* p. 104.

25. The reference to her mother's skeleton hand, another death image that underscores the political and physical death of slave owners further links the motherhood-motherland image. Through synecdoche, it connects them both to corruption although this is not to argue that the sexual and colonial elements do not also independently coexist.

26. For an expansion of seamstress apprenticeship, see the *New Yorker,* August 17, 1981, pp. 25–26.

27. For a source of this semiautobiographical incident, see "I picked up a stone and I threw it at the monkey. The monkey, seeing the stone, quickly moved out of its way. Three times I threw a stone at the monkey and three times it

moved away. The fourth time I threw the stone, the monkey caught it and threw it back at me. The stone struck me on my forehead over my right eye, making a deep gash. The gash healed immediately, but now the skin on my forehead felt false to me" (*At the Bottom*, pp. 43–44). Annie Drew, Jamaica Kincaid's mother, explained a family memory of a monkey anecdote that suggests Kincaid's reference to the monkey as a figure who works for justice. On one occasion, a monkey bit Annie Drew because she was playing with a dog. Monkeys hate dogs, and children were pulling the dog toward the monkey. The monkey would not tolerate being manipulated and fought back. Thus Kincaid observes in a slant way that the monkey always emblematizes mutability.

28. In numerous instances, Annie John's metaphoric and biological mother exemplifies a sturdy toughness that functions as the daughter's model of admirable behavior. In that sense, she resembles the women in Sylvia Wynter's novels, women "who seem to demonstrate the strength and enduring qualities of the folk culture, the women who provide support and sustenance for their men" (Chang, "Sylvia Wynter," p. 504).

29. The Red Girl and her consignment to the ocean link to the discussion at the end of *At the Bottom of the River* about ocean depths that frequently represent the unconscious. In *Annie John,* the Red Girl, who represents part of Annie John's imagination as well as her physical life, is temporarily relegated to the borders.

30. Conceivably, Jamaica Kincaid is referring to an abridged version of Bryan Edwards's notorious racist text *The History, Civil and Commercial of the British Colonies in the West Indies*. Edwards was a well-known planter and English politician. For another strictly autobiographical reference to Queen Victoria that underscores her commentary in *Annie John,* Jamaica Kincaid comments further on Queen Victoria:

"It went from colonialism to the modern world—that is, from 1890 to 1980—in five years. When I was growing up, we still celebrated Queen Victoria's birthday on May 24, and for us England (and I think this was true for V. S. Naipaul, too) and its glory was at its most theatrical, its most oppressive. Everything seemed divine and good only if it was English.

"So my education, which was very 'Empire,' only involved civilization up to the British Empire—which would include writing—so I never read anything past Kipling. Kipling wasn't even considered a serious writer" (Cudjoe, "An Interview with Jamaica Kincaid," p. 398).

31. Todorov talks extensively about Columbus as the signifier of colonial power and the anxieties of the colonizer in *The Conquest of America,* especially pp. 3–50.

32. Perry, "Interview with Jamaica Kincaid," p. 497.

33. In a reading at the University of Nebraska—Lincoln, November 9, 1990, Marlene Norbese Philips stated that "playing around with fiction and fact is a black thing."

34. In *The Conquest of America,* Todorov argues forcibly that discourse, in

this case specifically about colonial practices, is determined by the interlocutor (pp. 219–37). Note also that Miss Edwards is a mimic man, down to her name. See Ramraj, "The All-Embracing Christlike Vision," p. 128.

35. Valerie Smith, "Black Feminist Theory and the Representation of the 'Other,'" p. 55.

36. *Paradise Lost* is a clever choice on several fronts. Apart from the references to Milton and the implications of the British literary canon, paradise could also refer to Columbus's "most striking" belief in the earthly paradise. He was looking for this place when he stumbled on the Caribbean (Todorov, *The Conquest of America*, pp. 16–18).

37. Jamaica Kincaid mentions in Perry, "An Interview with Jamaica Kincaid" (pp. 496–97), that these two incidents about her grandfather and Columbus were originally separate. She cites this yoking as one means by which she draws autobiographical elements (chronologically displaced sometimes) into her fiction.

38. Ibid., p. 504.

39. Abrahams, *The Man-of-Words in the West Indies,* pp. 153 ff. and 178 ff. See also Dance, *Folklore from Contemporary Jamaicans,* pp. xix–xxv, 11–12, 16–17, and 23–26. Abrahams discusses the Anansi, or spider, tales and their significance. See also Meadows, "The Symbol's Symbol," pp. 272–90; Robert, *From Trickster to Badman,* pp. 25–26; and Tiffin "The Metaphor of Anancy in Caribbean Literature," pp. 15–52. For further insights about anancy tales, see Cartey, *Whispers from the Caribbean,* p. 280.

40. Jamaica Kincaid has read *Jane Eyre, Wide Sargasso Sea,* and, from the Belgian references, *Villette.* See Donna Perry, "An Interview with Jamaica Kincaid," p. 508. The teacher's Belgium rice that is mentioned earlier has a curiously double-edged touch since *Villette* is set in Belgium and Belgium instigated a particularly ruthless form of colonialism in the Congo (*AJ,* p. 83). As a trope of colonialism, Belgian rice is part of the resistance of colonized people.

41. For a compelling discussion of the bildungsroman, see Murdoch, "Severing the (M)other Connection," p. 326.

42. See, for example, Marilyn Lawrence, *The Anorexic Experience,* pp. 32–39; Abraham and Llewellyn-Jones, *Eating Disorders;* and Romeo, *Understanding Anorexia Nervosa.* For enuresis, see Warren R. Baller, *Bed-Wetting: Origins and Treatment* (New York: Pergamon Press, 1975).

43. Bloomfield, "Drill and Dance as Symbols of Imperialism," pp. 74–95. Jamaica Kincaid uses such colonial games and institutions as the Brownies to symbolize the colonial indoctrination of her childhood.

44. Annie John has recuperated a desirable subject position through a process of healing. Her illness has enabled her to change. In part, she creates gaps "in order that the repressed inscribe themselves there" (Féral, "Towards a Theory of Displacement," pp. 52–63).

45. See Grieve, *The Last Years of the English Slave Trade,* p. 156. For an important discussion of obeah in West Indian fiction that relates to Annie John's ritual,

see Ramchand, *The West Indian Novel and Its Background,* pp. 123–31, and especially p. 139.

46. Davies, "Writing Home," p. 65.

47. Robert, *From Trickster to Badman,* pp. 97, 100. For further discussion of the importance of "ancestral memories or longings" in twentieth-century West Indian writers, see Ramchand, "West Indian Literary History," p. 96.

48. Note also Brathwaite's complex conceptualization of "another" two mothers in Caribbean texts: "The influence of Africa, acting upon her particular centres in the creole context, creates another shifting of values (Garvey, Malcolm, Black Power) in the way say that the Euro-American step-mother continues to create effects upon the total creole society through power, patronage and the offerings of 'modernity' and 'progress'" (*The Development of Creole Society in Jamaica, 1770–1820* [Oxford: Clarendon Press, 1971], p. 6).

49. Kristeva, "My Memory's Hyperbole," p. 220. See also de Abruna argue that "displacement from an initial intimacy with her mother's realm is reflected in a growing away from the environment" (p. 274).

50. Cobham, "Revisioning Our Kumblas," p. 58.

51. Annie John's behavior is familiar in terms of Victor Turner's anthropological theories (*Dramas, Fields, and Metaphors,* p. 232).

52. According to Woodcock's criteria, Jamaica Kincaid fits squarely in the tradition of Caribbean literature, contrary to Kincaid's own view. Woodcock states that what Caribbean women writers "have in common is a concern for the pressures on women during adolescence, and a critique of male power." He uses texts by Zee Edgell and Erna Brodber to exemplify his point (Woodcock, "Post-1975 Caribbean Fiction," pp. 79–95). Moreover, Jamaica Kincaid's exposure of female experiences from *At the Bottom* to *Lucy* might have worked just as well as examples. Jamaica Kincaid stresses her views about a Caribbean tradition in Ferguson, "An Interview with Jamaica Kincaid."

53. Note, also, in connection with my argument about the speaker's multiple subjectivities here and elsewhere, Covi's deft analysis of Jamaica Kincaid's indeterminacy, her refusal to offer a fixed position, "to turn away from any definitive statement and to utter radical statements" ("Jamaica Kincaid and the Resistance to Canons," p. 345).

54. "From a psychoanalytic point of view," argues Bachelard, "we must say that all water is a kind of milk" (*Water and Dreams,* p. 117).

55. For the association of women with fluids and water in terms of a female symbol, see Sigmund Freud, *The Interpretation of Dreams,* p. 435. See also Irigaray, "Sexual Difference," pp. 118–30. Irigaray raises the issue of the angelic female body that is, in a sense, water or fluid denied. On the other hand, she poses "the fluid basis of life and language" as an alternative to forced aridity and further suggests that life and natural fluidity exist in language. See also Mangum, "Jamaica Kincaid," p. 262.

56. This is a paraphrase of Nelson Mandela's reply to the South African government's offer of conditional release in 1985: "I cannot sell my birthright."

57. C. L. R. James, "The Making of the Caribbean People," p. 189.

58. For information about the gendering of the bildungsroman and how female writers have subverted its frequently masculine assumptions in the past, see Abel, Hirsch, and Langland, *The Voyage of Fictions of Female Development,* especially p. 68; and Peixoto, *"Family Ties,"* pp. 287–303.

59. One example is Garis, "Through West Indian Eyes." See also a discussion of the "oneness of the sentiments" of narrator and author in Ramraj, "The All-Embracing Christlike Vision," pp. 133–34.

60. For an insightful view of an articulation of life through fiction (that could be applied to Kincaid's texts) and the relocation and exploration of subjectivities, see Lang, "Autobiography in the Aftermath of Romanticism," pp. 5, 12, 16.

61. See Cudjoe, "An Interview with Jamaica Kincaid," pp. 396–441.

CHAPTER 3

1. Watson, *The West Indian Heritage,* p. 178.

2. Cudjoe, "An Interview with Jamaica Kincaid," p. 404.

3. Jamaica Kincaid talks about her reasons for leaving Antigua in an interview with Garis, "Through West Indian Eyes," pp. 44, 70.

4. Césaire, *Discourse on Colonialism;* Fanon, *Black Skin, White Masks;* Cudjoe, *Resistance and Caribbean Literature.* Statistics that document the historical imbalance of power that led to the present situation are available in Patterson, *Slavery and Social Death,* p. 478.

5. Government corruption in Antigua has become so notorious that a British Commission of Inquiry headed by the queen's counsellor, Louis Blom-Cooper, had to be set up. That investigation, from May 16 to November 2, 1990, specifically concerned arms sold by the Israeli Defence Ministry to a fictitious Antiguan "Quarter Master General" (Blom-Cooper, *Guns for Antigua*). The local paper in St. John's, *Outlet,* has been uncovering similar decades-old scandals, including that of the Japanese nonleaded cars mentioned in *A Small Place.* This same newspaper carried an advertisement for *A Small Place* by a radical bookstore headed "Antigua! Antigua!" (*Outlet,* October 28, 1988, p. 5).

6. The sarcasm about religion is linked to the continual digs at Anglicanism and its appurtenances in *At the Bottom of the River* and *Annie John.* Anglican religion for Kincaid, or any form of patriotic national worship (including Brownies and Girl Guides), signifies popular complicity and colonial and postcolonial (in *A Small Place*) indoctrination.

7. Sewage is still such a major issue that conferences partly center on it, as do keynote speakers. While in Antigua in 1991, I attended a conference entitled *One Solution to Pollution Is: Youth with the Truth!* It was sponsored by the Baha'i' Community of Antigua in collaboration with the Environmental Awareness Group of Antigua at the Cortsland Hotel, St. John's, Antigua, January 26, 1991. One of the keynote speakers was the distinguished John Fuller. He spoke passionately of sewage being directly emptied into the Caribbean and of the damage

to the sea life. See also *The Revitalization of Downtown Saint John's Antigua and Barbuda*. For a general commentary by Jamaica Kincaid on English attitudes and their sense of historical responsibility, see "On Seeing England for the First Time." Although I saw this article after this manuscript was completed, it confirmed my overall appraisal of Jamaica Kincaid's analysis of colonialism.

8. Bachelard, *Water and Dreams,* p. 139.

9. Barthes, *Mythologies*.

10. The monkey tales and images change as Kincaid stamps her special brand of complex irony on the monkey tricksters who change shapes and size in popular folktales throughout the Caribbean. See, for example, Hodge, *Crick-Crack, Monkey*. Since the monkey is often the taleteller, Kincaid plays with that irony too. Here the colonizing representative calls pupils like Annie John "monkeys." On another occasion, in an interview with Cudjoe, Jamaica Kincaid calls herself a monkey, a curious reverse reappraisal. The narrator's mother's story in *At the Bottom of the River* and *Lucy* is one thing; the monkey's (the protagonist, Kincaid herself) is another. Kincaid also calls an Antigua resident "old monkey face." By continually shifting the metaphor's affiliation and refusing a simple closure, Kincaid insists on attentiveness to the symbol and suggests its chameleon, even treacherous quality. It can be two or more things at once. Yet it has deeply negative historical associations; it is used as a child's cruel taunt that in turn suggests how negatively the word is conceived, for the child conceals from her parents that she calls someone "monkey lettuce" (*New Yorker,* October 17, 1977, p. 28). In this instance, in a deliberate metonymic shift of signifiers from monkey to pupil, Kincaid overtly attacks racism, colonialism, and the ethnocentric (graphic) gaze.

11. For relevant discussion on the attachment of meaning, see Macdonell, *Theories of Discourse,* p. 11

12. Here the monkey matrix shifts again. The protagonist's acceptance of the designation monkey is intended to highlight colonial barbarity.

13. Kincaid's casual-sounding questions echo Virginia Woolf's equally artless device in *A Room of One's Own* down to (elsewhere) the use of a second person addressee: "You may be the sort of tourist who would wonder why a Prime Minister would want an airport named after him — why not a school, why not a hospital" (p. 3).

14. What Jamaica Kincaid does not specifically disclose is the fact that her "real" father is a worker at the Mill Reef Club. Her anger at the clubwoman involves a complex and doubled psychological attack on the (supposedly exploitative) treatment of her father. This association is as close as Kincaid ever comes to explaining any ties she feels for her biological father.

15. Once again sexuality becomes a veiled, dangerous issue. The hiding of culture in one's sexuality suggests the power of both and the refusal of the people to disclose themselves entirely. See also Hyam, "Empire and Sexual Opportunity," for the kind of sexual exploitation traditionally accepted in many colonized communities. In *At the Bottom of the River* and *Annie John,* the mother tries to forestall this gendered exploitation.

16. This crack is another piece in the overall picture of governmental corruption, in this case involving postal issues. Kincaid means to build a picture of a society run by corrupt politicians who mimic the British in their expropriation of resources, nest-feathering, and neglect of the population.

17. As Elizabeth Wilson has said in another context, "Sexual, racial and national 'politics' are interwoven by the author in such a way that each complements and comments on the other" ("Sexual, Racial, and National Politics," p. 51. As a common triad, this combination applies to the works of a wide range of male and female authors in the Caribbean literary tradition.

18. Said, *The World, the Text, and the Critic,* p. 53. Note further that Jamaica Kincaid speaks in an interview of getting her feisty spirit from her mother: "I know I must have gotten [sticking to your principles] from her. She was always very outspoken and had a great sense of right and wrong" Ferguson, "Interview with Jamaica Kincaid."

19. See *Outlet,* June 3, 1991. At its most fierce, death-threatening level, censorship forced Salman Rushdie into semipermanent hiding (Weatherby, *Salman Rushdie,* pp. 153–77).

20. Perry, "An Interview with Jamaica Kincaid," p. 498.

21. Mohanty and Mohanty, "Contradictions of Colonialism," p. 21.

22. An excellent abbreviated history of governmental ministers appeared in *Outlet* after the death of a politically questionable minister. See *Outlet,* May 31, 1991, pp. 1–2, 13–17.

23. I accept this contention as it fits the general picture of venality suggested in the local paper although I have been unable to find specific corroborating testimony. The corroborating documents, of course, are missing from the text but are continually intertextualized, specifically the Blom-Cooper report and the complete run of *Outlet* newspapers. For particular instances, see September 20, 1991, "Is This Man Fit to Hold Public Office," May 31, 1991. Note also that in terms of a boycott, Jamaica Kincaid was told she could not return to Antigua and that any plane on which she was on board would not be permitted to land. In April 1993, Jamaica Kincaid told me that the ban seems to have been as informally removed as it was instigated in the first place.

24. Perry, "An Interview with Jamaica Kincaid," p. 500.

25. Jamaica Kincaid, "On Seeing England for the First Time," pp. 3–11.

26. Woolf, *A Room of One's Own,* p. 24. For Kincaid's thoughts on Woolf, see Mendelsohn, "Leaving Home," p. 21.

27. The speaker's voice in *A Small Place* attempts calmness and distance, despite anger at what has taken place. In the main, Kincaid uses external evidence, facts that can be corroborated, telltale evidence like the library plaque to shore up her argument as a form of "object language." Another example of historical documentation is the Codrington estate connections, especially pp. 160 ff. There is much political debate around the Codrington family in Barbuda, especially the subtle notion of breeding strong slaves (Lowenthal and Clark, "Slave Breeding in Barbuda," pp. 510–35).

28. When I visited the newspaper offices of *Outlet,* a high administrative official strode in threateningly to inquire what was going to be printed about him.

29. Jamaica Kincaid speaks in the interview with Perry of their celebration of Queen Victoria's birthday without her (or many in the populace) knowing the queen was dead (Cudjoe, "An Interview with Jamaica Kincaid," pp. 397–98).

30. Quoted in Weatherby, *Salman Rushdie,* p. 31.

31. These texts are a very small example among many of Jamaica Kincaid's textual invocations: C. L. R. James, *A History of Negro Revolt,* p. 6; Fanon, *Black Skin, White Masks;* Césaire, *Discourse on Colonialism* and *Return to My Native Land;* Rodney, *West Africa and the Atlantic Slave Trade;* Woolf, *A Room of One's Own;* Gordimer, "A Lion on the Freeway"; Cudjoe, *Resistance and Caribbean Literature.* When I spoke to Annie Drew, Jamaica Kincaid's mother, she mentioned the extreme difficulty of rectifying political corruption that had become so ingrained.

32. Bennett, *Bondsmen and Bishops.*

33. Macdonell, *Theories of Discourse,* p. 47.

34. To the extent that Jamaica Kincaid tries to upgrade the status of black people by upgrading the need to rediscover lost history and culture, she ideologically connects to a global articulation on behalf of oppressed people. In reaction to white racism and cultural values imposed by whites, she exposes how black Antiguans have been brainwashed into Western ways of thinking. At some level she might agree with the Haitian poet Jean Price-Mars: "We belong to Africa by our blood" (Cashmore, *Dictionary of Race and Ethnic Relations,* p. 209).

35. Fanon, *The Wretched of The Earth,* p. 53; Ramchand, *The West Indian Novel and Its Background,* pp. 136 ff.

36. West, "Theory, Pragmatisms, and Politics," p. 32.

37. Narasimhaiah, *Awakened Conscience,* pp. 146–63.

38. Meese, *Crossing the Double Cross,* p. 44. See also, for example, James, "Introduction to Tradition and the West Indian Novel," in Harris, *Tradition,* pp. 69–75; for an elaboration of this point, see Jacobus, "The difference of View," pp. 49–62.

39. Spivak, "Three Women's Texts," p. 187.

40. Barbara Christian, "But What Do We Think We're Doing Anyway," p. 73.

41. Spivak, "Three Women's Texts," p. 87.

42. Carby, *Reconstructing Womanhood,* p. 95.

43. Ferguson, "Interview with Jamaica Kincaid."

44. Minh-Ha, *When the Moon Waxes Red,* pp. 193–94.

45. Connelly, review of *Memoirs of a Tourist,* by Stendhal, pp. 361–63.

CHAPTER 4

1. Jamaica Kincaid, *Lucy,* p. 11.
2. Said, *Orientalism,* p. 20.
3. Lorde, "Eye to Eye," p. 147.

4. Once again, one of Jamaica Kincaid's issues — her expatriation — ties her to the tradition of Caribbean writing. In Fido's words, "Migration is a central inspiration for [Caribbean women writers'] creative work" (Davies and Fido, "Talking It Over," p. ix). For an important bibliography, see Davies and Fido, *Out of the Kumbla*, pp. 1, 12–19.

5. See Adisa, "Island Daughter," p. 6.

6. For a political discussion of calypso in context, see Ramchand, *The West Indian Novel and Its Background*, pp. 132–37. See also Davis, *Emancipation Still Comin'*, pp. 44–45.

7. See chap. 3, note 27. The monkey image enables her texts to be viewed as loosely connecting sections in an ongoing autobiographical fiction. Here, Lewis metonymically connects monkeys to African-Americans in a well-worn usage. See Jordan, *White over Black*, pp. 228–29, 237.

8. By highlighting Lucy's naiveté about Sigmund Freud, Kincaid invites readings of the text based on unconscious motivation. In particular, Lewis's prior statement is notable.

9. See Jamaica Kincaid, "Biography of a Dress," pp. 93–100. The semifictional reminiscences in this article tend to confirm my evaluations of the mother-daughter-colonialism triangle in *Lucy* and elsewhere in Jamaica Kincaid's texts.

10. "The Daffodils" is a reminder that black Antiguan children are subjected to an ethnocentric education in which British cultural highlights — such as William Wordsworth's poem — are committed to memory. V. S. Naipaul mentions a similar experience. See Ramraj, "The All-Embracing Christlike Vision," p. 130.

11. Perry, "An Interview with Jamaica Kincaid," p. 501.

12. Ibid., p. 506.

13. Cudjoe, "An Interview with Jamaica Kincaid," p. 399.

14. Bachelard, *Water and Dreams*, p. 28.

15. Perowne, *The End of the Roman World*, p. xvii.

16. Charmet, *Paul Gauguin*. See also Anderson, *Gauguin's Paradise Lost*, pp. 157–86. Possibly Kincaid knows and silently alludes to the story of Gauguin's skirmish with sailors in Concarneau who laughed at Gauguin's Javanese mistress and the monkey he held by a string (Charmet, p. 75).

17. Since Jamaica Kincaid has read *Wide Sargasso Sea*, we could be hearing in Paul an echo of quests by protagonists like Rochester, who seeks Antoinette's hand in marriage so he can acquire her fortune. See Perry, "An Interview with Jamaica Kincaid," pp. 508.

18. At another level, Lucy's distance from and control of her own sexuality — her exposed desire — suggests an attempt by Kincaid to come to terms with sexuality and eroticism, either fictional, autobiographical, or both (Kristeva, "My Memory's Hyperbole," pp. 219–35).

19. Once again, Kincaid insists on the continuity and mutual allusiveness of her texts, as if they were to be treated as loosely fitting but connected sections of a personal and political saga. For this aspect, in the context of a travel narrative, see Pratt, *Imperial Eyes*. *Lucy* is such a text at one level as the saga of an expatriate.

20. Lucy wants to be treated as the picky-haired girl was—a slut, in the mother's terms in *At the Bottom of the River.* Thus the warnings in *At the Bottom* and the absence of slutlike behavior in *Annie John* (although further warnings occur) bear on the implied slutlike behavior of Myrna, who desires it and enjoys the attention. Hence, Annie John's mother stands reindicted while Lucy is sited on the "pro-slut," i.e., antiauthority, end of the continuum.

21. Beauvoir, *The Second Sex,* p. 3.

22. Jamaica Kincaid, "Ovando." See also Morrow and McGrath, *The New Gothic,* pp. 3–13.

23. Said, "Figures, Configurations, Transfigurations," p. 6.

24. Ferguson, "Interview with Jamaica Kincaid."

25. The references here are to Emily and Charlotte Brontë, *Jane Eyre,* and Blyton, *Here Comes Noddy.*

26. Belenky et al., *Women's Ways of Knowing,* pp. 83–86. Once again the mother-daughter relationship in the biological (as well as the colonial) sense asserts itself. Jamaica Kincaid recognizes this attentiveness to maternality and childhood even as "the stock in trade of West Indian writers." Thus she does in some ways identify herself within a Caribbean tradition while not stating so explicitly. She goes on: "Meryl [*sic*] Hodge's *Crick-Crack Money* [*sic*] is a wonderful book, and it's about a Caribbean childhood, too, not unlike mine. It's true that women sometimes fall victim to a kind of narcissism. Certainly it's true in the West Indies. I went to a conference on West Indian women writers, very learned, brilliant women. Many of them said, 'I know I should give my paper, but I'm going to tell you about myself instead.' It was at that moment that I realized that my mother wasn't that unusual" (Bonetti, "An Interview with Jamaica Kincaid," pp. 137–38).

27. Blue, like white, invokes transparency and suggests such cosmic borders as sea and sky.

28. Gay, *Freud,* p. 301.

29. Ibid., p. 299.

30. Wilentz, "English Is a Foreign Anguish," pp. 261–78.

31. Bakhtin, *The Dialogic Imagination,* p. 425.

32. For provocative readings of the philosophical importance of a camera, see Barrow, Armitage, and Tydeman, *Reading into Photography;* see also Burgin, *Thinking Photography,* pp. 46–47.

33. Cixous, "The Laugh of the Medusa," pp. 245–64; Féral, "Towards a Theory of Displacement," pp. 52–65.

34. See chap. 2, note 50. For a discussion of the implications of water, drought, and death, see Bachelard, *Water and Dreams,* pp. 65–69; for aridity as a metaphor, see Ramchand, *The West Indian Novel and Its Background,* p. 129.

35. For a riveting early account (or foreshadowing) of Peggy and Lucy, see "Jamaica Kincaid's New York," pp. 70–73.

36. Mohanty and Mohanty, "Contradictions of Colonialism"; Satya Mohanty, "Drawing the Color Line," pp. 311–43.

37. Hooks, "Choosing the Margin as a Space of Radical Openness," p. 23.

C H A P T E R 5

1. Jamaica Kincaid, "Ovando," pp. 75–83. In the introduction to *The New Gothic,* Morrow argues that Kincaid's "Ovando" is part of a new end-of-the-century exploration of the "bleaker facets of the human soul. . . . Hell is decidedly on earth, located within the vaults and chambers of our own minds" (p. xiv). Although my reading diverges somewhat from Morrow's, there are overlapping elements and certainly his contentions comprise one facet of Kincaid's narrative.

2. Jamaica Kincaid, *A Small Place,* pp. 9, 29.

3. See Ewen, *From Spaniard to Creole,* pp. 22–24.

4. Jamaica Kincaid is also insistent here on foregrounding the Amerindian encounter with Europe. For the importance of this approach, see the influential articles by Wilson Harris, *Tradition,* especially "Tradition and the West Indian Writer," pp. 28–47. See also Hulme, *Colonial Encounters,* especially pp. 59–65.

5. *Oxford English Dictionary.*

6. Ashdown, *Caribbean History in Maps,* p. 8; Bethell, ed., *Cambridge History of Latin America,* vol. 1, *Colonial Latin America,* pp. 164–66.

7. Watson, *The West Indian Heritage,* p. 3. For a description of the original encounters based on firsthand sources, see Tyler, *Two Worlds,* pp. 206–44. See also Fernandez, "Dreams of Two Americas," especially pp. 122–25.

8. Parry and Keith, *The New Iberian World,* pp. 255–57. See also *A Letter to Ferdinand and Isabella, 1503,* pp. 69–71.

9. Helps, *The Spanish Conquest in America,* p. 126.

10. Las Casas, *History of the Voyage and Discoveries the Spaniards have made in the East Indies.*

11. Ibid., p. 81.

12. Helps, *The Spanish Conquest in America,* p. 162.

13. Irving, *The Life and Voyages of Christopher Columbus,* p. 118.

14. See Helps, *The Spanish Conquest in America,* p. 121, for an alternate interpretation.

15. Hazard, *Santo Domingo,* p. 30.

16. Irving, *The Life and Voyages of Christopher Columbus,* p. 442.

17. Helps, *The Spanish Conquest in America,* p. 133.

18. Irving, *The Life and Voyages of Christopher Columbus,* p. 433.

19. Parry and Keith, *The New Iberian World,* p. xiii.

20. Irving, *The Life and Voyages of Christopher Columbus,* pp. 528–29. See also Elliott, *Imperial Spain.*

21. Irving, *The Life and Voyages of Christopher Columbus,* pp. 533–34. See Reuel K. Wilson, "The Letters of Bruno Schulz, Jerzy Stempowski, and especially Julian Tuwim," pp. 132–34.

22. Irving, *The Life and Voyages of Christopher Columbus,* p. 534.

23. Helps, *The Spanish Conquest in America,* pp. 145–46.

24. Ibid., p. 147.

25. Ewen, *From Spaniard to Creole,* pp. 26–27; see also Tyler, *Two Worlds,* p. 237.

26. Hazard, *Santo Domingo,* p. 36.

27. Ibid., p. 40.

28. Tyler, *Two Worlds,* p. 71–73.

29. Ibid., p. 101.

30. Ibid., p. 153.

31. To take an example from another part of the world, there was a time when the Vietnamese were unprepared, too.

32. Johnson, *The Devil, The Gargoyle, and the Buffoon,* p. 158.

33. Ibid., p. 157.

34. Ibid., p. 165.

35. Ibid.

36. A good example of this is the expectations that "explorers" bring to other peoples' countries. To take one typical instance, when Mungo Park arrived he expected (and received) warm hospitality. His visit, of course, paralleled the devastation of African cultures and populations (Hibbert, *Africa Explored,* p. 68).

37. Irving, *The Live and Voyages of Christopher Columbus,* p. 531. See also Todorov, *The Conquest of America.*

38. Kincaid, *A Small Place,* p. 9; Todorov, *The Conquest of America.*

39. See, for example, Harris, *Tradition,* pp. 72–73.

40. For an elaboration, see, for example, Hulme, *Colonial Encounters.*

41. Ovando, moreover, lies on broken glass bottles, manufactured by a First World company. Silent, oblique, grim witticisms against such signs of imperialism as North American brands of pop, are scattered throughout the text.

42. I thank Robert Haller for a discussion of this point.

43. Grimal, *The Dictionary of Classical Mythology,* p. 302.

44. See Todorov, *The Conquest of America,* p. 27.

45. Irving, *The Life and Voyages of Christopher Columbus,* p. 92. See also Asante ". . . And Then There Was Columbus," p. 144.

46. Irving, *Life and Voyages of Christopher Columbus,* p. 440.

47. For evidence of this corruption, despite severe press censorship in Antigua, see *Outlet,* especially the following issues, October 26, 1990; December 21, 1990; and especially May 31, 1991.

48. Jamaica Kincaid's explanation of Ovando's rotten body (conceived broadly) strikingly contrasts with Wilson Harris's discussion of a "magic corpse," almost as if Kincaid contrasts Ovando with this mystical Caribbean conception (Harris, "Metaphor and Myth," p. 11).

49. *Encyclopedia Americana.* See also Nichols and Cooke, *The Oxford Book of Invertebrates,* pp. 96–101.

50. *Encyclopedia Americana.*

51. Ibid.

52. Ibid.

53. Hall, "Cultural Identity and Cinematic Representation," pp. 70–73.

54. See also Garis, "Through West Indian Eyes," pp. 78–79.

55. Perry, "An Interview with Jamaica Kincaid," p. 501.

56. Cudjoe, "Interview with Jamaica Kincaid," p. 408.

57. Ibid., p. 140. Kincaid stresses the narrator's refusal to allow the situation to be naturalized. She insists on foregrounding race (appearances) as well as colonial and gender issues. For a telling comment on this scenario, see Chandra T. Mohanty, Introduction, "Cartographies of Struggle," p. 18.

58. Cudjoe, "Interview with Jamaica Kincaid," p. 410.

59. Ibid.

60. Jamaica Kincaid, "Antigua Crossings," p. 48.

61. Cudjoe, "Interview with Jamaica Kincaid," pp. 405–6.

62. See, for example, Rodway, *The West Indies and the Spanish Main;* Hazard, *Santo Domingo,* pp. 18–48; and Cudjoe, "Interview with Jamaica Kincaid," p. 403.

63. Perry, "An Interview with Jamaica Kincaid," p. 501.

64. National Public Radio, p. 22.

65. Ashcroft, Griffiths, and Tiffin, *The Empire Writes Back,* p. 150.

66. Cudjoe, "Interview with Jamaica Kincaid," p. 406.

67. Perry, "An Interview with Jamaica Kincaid," p. 501.

68. Ibid., p. 509; see also pp. 500, 502.

69. Ibid., p. 502.

70. Kincaid, *At the Bottom of the River,* p. 76.

71. Ibid., pp. 76–77.

72. Hutcheon, *Narcissistic Narrative,* p. 61.

73. Retamar, *Caliban and Other Essays,* p. 36.

74. Wilson Harris discusses the particular relation in Caribbean literature of creativity to violence in "Adversarial Contexts and Creativity," pp. 124–28.

CONCLUSION

1. Minh-Ha, *When the Moon Waxes Red,* p. 191.

2. Said, *Culture and Imperialism,* p. x.

3. *Christian Science Monitor,* May 2, 1985, p. 2.

4. Perry, "An Interview with Jamaica Kincaid," p. 494.

5. Bonetti, "An Interview with Jamaica Kincaid," p. 126.

6. *Christian Science Monitor,* May 2, 1985, p. 42.

7. Wilson Harris, "The Narrative Phenomenon," p. 150.

8. Hooks, *Yearning,* p. 150.

9. C. L. R. James, *The Black Jacobins.*

10. Fraser, *Unruly Practices,* p. 63.

11. Retamar, *Caliban and Other Essays,* p. 36.

12. Guha, *Selected Subaltern Studies,* pp. 72, 77.

13. Moira Ferguson, "An Interview with Jamaica Kincaid."

Bibliography

PRIMARY SOURCES: THE TEXTS OF JAMAICA KINCAID

Books

At the Bottom of the River. New York: Farrar, Straus, Giroux, 1978.
Annie John. New York: New American Library, 1983.
And Eric Fischl. *Annie, Gwen, Lily, Pam and Tulip.* New York: Whitney Museum of American Art, 1986; Alfred A. Knopf in association with the Whitney Museum, 1989.
A Small Place. London: Virago Press, 1988.
Lucy. New York: Farrar, Straus, Giroux, 1990.

Short Stories

"The Fourth." *New Yorker,* 19 July 1976.
"Dates and Comment." *New Yorker,* 17 October 1977.
"Girl," *The New Yorker,* 26 June 1978. Rpt. In *Wayward Girls, Wicked Women: An Anthology of Stories,* ed. Angela Carter. London: The Women's Press. 1987. In *Green Cane and Juicy Flotsam: Short Stories by Caribbean Women,* ed. Carmen C. Esteves and Lizabeth Paravisini-Gebert. New Brunswick, N.J.: Rutgers Univ. Press, 1991.
"In the Night." *New Yorker,* 24 July 1978.
"Wingless." *New Yorker,* 29 January 1979.
"Holidays." *New Yorker,* 27 August 1979.
"At Last." *New Yorker,* 17 December 1979.
"The Letter from Home." *New Yorker,* 20 April 1981.
"The Apprentice." *New Yorker,* 17 August 1981.
"What I have Been Doing Lately." *The Paris Review* 23 (1981).

"At the Bottom of the River." *New Yorker,* 3 May 1982. Excerpt in Mordecai and Wilson, eds., *Her True-True Name.*
"Notes and Comment." *New Yorker,* 3 January 1983.
"Figures in the Distance." *New Yorker,* 9 May 1983.
"The Red Girl." *New Yorker,* 8 August 1983.
"Columbus in Chains." *New Yorker,* 10 October 1983.
"The Circling Hand." *New Yorker,* 21 November 1983.
"Gwen." *New Yorker,* 16 April 1984.
"Somewhere Belgium." *New Yorker,* 14 May 1984.
"The Long Rain." *New Yorker,* 30 July 1984.
"A Walk to the Jetty." *New Yorker,* 5 November 1984.
"Poor Visitor." *New Yorker,* 27 February 1989.
"Mariah." *New Yorker,* 26 June 1989. Rept. In *Stories from the American Mosaic,* ed. Scott Walker. Saint Paul: Graywolf Press, 1990.
"The Tongue." *New Yorker,* 9 October 1989.
"Cold Heart." *New Yorker,* 25 June 1990.
"Lucy." *New Yorker,* 24 September 1990.
"My Mother." In *Caribbean New Wave: Contemporary Short Stories,* ed. Stewart Brown. London: Heinemann, 1990.
"The Finishing Line." *New York Times Book Review,* 2 December 1990.
"Have Yourself a Gorey Little Christmas: Nine Writers Create Stories for Edward Gorey's Christmas Illustrations." *New York Times Book Review,* 2 December 1990.

Shorter Fiction, Essays, and Nonfiction

"Erotica." *Ms.* January 1975.
"Jamaica Kincaid's New York." *Rolling Stone,* October 6, 1977.
"Antigua Crossings." *Rolling Stone,* June 19, 1978.
"The Ugly Tourist." From *A Small Place. Harper's,* September 1988.
"Ovando." *Conjunctions,* vol. 10, 1989.
"On Seeing England for the First Time." *Translations* 1, no. 51, 1991. Foreword to *Babouk,* by Guy Endore. New York: Monthly Review Press, 1991. With Ellen Pall. "Out of Kenya." *New York Times,* 16 September 1991.
"Biography of a Dress." *Grand Street* 11, no. 3, 1992.

Interviews

Bonetti, Kay. "An Interview with Jamaica Kincaid." *The Missouri Review* 15 (1992).
The Christian Science Monitor, May 2, 1985.

Cudjoe, Selwyn R. "Interview with Jamaica Kincaid." *Callaloo* 12 (1989).

Edwards, Audrey. "Jamaica Kincaid Writes of Passage." *Essence,* May 1991.

Ferguson, Moira. "Interview with Jamaica Kincaid." *Kenyon Review,* Summer 1994.

Fugard, Athol. "Interview with South African Playwright." *Interview* 20 (August 1990).

Garis, Leslie. "Through West Indian Eyes." *New York Times Magazine,* October 11, 1990.

"Interview." *New Yorker,* 17 August 1981.

National Public Radio, November 4, 1990. Transcript.

O'Conner, Patricia T. "My Mother Wrote My Life." *New York Times Book Review,* 7 April 1985.

Perry, Donna. "Interview with Jamaica Kincaid." In Gates, ed., *Reading Black, Reading Feminist.*

S E C O N D A R Y   S O U R C E S

Books

Abel, Elizabeth, Marianne Hirsch, and Elizabeth Langland, eds. *The Voyage Out: Fictions of Female Development.* Hanover and London: Univ. Press of New England, 1983.

Abraham, Suzanne, and Derek Llewellyn-Jones. *Eating Disorders: The Facts.* Oxford: Oxford Univ. Press, 1984.

Abrahams, Roger D. *The Man-of-Words in the West Indies: Performance and the Emergence of Creole Culture.* Baltimore and London: Johns Hopkins Univ. Press, 1983.

Andersen, Wayne. *Gauguin's Paradise Lost.* New York: Viking, 1971.

Arbuthnot, John. *The History of John Bull.* Ed. Alan W. Bower and Robert A. Erickson. Oxford: Clarendon Press, 1976.

Ashcroft, Bill, Gareth Griffiths, and Helen Tiffin. *The Empire Writes Back: Theory and Practice in Post-Colonial Literatures.* London and New York: Routledge, 1989.

Ashdown, Peter. *Caribbean History in Maps.* Trinidad and Jamaica: Longman Caribbean, 1979.

Bachelard, Gaston. *Water and Dreams: An Essay on the Imagination of Matter.* Trans. Edith R. Farrell. Dallas: Dallas Institute of Humanities and Culture, 1942.

Bailey, Greg. *The Mythology of Brahma.* Delhi: Oxford Univ. Press, 1983.

Bakhtin, M. M. *The Dialogic Imagination: Four Essays.* Ed. Michael Holquist. Trans. Caryl Emerson and Michael Holquist. Austin: Univ. of Texas Press, 1981.

Barrow, Thomas F., Shelley Armitage, and William E. Tydeman, eds. *Reading into Photography: Selected Essays, 1959–1980*. Albuquerque: Univ. of New Mexico Press, 1982.

Barthes, Roland. *Mythologies*. Trans. Annette Lavers 1957. Rpt. London: Paladin Grafton Books, 1972.

Beauvoir, Simone de. *The Second Sex*. Trans. and ed. H. M. Parshley. New York: Vintage Books, 1952.

Belenky, Mary Field, Blythe McVicker Clinchy, Nancy Rule Goldberger, and Jill Mattuck Tarule. *Women's Ways of Knowing: The Development of Self, Voice, and Mind*. New York: Basic Books, 1969.

Belsey, Catherine, and Jane Moore, eds. *The Feminist Reader: Essays in Gender and the Politics of Literary Criticism*. Oxford: Basil Blackwell, 1989.

Bennett, J. Harry, Jr. *Bondsmen and Bishops: Slavery and Apprenticeship on the Codrington Plantation of Barbados, 1710–1838*. Berkeley: Univ. of California Press, 1958.

Bethell, Leslie, ed. *The Cambridge History of Latin America*. Vol. 1, *Colonial Latin America*.

Bhabha, Homi K., ed. *Nation and Narration*. London and New York: Routledge, 1990.

Blom-Cooper, Louis. *Guns for Antigua: Report of the Commission of Inquiry into the Circumstances Surrounding the Shipment of Arms from Israel to Antigua and Transhipment on 24 April 1989 en Route to Columbia*. Antigua and Barbuda: Duckworth, 1990.

Blyton, Enid. *Here Comes Noddy*. London: Sampson Lowe, Marston & Co., and Richards Press, 1951.

Burgin, Victor. *Thinking Photography*. New York: Macmillan, 1982.

Carby, Hazel V. *Reconstructing Womanhood: The Emergence of the Afro-American Woman Novelist*. New York and Oxford: Oxford Univ. Press, 1987.

Cartey, Wilfred. *Whispers from the Caribbean: I Going Away, I Going Home*. Los Angeles: Center for Afro-American Studies, 1991.

Cashmore, E. Ellis. *Dictionary of Race and Ethnic Relations*. London: Routledge, 1984.

Castle, Terry. *Masquerade and Civilization: The Carnivalesque in Eighteenth-Century English Culture and Fiction*. Stanford: Stanford Univ. Press, 1986.

Césaire, Aimé. *Discourse on Colonialism*. New York: Monthly Review Press, 1972.

Charmet Raymond. *Paul Gauguin*. New York: Barnes & Noble, 1966.

Chodorow, Nancy. *The Reproduction of Mothering: Psychoanalysis and the Society of Gender*. Berkeley: Univ. of California Press, 1978.

Cudjoe, Selwyn R. *Resistance and Caribbean Literature*. Athens: Ohio Univ. Press, 1980.

————, ed. *Caribbean Women Writers: Essays from the First International Conference*. Wellesley, Mass.: Calaloux Publications, 1990.

Dalsimer, Katherine. *Female Adolescence: Psychoanalytic Reflections on Works of Literature*. New Haven and London: Yale Univ. Press, 1986.

Dance, Daryl C. *Folklore from Contemporary Jamaicans.* Knoxville: Univ. of Tennessee Press, 1985.

——, ed. *Fifty Caribbean Writers: A Bio-bibliographical Critical Sourcebook.* New York: Greenwood Press, 1986.

Davies, Carole Boyce, and Fido, Elaine Savory, eds. *Out of the Kumbla: Caribbean Women and Literature.* Trenton: Africa World Press, 1990.

Davis, Kortright. *Emancipation Still Comin': Explorations in Caribbean Emancipatory Theology.* Maryknoll, N.Y.: Orbis Books, 1990.

DeKoven, Marianne. *Rich and Strange: Gender, History, Modernism.* Princeton: Princeton Univ. Press, 1991.

Dixon, Bob. *Catching Them Young: Sex, Race, and Class in Children's Fiction. Political Ideas in Children's Fiction.* Vol. 2. London: Pluto, 1977.

Edwards, Bryan. *The History, Civil and Commercial of the British Colonies in the West Indies.* 2 vols. London, 1793.

Ehrenzweig, Anton. *The Order of Art.* Berkeley: Univ. of California Press, 1967.

Elliott, J. H. *Imperial Spain, 1469–1716.* New York: St. Martin's Press, 1964.

Ewen, Charles R. *From Spaniard to Creole: The Archaeology of Cultural Formation at Puerto Real, Haiti.* Tuscaloosa and London: Univ. of Alabama Press, 1991.

Fanon, Frantz. *Black Skin, White Masks.* Trans. Charles Lam Markmann 1952. Rpt. London and Sydney: Pluto Press, 1986.

——. *The Wretched of the Earth.* Trans. Constance Farrington. New York: Grove Press, 1963.

Fraser, Nancy. *Unruly Practices: Power, Discourse, and Gender in Contemporary Social Theory.* Minneapolis: Univ. of Minnesota Press, 1989.

Freud, Anna. *The Writings of Anna Freud.* Vol. 2. *The Ego and the Mechanisms of Defense.* New York: International Universities Press, 1966.

Freud, Sigmund. *The Interpretation of Dreams.* Trans. James Strachey. New York: Discus Books, 1965.

Gates, Henry Louis, Jr., ed. *Reading Black, Reading Feminist: A Critical Anthology.* New York: Meridian, 1990.

Gay, Peter. *Freud: A Life for Our Time.* London: J. M. Dent, 1989.

Giddings, Paula. *When and Where I Enter: The Impact of Black Women on Race and Sex in America.* Toronto: Bantam Books, 1984.

Gilbert, Sandra, and Susan Gubar. *The Madwoman in the Attic: Women Writers and the Literary Imagination.* New Haven: Yale Univ. Press, 1979.

Goodison, Lorna. *I Am Becoming My Mother.* London–Port of Spain: New Beacon Books, 1986.

Grieve, Averil Mackenzie. *The Last Years of the English Slave Trade: Liverpool, 1750–1807.* New York: Frank Cass, 1968.

Grimal, Pierre. *The Dictionary of Classical Mythology.* Trans. A. R. Maxwell-Hyslop. New York: Basil Blackwell, 1986.

Guha, Ranajit. *Selected Subaltern Studies.* Oxford: Oxford Univ. Press, 1988.

Harris, Wilson. *The Sleepers of Roraima: A Caribbean Trilogy.* London: Faber and Faber, 1970.

———. *Explorations: A Selection of Talks and Articles, 1966–1981.* Aarhus, Denmark: Dangaroo Press, 1981.

———. *Tradition: The Writer and Society.* London: New Beacon Books, 1967.

Hart, Patricia. *Narrative Magic in the Fiction of Isabel Allende.* London and Toronto: Associated Univ. Presses, 1987.

Hazard, Samuel. *Santo Domingo, Past and Present: With a Glance at Hayti.* New York: Harper & Brothers, 1873.

Helps, Arthur, Sir. *The Spanish Conquest in America.* New York: AMS Press, 1966.

Hibbert, Christopher. *Africa Explored: Europeans in the Dark Continent 1769–1889.* London: Penguin, 1982.

Highfield, Roger, ed. *Spain in the Fifteenth Century 1369–1516.* Trans. Frances M. López-Morillas. London: Macmillan, 1972.

Hirsch, Marianne. *The Mother/Daughter Plot: Narrative, Psychoanalysis, Feminism.* Bloomington and Indianapolis: Indiana Univ. Press, 1989.

Hodge, Merle. *Crick Crack, Monkey.* London: Heinemann, 1970.

Holland, Barron. *Popular Hinduism and Hindu Mythology: An Annotated Bibliography.* Westport, Conn.: Greenwood Press, 1979.

hooks, bell. *Yearning: Race, Gender, and Cultural Politics.* Boston: South End Press, 1990.

Hulme, Peter. *Colonial Encounters: Europe and the Native Caribbean, 1492–1797.* London and New York: Methuen, 1986.

Hutcheon, Linda. *Narcissistic Narrative: The Metafictional Paradox.* Ontario: Wilfrid Laurier Univ. Press, 1980.

Irving, Washington. *The Life and Voyages of Christopher Columbus.* Ed. John Harmon McElroy. Boston: Twayne, 1981.

James, C. L. R. *A History of Negro Revolt.* New York: Haskell House, 1969.

———. *The Black Jacobins: Toussaint L'Ouverture and the San Domingo Revolution.* New York: Vintage Books, 1963.

Johnson, Lemuel A. *The Devil, the Gargoyle, and the Buffoon: The Negro as Metaphor in Western Literature.* Port Washington, N.Y.: Kennikat Press, 1971.

Jordan, Winthrop. *White over Black: American Attitudes toward the Negro, 1550–1812.* Chapel Hill: Univ. of North Carolina Press, 1968.

Joseph, Gloria I., and Jill Lewis, eds. *Common Differences: Conflicts in Black and White Feminist Perspectives.* New York: Anchor Press, 1981.

Kingsley, Charles. *The Water-Babies: A Fairy-Tale for a Land-Baby.* London: J. M. Dent, 1890.

Kinsley, David R. *Hinduism: A Cultural Perspective.* Englewood Cliffs, N.J.: Prentice-Hall, 1982.

Kloepfer, Deborah Kelly. *The Unspeakable Mother: Forbidden Discourse in Jean Rhys and H.D.* Ithaca and London: Cornell Univ. Press, 1989.

LaPlanche, J., and J. B. Pontalis. *The Language of Psycho-Analysis.* Trans. Donald Nicholson-Smith. New York: Norton, 1973.

Las Casas, Bartolomé de. *History of the Voyage and Discoveries the Spaniards have made in the East Indies.* Trans. in part and ed. Andrée Collard. New York: Harper Torchbooks, 1971.

Lawrence, Karen R. *Decolonizing Tradition: New Views of Twentieth Century "British" Literary Canons.* Urbana: Univ. of Illinois Press, 1992.

Lawrence, Marilyn. *The Anorexic Experience.* London: Women's Press, 1984.

Lyotard, Jean-François. *The Postmodern Condition: A Report on Knowledge.* Minneapolis: Univ. of Minnesota Press, 1991.

Macdonell, Diane. *Theories of Discourse.* Oxford: Basil Blackwell, 1986.

Macherey, Pierre. *A Theory of Literary Production.* Trans. Geoffrey Wall. New York: Routledge, 1978.

Mangan, J. A., ed. *Making Imperial Mentalities: Socialisation and British Imperialism.* Manchester and New York: Manchester Univ. Press, 1990.

Mark Twain. *King Leopold's Soliloquy to the Belgians.* New York: International Publishers, 1961.

Marks, Elaine, and Isabelle de Courtivron, eds. *New French Feminisms: An Anthology.* New York: Schocken Books, 1981.

Meese, Elizabeth. *Crossing the Double Cross: The Practice of Feminist Criticism.* Chapel Hill: Univ. of North Carolina Press, 1986.

Minh-Ha, Trinh T. *When the Moon Waxes Red: Representation, Gender and Cultural Politics.* New York and London: Routledge, 1991.

Moffatt, James, and Millar Patrick. *Handbook to the Church Hymnary with Supplement.* London: Oxford Univ. Press, 1935.

Moi, Toril, ed. *The Kristeva Reader.* New York: Columbia Univ. Press, 1986.

———, ed. *French Feminist Thought: A Reader.* Oxford: Basil Blackwell, 1987.

Mordecai, Pamela, and Betty Wilson, eds. *Her True-True Name: An Anthology of Women's Writings from the Caribbean.* London: Heinemann, 1989.

Morrow, Bradford, and Patrick McGrath. *The New Gothic: A Collection of Contemporary Gothic Fiction.* New York: Random House, 1991.

Narasimhaiah, C. D. *Awakened Conscience: Studies in Commonwealth Literature.* Hong Kong, Singapore, Kuala Lumpur: Heinemann Educational Books, 1978.

Nasta, Susheila, ed. *Motherlands: Black Women's Writing from Africa, the Caribbean and South Asia.* New Brunswick, N.J.: Rutgers Univ. Press, 1991.

Nichols, David, and John A. L. Cooke. *The Oxford Book of Invertebrates: Protozoa, Sponges, Coelentereaes, Worms, Molluscs, Echinoderms, and Anthropods (Other than Insects).* London: Oxford Univ. Press, 1971.

North, Louise McCoy. *The Psalms and Hymns of Protestantism: From the Sixteenth to the Nineteenth Century.* Madison, N.J.: Univ. of Madison, 1936.

Nowell, Charles E., trans. *A Letter to Ferdinand and Isabella 1503.* Rpt. Minneapolis: Univ. of Minnesota Press, 1965.

Paravisini-Gebert, Lizabeth, and Olga Torres-Seda. *Caribbean Women Novelists: An Annotated Critical Bibliography.* Westport, Conn., and London: Greenwood Press, 1993.

Parry, John H., and Robert G. Keith. *New Iberian World: A Documentary History of the Discovery and Settlement of Latin America to the Early 17th Century.* New York: Times Books: Hector & Rose, 1984.

Patterson, Orlando. *Slavery and Social Death: A Comparative Study.* Cambridge: Harvard Univ. Press, 1982.

Perowne, Stewart. *The End of the Roman World.* New York: Crowell, 1967.

Petersen, Kirsten Holst, and Anna Rutherford, eds. *A Double Colonization: Colonial and Post-Colonial Women's Writing.* Oxford: Dangaroo Press, 1986.

Pope, Clifford H. *The Reptile World: A Natural History of the Snakes, Lizards, Turtles, and Crocodilians.* New York: Knopf, 1966.

Pratt, Mary Louise. *Imperial Eyes: Travel Writing and Transculturation.* New York: Routledge, 1992.

Ramchand, Kenneth. *The West Indian Novel and Its Background.* London: Heinemann, 1970.

Ray, Sheila G. *The Blyton Phenomenon: The Controversy Surrounding the World's Most Successful Children's Writer.* London: Andre Deutsch, 1982.

Retamar, Roberto Fernández. *Caliban and Other Essays.* Minneapolis: Univ. of Minnesota Press, 1989.

The Revitalization of Downtown Saint John's Antigua and Barbuda: First Phase Action Plan. General Secretariat Organization of American States, 1986.

Roberts, John W. *From Trickster to Badman: The Black Folk Hero in Slavery and Freedom.* Philadelphia: Univ. of Pennsylvania Press, 1989.

Rodney, Walter. *West Africa and the Atlantic Slave Trade.* East African Publishing House: Historical Association of Tanzania Paper no. 2, 1967.

Rodway, James. *The West Indies and the Spanish Main.* London: Fisher Unwin, 1896.

Romeo, Felicia. *Understanding Anorexia Nervosa.* Springfield, Ill.: Charles Thomas, 1986.

Routley, Erik. *An English-Speaking Hymnal Guide.* Collegeville, Minn.: Liturgical Press, 1979.

Rubin, Nancy. *Isabella of Castile: The First Renaissance Queen.* New York: St. Martin's, 1991.

Sahi, Jyoti. *The Child and the Serpent: Reflections on Popular Indian Symbols.* London: Routledge & Kegan Paul, 1980.

Said, Edward. *Orientalism.* New York: Vintage Press, 1979.

——. *The World, the Text, and the Critic.* Cambridge: Harvard Univ. Press, 1983.

——. *Culture and Imperialism.* New York: Knopf, 1993.

Sangari, KumKum, and Sudesh Vaid, eds. *Recasting Women: Essays in Colonial History.* New Delhi: Kali for Women Press, 1989.

Savacou 13 (special issue "Caribbean women"), ed. Lucille Mathurain Mair. Gemini, 1977.

Schulz, Bruno. *The Street of Crocodiles.* Trans. Celina Wieniewska. New York: Penguin Books, 1934.

Smith, Barbara Herrnstein. *On the Margins of Discourse: The Relation of Literature to Language.* Chicago: Univ. of Chicago Press, 1978.

Snodgrass, Robert Evans. *The Thorax of Insects and the Articulation of Wings.* Washington, D.C.: Government Printing Office, 1909.

Todorov, Tzvetan. *The Conquest of America: The Questions of the Other.* Trans. Richard Howard. New York: Harper & Row, 1982.

Turner, Victor. *Dramas, Fields, and Metaphors: Symbolic Action in Human Society.* Ithaca: Cornell Univ. Press, 1974.

Tyler, S. Lyman. *Two Worlds: The Indian Encounter with the European 1492–1509.* Salt Lake City: Univ. of Utah Press, 1988.

Wall, Cheryl A., ed. *Changing Our Own Words: Essays on Criticism, Theory, and Writings by Black Women.* New Brunswick, N.J.: Rutgers Univ. Press, 1989.

Watson, Jack B. *The West Indian Heritage: A History of the West Indies.* London: Jack Murray, 1979.

Weatherby, W. J. *Salman Rushdie: Sentenced to Death.* New York: Cornell Univ. Press, 1990.

Wilson, Samuel M. *Hispaniola: Caribbean Chiefdoms in the Age of Columbus.* Tuscaloosa and London: Univ. of Alabama Press, 1990.

Woolf, Virginia. *A Room of One's Own.* 1929. Rpt. New York: Harcourt Brace Jovanovich, 1957.

Articles

Adisa, Opal Palmer. "Island Daughter." Review of *Lucy* in *Women's Review of Books,* vol. 8.

"An Interview with Bruno Schulz." *Pequod: A Journal of Contemporary Literature and Literary Criticism,* nos. 16 and 17 (1984): 144–48.

Asante, Molefi Kete. ". . . And Then There Was Columbus." *Essence,* October 1991.

Bhabha, Homi K. "Signs Taken for Wonders: Questions of Ambivalence and Authority under a Tree outside Delhi, May 1817." In *"Race," Writing and Difference,* ed. Henry Louis Gates, Jr., pp. 163–84. Chicago: Univ. of Chicago Press, 1985.

Bloomfield, Anne. "Drill and Dance as Symbols of Imperialism." In Mangan, ed., *Making Imperial Mentalities,* pp. 74–95.

Brown, Russel E. "Bruno Schulz's Sanatorium Story." *Polish Perspective: Quarterly Review* 30 (1987): 35–46.

Chang, Victor L. "Sylvia Wynter." In Dance, ed., *Fifty Caribbean Writers,* pp. 498–507.

Christian, Barbara. "But What Do We Think We're Doing Anyway: The State of Black Feminist Criticism(s) or My Version of a Little Bit of History." In Wall, ed., *Changing Our Own Words,* pp. 58–74.

——. "Gloria Naylor's Geography." In Gates, ed., *Reading Black, Reading Feminist,* pp. 348–73.

Cixous, Hélène. "The Laugh of the Medusa." In Marks and Courtivron, eds., *New French Feminisms,* pp. 245–64.

Cobham, Rhonda. "Getting Out of the Kumbla." Review of *Jane and Louisa Will Soon Come Home,* by Erna Brodber. *Race Today* 14 (December 1981/January 1982): 33–34.

———. "Revisioning Our Kumblas: Transforming Feminist and Nationalist Agendas in Three Caribbean Women's Texts." *Callaloo* 16 (Winter 1993): 58.

Connelly, Steven E. Review of *Memoirs of a Tourist* by Stendhal. *Journal of Mind and Behavior* 8, no. 2 (1987): 361–63.

Covi, Giovanna. "Jamaica Kincaid and the Resistance to the Canons." In Davies and Fido, eds., *Out of the Kumbla,* pp. 345–54.

Davies, Carole. "Mothering and Healing in Recent Black Women's Fiction." *Sage: A Scholarly Journal on Black Women* 2, no. 1 (1985): 41–43.

Davies, Carole Boyce, and Elaine Savory Fido, eds. "Writing Home: Gender and Heritage in the Works of Afro-Caribbean/American Women Writers." In Davies and Fido, eds., *Out of the Kumbla,* pp. 59–73.

de Abruna, Laura Niesen. "Family Connections: Mother and Mother Country in the Fiction of Jean Rhys and Jamaica Kincaid." In Nasta, ed., *Motherlands,* pp. 257–89.

Dutton, Wendy. "Merge and Separate: Jamaica Kincaid's Fiction." *World Literature Today* 63 (1989): 406–10.

Féral, Josette. "Towards a Theory of Displacement." *Sub-Stance* 32 (1981): 52–65.

Ferguson, Moira. "*Lucy* and the Mark of the Colonizer." *Modern Fiction Studies* (Spring 1994).

———. "Annie John: Confrontation with Three Parents." *African-American Review,* forthcoming.

Fernandez, Pablo Armano. "Dreams of Two Americas." In *Reinventing the Americas: Comparative Studies of Literature of the United States and Spanish America,* ed. Bell Gale Chevigny and Gari Laguardia, pp. 122–25. Cambridge: Cambridge Univ. Press, 1986.

Gardiner, Judith Kegan. "On Female Identity and Writing by Women." In *Writing and Sexual Difference,* ed. Elizabeth Abel, pp. 177–91. Chicago and London: Univ. of Chicago Press, 1982.

Gilkes, Michael. "The Madonna Pool: Woman as 'Muse of Identity.'" *Journal of West Indian Literature* 1, no. 2 (1987): 1–19.

Gordimer, Nadine. "A Lion on the Freeway." In her *A Soldier's Embrace,* pp. 24–27. New York: Viking, 1975.

Guha, Ranajit. "The Prose of Counter-Insurgency." In his *Selected Subaltern Studies.*

Hall, Stuart. "Cultural Identity and Cinematic Representation." *Third Scenario: Theory and the Politics of Location. Framework* (London) 36 (1989): 68–81.

———. "Minimal Selves." *Identity Documents 6,* pp. 44–46. London: Institute of Contemporary Arts, 1987.

Harris, Wilson. "Metaphor and Myth." In *Myth and Metaphor,* ed. Robert Sellick, pp. 1–14. Adelaide: Centre for Research in the New Literatures in English, 1982.

——. "Adversarial Contexts and Creativity." *New Left Review* 54 (1986): 124–28.

——. "The Native Phenomenon." In *Common Wealth* (Papers delivered at the Conference of Commonwealth Literature, Aarhus University, Aarhus, Denmark, April 26–30, 1971), ed. Anna Rutherford. Aarhus: Akademisk Boghandel, n.d., pp. 144–50.

Hector, Tim. "Reuben Henry Harris — End of an Era?" *Outlet,* May 31, 1991.

——. "Is This Man Fit to Hold Public Office?" *Outlet,* September 20, 1991.

——. "*A Small Place:* A Large Vision." *Outlet,* August 26, 1988.

hooks, bell. "Choosing the Margin as a Space of Radical Openness." *Framework* (London) 36 (1989): 15–23.

Hyam, Ronald. "Empire and Sexual Opportunity." In his *Empire and Sexuality: The British Experience,* pp. 88–114. Manchester: Manchester Univ. Press, 1990.

Insanally, Annette. "Sexual Politics in Contemporary Female Writing on the Caribbean." In Lowell Fiet, ed., *West Indian Literature and Its Political Context,* pp. 79–91. Rio Piedras, Puerto Rico: Univ. of Puerto Rico, 1988.

Irigaray, Luce. "This Sex Which Is Not One." In Marks and de Courtivron, eds., *New French Feminisms,* pp. 99–106.

——. "Sexual Difference." In Moi, ed., *French Feminist Thought,* pp. 118–30.

Ismond, Patricia. "Jamaica Kincaid: First They Must Be Children." *World Literature Written in English* 282 (1988): 336–41.

Jacobus, Mary. "The Difference of View." In Belsey and Moore, eds., *The Feminist Reader,* pp. 49–62.

James, C. L. R. "The Making of the Caribbean People." In his *At the Rendezvous of Victory: Selected Writings,* pp. 173–90. London: Allison and Busby, 1984.

James, Louis. "Reflections, and *The Bottom of the River:* The Transformation of Caribbean Experience in the Fiction of Jamaica Kincaid." *Wasafiri* 8–9 (Winter 1988–89): 15–17.

Joseph, Gloria I. "Black Mothers and Daughters: Traditional and New Perspectives." In Patricia Bell-Scott, *Double Stitch: Black Women Write about Mothers and Daughters.* Boston: Beacon Press, 1991.

Joseph, Gloria I., and Jill Lewis. "Black Mothers and Daughters: Their Roles and Functions in American Society." In Joseph and Lewis, eds., *Common Differences,* pp. 75–148.

Katrak, Ketu H. "Decolonizing Culture: Toward a Theory for Postcolonial Women's Texts." *Modern Fiction Studies* 35 (1989): 161–62.

Kristeva, Julia. "My Memory's Hyperbole." In *The Female Autograph,* ed. Domna Stanton, pp. 219–35. Chicago and London: Univ. of Chicago Press, 1984.

——. *Revolution in Poetic Language.* In Moi, ed., *The Kristeva Reader,* pp. 89–136.

Lang, Candace. "Autobiography in the Aftermath of Romanticism." *Diacritics* 12 (1982): 2–16.

Lorde, Audre. "Eye to Eye: Black Women, Hatred, and Anger." In her *Sister Out-*

sider: Essays and Speeches, pp. 145–75. Trumansburg, N.Y.: Crossing Press, 1984.

Lowenthal, David, and Colin Clark. "Slave Breeding in Barbuda." *Annals of the New York Academy of Sciences* 292 (1977): 510–35.

Mangum, Bryant. "Jamaica Kincaid." In Dance, ed., *Fifty Caribbean Writers,* p. 262.

Meadows, Patrick Alan. "The Symbol's Symbol: Spider Webs in French Literature." *Symposium: A Quarterly Journal in Modern Foreign Literature* 44 (1990): 272–90.

Mendelsohn, Jane. "Leaving Home: Jamaica Kincaid's Voyage round Her Mother." *Voice Literary Supplement,* October 1990, 21.

Mohanty, Chandra T., and Satya P. Mohanty. "Contradictions of Colonialism." Review of Kumkum Sangari and Sudesh Vaid, eds., *Recasting Women.* In *Women's Review of Books* 7, no. 6 (1990): 19–21.

———. Introduction. "Cartographies of Struggle: Third World Women and the Politics of Feminism." In *Third World Women and the Politics of Feminism,* ed. Ann Russo and Lourdes Torres, pp. 1–44. Bloomington: Indiana Univ. Press, 1991.

Mohanty, Satya P. "Drawing the Color Line: Kipling and the Culture of Colonial Rule." In *The Bounds of Race: Perspectives on Hegemony and Resistance,* ed. Dominick LaCapra, pp. 311–43. Ithaca and London: Cornell Univ. Press, 1991.

Mordecai, Pamela C. "The West Indian Male Sensibility in Search of Itself: Some Comments on *Nor Any Country, The Mimic Men,* and *The Secret Ladder.*" *World Literature Written in English* 21 (1982): 629–44.

Morris, Ann R., and Margaret M. Dunn. "'The Bloodstream of Our Inheritance': Female Identity and the Caribbean Mothers'-Land.'" In Nasta, ed., *Motherlands,* pp. 219–37.

Murdoch, H. Adlai. "Severing the (M)other Connection: The Representation of Cultural Identity in Jamaica Kincaid's *Annie John.*" *Callaloo* (Spring 1988): 325–40.

Natov, Roni. "Mothers and Daughters: Jamaica Kincaid's Pre-Oedipal Narrative." *Children's Literature* 18 (1990): 1–16.

Peixoto, Marta. "*Family Ties:* Female Development in Clarice Lispector." In Abel, Hirsch, and Langland, eds., *The Voyage,* pp. 287–303.

Perry, Donna. "Initiation in Jamaica Kincaid's *Annie John.*" In Cudjoe, ed., *Caribbean Women Writers,* pp. 245–53.

Ramraj, Victor. "The All-Embracing Christlike Vision: Tone and Attitude in the Mimic Men." In *Commonwealth,* ed. Anna Rutherford, pp. 125–34. Papers Delivered at the Conference of Commonwealth Literature, Aarhus University, April 26–30, 1971, Akademisk Boghandel, Universitetsparken, Aarhus, Danmark.

Ramchand, Kenneth. "West Indian Literary History: Literariness, Orality and Periodization." *Callaloo* (Winter 1988): 95–111.

Rubin, Muriel Lynn. "Adolescence and Autobiographical Fiction: Teaching *Annie John* by Jamaica Kincaid." *Wasafiri* 8 (Spring 1988): 11–14.

Said, Edward. "Figures, Configurations, Transfigurations." *Race and Class: A Journal of Black and Third World Liberation* 32 (July–September 1990): 1–16.

Slemon, Stephen, and Helen Tiffin. Introduction. *After Europe: Essays in Post-Colonial Criticism.* Oxford: Dangaroo Press, 1989.

Smith, Valerie. "Black Feminist Theory and the Representation of the 'Other.'" In Wall, ed., *Changing Our Own Words,* pp. 38–57.

Soyinka, Wole. "The Critic and Society: Barthes, Leftocracy and Other Mythologies." In *Black Literature and Literary Theory,* ed. Henry Louis Gates, Jr., pp. 27–57. New York and London: Methuen, 1984.

Spivak, Gayatri Chakravorty. "Three Women's Texts and a Critique of Imperialism." In Belsey and Moore, eds., *The Feminist Reader,* pp. 175–95.

Tapping, Craig. "Children and History in the Caribbean Novel: George Lamming's *In the Castle of My Skin* and Jamaica Kincaid's *Annie John.*" *Kunapipi* 11, no. 2 (1989): 51–59.

Tiffin, Helen. "Decolonization and Audience: Erna Brodber's *Myal* and Jamaica Kincaid's *A Small Place.*" *SPAN: Journal of the South Pacific Association for Commonwealth Literature and Language Studies* 30 (April 1990): 27–38.

Warren, Allen. "'Mothers for the Empire'?" The Girl Guides Association in Britain, 1909–1939." In Mangan, ed., *Making Imperial Mentalities,* pp. 96–109.

West, Cornel. "Theory, Pragmatisms, and Politics." In *Consequences of Theory,* ed. Jonathan Arac and Barbara Johnson, p. 32. Baltimore and London: Johns Hopkins Univ. Press, 1991.

Wilentz, Gay. "English Is a Foreign Anguish: Caribbean Writers and the Disruption of the Colonial Canon." In Karen R. Lawrence, ed., *Decolonizing Tradition,* pp. 261–78.

Wilson, Betty. "Sexual, Racial and National Politics: Jacqueline Manicom's *Mon Examen de Blanc.*" *Journal of West Indian Literature* 1, no. 2 (1987): 50–57.

Wilson, Reuel K. "The Letters of Bruno Schulz, Jerzy Stempowski, and Especially Julian Tuwim." *World Literature Today,* Spring 1990, p. 246.

Woodcock, Bruce. "Post-1975 Caribbean Fiction and the Challenge to English Literature." *Critical Quarterly* 28 (1986): 79–95.

Index